UMA THURMAN

Also available from Aurum Press

UMA THURMAN
The Biography

BRYONY SUTHERLAND & LUCY ELLIS

AURUM PRESS

First published in Great Britain 2004 by Aurum Press Ltd
25 Bedford Avenue, London WC1B 3AT

A catalogue record for this book is available
from the British Library.

ISBN 1 84513 006 5

10 9 8 7 6 5 4 3 2 1
2008 2007 2006 2005 2004

Designed and typeset by M Rules
Printed and bound in Great Britain by
MPG Books Ltd, Bodmin

'Make it magnificent'

CONTENTS

ACKNOWLEDGEMENTS

Atomic are indebted to the following people whose interviews, contacts, research and other assistance made this book possible:

Dr Joan Ashcroft MB BS BSc, Sue Baker, Carolyn Boucher, Barry Edelstein, Clare Ellis, Hilary Field, Steven Field, Gary Gilbert, Matt Gross, Steve Gross, Craig Hefner, Deborah Holman, Rob Kerr, Jeroen Krabbé, Jeremy Marshall, Natalia Marshall, Michele Martin, Deane Merrill, Susan Minall, Derek Moore, Gill Moore, Henrik Mosén, Debbie Murray, Tim Murray, John Neville, Marie Outhwaite, Gert Påhlsson, Richard Rees, David Rowland, Gwen Rudman, Trevor Smith, Sher Sweet and Suresh Tolat.

Also to the following companies: ARM Direct, C'Est La Vie DVD, Feats Press, OCD Action and *RRP* magazine.

Special thanks go to our tireless editor Karen Ings, Bill McCreadie and all at Aurum Press and Trafalgar Square. Also to our favourite picture researcher, Nikki Lloyd – we promise we'll make that coffee soon!

In a professional sense we would like to thank Simon Bennett (Denton Wilde and Sapte), Steven Gordon (Martin Greene), John Prater (Kenneth Prater Photography) and everyone at the Society Of Authors who has helped us over the years.

Personally we send our love and thanks to our husbands and families, Belinda Farley, and to Finlay's triumvirate of carers: Kyoko Barrio, Barbara Newson and Sylvia Sutherland.

And finally, in remembrance of the unfortunate chicken that met its maker under Uma's wheels during the filming of *Kill Bill*.

Bryony Sutherland & Lucy Ellis, July 2004

PICTURE CREDITS

NOT SO PLEASANTLY DUMB

'Uma is not conventionally beautiful. But it's an amazing face to work with. One moment, she can look like Marlene Dietrich, the next like Bette Davis.'

JAMES IVORY, DIRECTOR, *THE GOLDEN BOWL*

In the Swedish port of Trelleborg stands a magnificent statue of a woman. Tall, striking and entirely naked, the effigy depicts Birgit Holmquist, a native beauty who would one day marry a German baron and travel the world. Her stance is open yet poised for flight, her seaward gaze wistful and otherworldly.

Years later, an unknown teenage actress would ensnare the attentions of a million movie buffs, arising radiant, serene and wholly unclothed from a scallop shell in Terry Gilliam's cult fantasy *The Adventures Of Baron Munchausen*. Although essentially recreating Botticelli's *Birth Of Venus* for the big screen, the scene unknowingly mirrored Birgit's silent, brazen statement to her Swedish hometown. The ingénue gracefully ascending into the public's consciousness some fifty-nine years later was none other than her granddaughter, Uma Thurman.

No journalist interviewing or writing about Thurman is able to avoid passing comment on the actress's extraordinary looks. All too often her considerable talents are skimmed over in favour of rapturous appreciation of her curvaceous 6-foot frame, impossibly long limbs and flawless complexion. Her face alone stops traffic: the bone structure sharp, the nose regal, the aquamarine eyes spaced so unnervingly far apart it is almost impossible to focus on both simultaneously.

Oddly, there's something about this very exotic combination which provides a completely blank canvas for her work. Uma can look exquisite, or, with an imperceptible shift in her features, repulsive. She's ideal fare for a costume drama, virginally innocent in a bodice-ripper, cute in a romantic comedy, vampishly seductive in a blockbuster, petrifyingly heroic in a revenge epic. She's also the kind of Hollywood A-lister who can blend invisibly into a crowd, conducting her everyday affairs largely unnoticed despite her supermodel proportions.

Unquestionably, behind the beauty there are brains. In the year she arose naked from the scallop shell, eighteen-year-old Uma commented, 'Because of the way I look, people think I should be quite simple, but fortunately I'm not so pleasantly dumb.' Indeed, just a passing glance at her immediate gene pool and influences (the Baroness and her Baron; an off-Broadway actress; a model-turned-psychotherapist; a celebrated professor and Tibetan Buddhist monk; a revolutionary narcophilosopher) strongly suggests that this is no blonde bimbo. And you don't go through marriages to such brilliant actors as Gary Oldman and Ethan Hawke without picking up a thing or two.

Understandably, Uma detests the all-too-easy label of 'thinking man's sex symbol'. 'It's primarily condescending,' she says. 'Always that thing of "but she's intelligent", with these quotes around it. Like it's such a big deal that an actress has half a brain.'

It is an issue she has not allowed to cloud her career. 'I wasn't discovered at McDonald's or Howard Johnson's,' she laughs. 'My background prepared me for life and gave me a fairly open, free-thinking attitude to life and this business we're in. Common sense is highly underrated, don't you think?'

Somehow, neither common sense nor the experience garnered from exposure in over thirty films has made her comfortable with fame. 'I still don't feel completely at ease having attention focused on myself,' she confessed in 2003. 'Although, I am aware that's something of a contradiction for me as an actor, whose profession invites people to focus on you!' According to her close friend Natasha Richardson, the intimidating persona Uma often presents to the public hides a 'real vulnerability', and, in private, she finds it difficult to let her guard down.

Probably because of her ongoing need to challenge people's perceptions, the actress's film choices have always been intriguing. More than any other performer of her generation, Uma tests herself each and every time to try something different.

'I have to keep interested,' she explains. 'I can't imagine playing the same genre or the same kind of role over and over again. I've always tried to do the opposite to what I just did, and I don't know if working that way has helped my career, but I needed to do it. But it's been hard having such a schizophrenic career.'

This diversity has led to some impressive pairings, both with her directors (Terry Gilliam, Stephen Frears, Gus Van Sant, Joel Schumacher, Woody Allen, James Ivory, Quentin Tarantino) and her co-stars (Robert De Niro, Vanessa Redgrave, John Malkovich, Richard Gere, Liam Neeson, John Travolta, Ralph Fiennes, Gérard Depardieu, Ethan Hawke).

In fact, Uma has often chosen to stay in the background, usually at the expense of first billing, in order to fulfil her desire for constant creative change: 'I like to move laterally. I'm very comfortable sliding from side to side,' she says by way of explanation.

The downside to this is that besides the handful of obvious titles like *Pulp Fiction*, *Kill Bill* and *Dangerous Liaisons*, the average viewer might be hard pressed to name more than a fraction of Thurman's considerable CV, despite having the distinct impression that she is an actress of quality. 'I have a mixed career, but a number of times I've been asked to play very cool characters,' she admits.

There are benefits to this conscious decision to avoid the limelight in the majority of her work. When Uma has a hit, it sticks, and the box-office success allows her to experiment further with the benefit of a high degree of recognition. When one of Uma's films bombs – and several have, significantly – somehow she either does not seem sufficiently attached to the project for it to affect her career, or her own performance remains blameless, and she sails on to the next project without a backwards glance. (Apparently, Uma's favourite fortune-cookie message is: 'Remember the lesson, forget the experience.')

Equally, Uma's unusual need to skip from genre to genre means that she has already proved herself in a huge variety of 'character' roles, ensuring a far easier shift to meatier parts as she matures. She's rarely played 'the girlfriend' or relied solely on her looks, so it's likely she will be with us for many years to come.

'I remember thinking that I didn't want to be the flavour of the month,' she reflects on her eighteen-year career. 'I've always tried to define myself as more than one thing, and it's important to me to have the courage to fail, to keep trying different kinds of roles.

'I wanted to know what comedy was like, what a thriller was like, what action was like, what dancing and singing were like. From a craftsman's point of view, I wanted to try to perfect myself in as many directions as I could.'

As a craftsman, Uma remains unsurpassed in her generation. As an individual, her story is unique, as full of hits and misses as her work to date and easily as fascinating. As the actress herself admits: 'Sometimes you get to paint with a role. Sometimes you can only plaster.'

1

YOU'RE NOBODY TILL SOMEBODY LOVES YOU

'*Remember: the hallucinations which you may now experience, the visions and insights, will teach you much about yourself and the world. The veil of routine perception will be torn from your eyes.*'

THE TIBETAN BOOK OF THE DEAD

'*I find this obsession with lineage ridiculous and rather pathetic.*'

UMA THURMAN

The open arms of the *Famntaget* statue have welcomed ships to the southern Swedish port of Trelleborg for the last seventy-four years, night and day, rain or shine. Commissioned by Albert Emil Fredrik Holmquist, a rubber-factory union manager, and his wife Julie, their daughter Birgit Olga's naked beauty was immortalized in bronze by the noted sculptor Axel Ebbe in 1930.

It was the first of many highly unusual 'life decisions' made by Uma Thurman's ancestors, placing a typically indelible mark on the world and inviting praise, criticism, and even scorn.

Five years later, Birgit would further attract public speculation when she married her titled German lover, Baron Friedrich Karl Johannes von Schlebrügge, on 12 March 1935. Hailing from Westphalia, the former province of Prussia, and twenty-five years her senior, the monacled Baron already had quite a past.

This was his second marriage, and he had previously been jailed by the Nazis for refusing to betray his Jewish business partners. This dangerous sense of loyalty appealed to Birgit; a chance meeting in Berlin was all it took for the two of them to fall in love. They decamped to Sweden and married in Birgit's home town.

In 1941 the von Schlebrügges had travelled a unique path to Mexico

City, Mexico, where they welcomed the birth of a daughter, Nena Birgitte Caroline. The family then moved on to Peking, but sadly Birgit and her Baron divorced when Nena was only six. Birgit wisely decided to take her daughter back to Sweden and eventually they settled in Stockholm, which, although many miles away from Trelleborg, offered some of the familiarity of home. There the pair lived without incident for nearly a decade.

When Nena hit her teens, her confidence was somewhat undermined by the fact that she suddenly shot up to nearly 6 feet tall. Mortified, she convinced herself she was 'an ugly duckling' and that none of the boys would ever look at her.

Not so. In 1955 the celebrated British *Vogue* photographer Norman Parkinson just happened to be passing the playground of Nena's school. He stopped in his tracks when he caught sight of her. Nena was tall and slender, with golden hair, enormous far-apart eyes, a high forehead and angular cheekbones. He wasted no time in inviting the stunning teenager to accompany him to London.

'The idea of being a model would never have occurred to me,' Nena recalls. 'But it so happened that I was sixteen and I'd started to feel very restless.'

Having modelled and travelled extensively herself, Birgit was not going to stand in her daughter's way, so off Nena went to London, where she signed with the prestigious Ford modelling agency. The weekly wage went some way to restoring Nena's faith in herself, and within the year she relocated across the Atlantic Ocean to Manhattan. There Nena fully asserted her independence as a woman, rising rapidly through the ranks of the city's top fashion models, and posing for high-profile work such as Parkinson's own *You Can Be A Walkin' Talkin' Swimmin' Doll*.

As the late 1950s lurched into the Swinging Sixties, Nena found her model status allowed her free entry to the best parties.

'Salvador Dalí and I became great buddies,' she says. 'I would sit around at the St Regis with him and meet weird people.' Indeed, it was the surrealist Spanish painter and sculptor who would introduce Nena to her first husband, psychedelic guru and LSD proponent Timothy Leary.

*

Dr Timothy Leary PhD encompassed many disciplines: psychologist, philosopher, Harvard professor, author and revolutionary. Nicknamed the 'Galileo of Consciousness', his main distinction came from going public with his observations of the mind as altered by narcotics.

In the spring of 1962, Leary established research into psychedelic drugs at the Castalia Institute in Millbrook, New York. Outwardly Baroque in appearance, inside the institute resembled a Middle Eastern temple, and it provided a haven for the hip and elite to escape real life and experiment as they pleased. By 1963, Leary (dismissed that year from Harvard) had allegedly shared drug experiences with the likes of Marilyn Monroe, Allen Ginsberg, Cary Grant, Charles Mingus, Willem de Kooning, Aldous Huxley, Thelonious Monk and William S. Burroughs. Three years later, he would coin his infamous slogan: 'Tune in, turn on, drop out'.

As an estimated 3.6 million Americans began to experiment with LSD, in part because of Leary's highly publicized advocation, Richard Nixon proclaimed him 'the most dangerous man in America'. Leary's response was to warn the public: 'Acid is not for every brain – only the healthy, happy, wholesome, handsome, hopeful, humorous, high-velocity should seek these experiences.'

'There were some 150 of us, all high on LSD, or pot, or both,' recalled Michael Hollingshead of the von Schlebrügge–Leary nuptials in his book *The Man Who Turned On The World*. The ceremony was held in the Episcopal church in the scenic village of Millbrook early one afternoon in 1964, and a Swedish-style buffet greeted the guests afterwards. 'It was a brilliant festive occasion with everyone dressed up so brightly that it was like watching an idyllic pageant from Elizabethan England,' Hollingshead remembers. The girls wore glittering saris and carried flowers, the men wore a variety of colourful robes and eye-catching costumes. Catching a glimpse of the spirited crowd was like peeking into a 'kaleidoscopic garden party of glorious humanity'.

The joyful event was preserved for posterity in a fifteen-minute documentary, *You're Nobody Till Somebody Loves You*, directed by D. A. Pennebaker with music by Monte Rock III, Maynard Fergusson and Charles Mingus. Don Snyder took the photographs. Wedding gifts included hashish, magic mushrooms, cocaine and, of course, LSD. The happy couple honeymooned in New Delhi and Nepal.

It was an awfully long way from Stockholm.

Like her mother before her, Nena had wed a man over twenty years her senior and very much set on his own collision course through life. He also had two children from a previous marriage. Away from the surreal sanctuary of Millbrook, things seemed different; by the time Nena and Tim returned from their honeymoon, the marriage was already faltering. In the end it lasted just less than a year, and Leary would move to Mexico with his children and new love, Rosemary

Woodruff, the week after Christmas 1965. The following year he would be arrested and imprisoned on drug charges pertaining to his daughter's possession of marijuana.

Far from being broken-hearted, Nena was astute enough to recognize that 'Leary was the missing daddy I was trying to supply myself with. Once I understood it was a "daddy trip", it was over.' The divorce was amicable and Nena would stay in touch with her ex.[*]

*

On 14 October 1942, Elizabeth Farrar and Beverley Thurman welcomed their son into the world. Robert Alexander Farrar Thurman was born in New York City and grew up in a warm, romantic household filled to the brim with creative influences. His mother was an actress who had dropped out of college to pursue her dream; his father, a medical student, had also abandoned his studies to follow his sweetheart to New York.

During the course of her adventures, Elizabeth would become a moderately successful off-Broadway actress, at one point sharing a flat with Bette Davis. Beverley would eventually become an editor for the Associated Press. Between them they brought up their children in a highly literary environment, encouraging their aspirations and imaginations in equal measure.

Weekly dramatic readings were held at the Thurman residence, conducted by Augustin Duncan, brother to the famous dancer Isadora. Robert and his brothers took part, and he developed key oratorical skills while performing Shakespeare in his front room, also gaining an erudite background. 'I was Mr Establishment, the golden-boy-ish type of thing,' he laughs today. Robert grew into a fine-looking young man with wavy, reddish-blond hair, a booming voice, an intense, charismatic presence and a sparkling wit.

He also had a strong rebellious streak. In April 1958, during his senior year at Phillips Exeter, he and a pal zoomed off on their motorbikes on a dare to join Fidel Castro's revolution. Apprehended at Miami, they returned shamefaced and were abruptly expelled without attaining their high-school diplomas. Rapidly developing a 'playboy' attitude to life while conversely wishing to continue his education, Robert spent a year in Mexico before entering Harvard on a scholarship in 1959.

---

[*] It has been said that Leary is Uma's godfather, but the authors could find no evidence to back up this claim.

It was at that prestigious university that Robert met Christophe de Menil, the Texan oil heiress to a considerable fortune and fine-art collection. Robert was nineteen and just beginning his studies, while Christophe was twenty-six, but that didn't stop the pair falling in love and marrying, and soon producing a baby.

A fluke accident that same year caused his life to change immeasurably. One day, while changing a flat tyre, the tyre iron slipped and pierced his left eyeball. Robert was fortunate to escape with his life, but the eye was destroyed and he would either have to wear a glass replacement or simply have an empty socket for the rest of his days.

'It woke me to the idea that life is very brief and it could end at any time – what would have been the point of just fooling around?' he later recalled. 'That made me drop my playboy side and get serious about trying to find the meaning of life.'

Further fuelled by his recent studies of Buddhist texts, Robert told Christophe he wanted to travel to the East. Apprehensive about leaving all she knew behind, Christophe protested, but it was too late. 'I then started identifying with Buddha, left my wife and child and went over there. I was very sad about that, but I felt – even as a father – what's the use of not being enlightened?' he later remarked.

Shelving fatherhood, his short marriage and a promising Harvard education, Robert travelled to India via Turkey and Iran. His mother was horrified, but his father, a more spiritual soul, quietly encouraged him, telling him it was 'what I always wanted to do'. This was the last piece of fatherly support Robert would receive, as Beverley died suddenly soon after.

Robert fell into an unstable, beggar-like existence on his path to enlightenment. 'I had an empty [eye] socket, long hair and a scraggly beard. I wore black baggy Afghani pants, a T-shirt with a white shawl thrown around me and leather sandals.' Any ties to his playboy existence snapped for good as soon as he encountered the Tibetans, for then he knew he had found his spiritual home.

*

Tibet is as much a major religious enclave as it is a country. Tibetan Buddhism is a distinctive form of the religion found in Tibet, Mongolia and adjacent regions.

Buddhism itself arose from the teachings of Buddha (meaning 'enlightened') in India during 6–5 BC, following the fundamental doctrine of the Four Noble Truths (existence is suffering; suffering has a cause within the self; one may be freed of suffering; following the precepts of the Eightfold Path ends suffering and leads to nirvana). Essentially, the religion teaches that the elimination of the self and all earthly desires is the highest goal and leads to enlightenment.

Tibetan Buddhism originated in Tibet around AD 7 and was derived from Indian Mahayana Buddhism, also embodying elements of Tantric Buddhism and the native Tibetan religion, Bon. In the fifteenth century the lama (meaning 'monk' or 'teacher') Tsong-kha-pa began the Yellow Hat Sect, which introduced reforms and scrupulous discipline within the monasteries.

Within the next 150 years, the Dalai Lama (meaning 'ocean of wisdom') would become the traditional spiritual leader of the country. The line of Dalai Lamas had begun in the fourteenth century, with each considered to be the reincarnation of his predecessor.

The present Dalai Lama is the fourteenth incarnation, enthroned at the tender age of four against a dangerous backdrop of political unrest. Growing into a most modern young man whose interests included technology and state affairs, he was forced to shoulder the additional responsibility of being made secular head of state at just fifteen years of age, as Communist China invaded Tibet in October 1950.

Matters came to a head with the Tibetan Uprising of 1959, when some 87,000 Tibetans died during the abortive revolt against Chinese domination. The Dalai Lama fled to India amid a mass exodus of an estimated 80,000. Since then, China has actively suppressed Tibetan Buddhism, torturing and killing Tibet's peaceful population.

*

After a spell in Tibet, Robert Thurman understood the kind of life he felt he should be living. Returning briefly to America to attend his father's funeral, he met a Mongolian monk living in New Jersey. The lama challenged him to find enlightenment, and Robert was hooked. They studied together and Robert learned to speak Tibetan fluently in ten weeks flat.

Robert accompanied his guru to Dharamsala in India soon afterwards, where he was introduced to the exiled Dalai Lama. A strange but mutually beneficial relationship blossomed, whereby the young refugee exchanged spiritual teaching for the remains of a Harvard education. In 1965, at the age of twenty-four, Robert became the first Westerner to be ordained a Tibetan Buddhist monk. The ceremony was conducted personally by the Dalai Lama, by now a very dear friend. Robert shaved his head, wore a maroon robe and adopted a new name, Tenzin.

It has been said that Tibetan Buddhism is the hardest Buddhist route for a Westerner to follow, with its prostrations, visualizations, guru worship and deity yoga. The Geluk grouping, which is the Dalai Lama's order, is popularly considered to be the most philosophical and scholarly. To Robert, Buddhist enlightenment meant 'the tolerance of cognitive dissonance, the ability to cope with the beauty of complexity', a concept he grasped with typical boundless enthusiasm, and he determined to spread the word around the world.

Returning to America in his monk's garb, Robert was received with disbelief, amusement and respect in equal measure. Moreover, the timing of his homecoming was crucial in a land that was already changing dramatically.

'It was the mid-1960s and all my contemporaries were freaking out over the civil rights movement or the Vietnam War. I felt that I was hiding out from the real burdens,' he admits. Further persuaded by his religious elders that a 'white geshe' was probably not what New York needed just then, Robert shed his robes and decided to become a professor, lecturing on the dharma (Buddhist truth) and spreading enlightenment in a more conventional manner.

In time, Robert would become the Jey Tsong Khapa Professor of Indo-Tibetan Buddhist Studies and head of the Columbia Center for Buddhist Studies at Columbia University. He would write many books, including *Essential Tibetan Buddhism*, *Inner Revolution: Life, Liberty, And The Pursuit Of Real Happiness* and *The Politics Of Enlightenment: A Handbook For The Cool Revolution*, and translate major religious texts such as *Holy Teaching Of Vimalakirti: A Mahayana Scripture* and *The Tibetan Book Of The Dead*. In 1987 he would co-found Tibet House, the Dalai Lama's cultural outpost in America, and a decade later he would be selected by *Time* magazine as one of the world's twenty-five most influential people.

*

Back in 1966, Robert Thurman re-enrolled at Harvard for a master's degree in East Asian Studies. Among his mentors was a certain Timothy Leary, and the two became close, enthusiastically exchanging theories on life and the universe.

One day Leary invited his prize pupil to speak at the Hitchcock estate in Millbrook. When Robert arrived at the party, the beautiful Nena was present in the audience, unhappy in her failed marriage to Leary and seeking spiritual guidance. In spite of his shaved head and missing eye, Nena found Robert utterly beguiling in a both physical and mystical sense, and the two became inseparable.

They married in 1967 after Nena obtained a divorce from Leary, and settled in Amherst, Massachusetts, while Robert completed his master's over the next two years.

Against this backdrop of religious instruction, academia and a plethora of exotic 1960s influences, their first child together was born in 1968. The Thurmans named their son Ganden, which means 'joy' in Tibetan and is also the name for the western heavens where the Maitreya Buddha (the Future Buddha) resides.

*

Their second child, Uma Karuna Thurman, was born on 29 April 1970 in Boston, Massachusetts.

'She was absolutely perfect, radiant from birth,' says her father, 'a little postmature, so there wasn't a wrinkle on her skin, and her hair was fully grown in.'

Her name was perhaps even more unusual than her older brother's. Uma (actually 'UmA') is the Hindu goddess of light and beauty in Indian mythology, and the mother of Ganesha, the elephant-headed god. Various translations include 'The Middle Way', 'Bestower of Blessings', 'The Bright One' and 'May She Not Suffer', the latter referring to the fact that the goddess is the reincarnation of Parvati, who had committed suicide in her previous life.

'It's a primal sound,' Uma herself once offered. 'It means "horse" in Japanese, "grandmother" in some other language, it's the feminine prefix in another.' As a single Sanskrit word, *uma* means splendour, light, fame and tranquillity – all notably fitting descriptions for the woman she would one day become. Her middle name, Karuna, is one of the four sublime abodes in Buddhism, meaning 'compassion'.

And so Uma was welcomed back to the Thurmans' home in Amherst, where her father had taken on the post of professor of religion at Amherst College.

2

THE QUEST FOR THE MIDDLE WAY

'My mum, dad and brothers are completely eccentric. In fact, they're not unlike the Munsters.'

UMA THURMAN

Amherst lies in the centre of the Pioneer Valley of western Massachusetts, among steep mountains, rolling hills, streams, forests and abundant vegetation. It is an area of spectacular natural beauty, and is protected by over fifty conservation orders.

The fast-flowing streams of Colonial Amherst and the nearby arsenal in Springfield drew white settlers to the region, bringing technology that catapulted the Pioneer Valley into the Industrial Revolution ahead of the surrounding territories. The juxtaposition of water with guns is a strange but accurate metaphor for the cultural diversity Amherst enjoys to this day.

Railways built in the mid-to-late 1800s helped Amherst's local businesses thrive in sectors such as farming, cotton factories and brick-making. But by the mid-1900s, Amherst had emerged as a major centre for education, with five prestigious colleges. The town's literary ambience was amply assisted by the presence of such luminaries as Noah Webster, the author of the first American dictionary, and the poets Emily Dickinson and Robert Frost.

To put into perspective the importance of education in this relatively small American town, today Amherst has a population of around 35,000 and is home to the University of Massachusetts at Amherst, which tutors some 24,000 students.

Robert Thurman would teach at the historic Amherst College,

founded in 1821, for the next fifteen years. His life's work and passion spilled over from his studies and teaching, and he would frequently open his home to numerous dharma students, occasional Tibetan refugees, and eminent international holy men (including, of course, the Dalai Lama when he happened to be visiting the East Coast). Filled with gossip, debate, guests, dogs and now babies, the Thurmans' enormous, ramshackle Victorian house soon became the talk of the town.

Needless to say, Uma's upbringing was always going to be bohemian, and Amherst was only the beginning. As she grew up, family summers would be spent at the country retreat of Woodstock, New York, traditionally a mecca for painters, writers, musicians, nature lovers, free thinkers and free spirits. Twice in her young life, the whole family was uprooted and spent a year on a pilgrimage to India, the first time when she was only a year old.

Uma would grow up thinking that relocation (the Thurmans continued to move around, even within the limits of Amherst) and the constant stream of poets, priests, writers and artists that invaded her life were normal. Although Robert's religious lifestyle dominated the Thurmans' lives, Nena had retained many of her quirkier acquaintances, now in effect family friends.

In 1972 both of Uma's parents could be seen in the cult piece *Ciao Manhattan*. The film was an ambiguous and rambling documentary following the life of Edie Sedgewick, a young model and acolyte of Andy Warhol's Factory scene, who would die from a drug overdose three months after its completion. *Ciao Manhattan* veritably overflows with startling cameos from some of the most interesting personalities of 1960s underground culture; alongside Uma's parents, the line-up includes Roger Vadim, Susan Hoffman, Andy Warhol and a sometimes naked Allen Ginsberg.*

*

In 1973 Nena gave birth to the Thurmans' third child, a boy they named Dechen, meaning 'great bliss' in Tibetan. The new life compensated a little for the sad death of her mother, Birgit, in April that year in Stockholm. Another son, Mipam (after Mipam Rinpoche, a famous nineteenth-century lama), would complete the family five years later. Uma's status as only daughter was sealed.

---

* For the modern viewer, Nena Thurman's resemblance to Uma is extraordinary and quite uncanny.

In 1975 five-year-old Uma enrolled in kindergarten at Wildwood Elementary School, Amherst. A friendly and welcoming school immensely proud of its multi-ethnic community, it seemed like the ideal place for the daughter of a scholar to start her own education.

But for Uma, it was hell from the word go. 'My mother gave me a lot of her Swedish, European feeling and sense of separation from America,' she recalls of this period. Although Wildwood prided itself on its multiculturalism and diversity, there weren't many families like Uma's waiting at the school gates. From the very beginning, her peers sneered at her rhyming name, the double whammy of 'Uma Karuna', completely unable in their childishness to comprehend why a classmate should be named after a Hindu goddess.

But it wasn't just the name or the teasing. Uma had never really examined herself critically until a classmate said he didn't like her nose, giving her the cruel nickname of 'Piggy'.

'I had to go to a mirror and look at it,' she recalls. 'I couldn't picture myself in my own head. I had no image beyond a stick figure.' And when she analysed her appearance, she didn't like what she saw.

'I was severely odd-looking,' she continues. 'I had a big nose and a big mouth and these far-apart eyes which looked like I had two fish swimming in my ears. I had an odd name and I always had these big knots in my hair that made it stick out, giving me a very odd-shaped head, like a hammerhead shark.'

Sadly for Uma, the little boy's taunts started a trend. 'I was constantly told I was ugly by the other kids,' she says. 'I wasn't a mean person as a kid, or dumb, and something has to be said to justify excluding you.'

The death of Uma's grandmother, her growing insecurities and the unkind treatment at school combined to trigger a staggering development in the little girl's psyche. 'Mortality brought home the idea that things and people pass, that I hadn't arrived at any kind of resting place and indeed there might not be one at all,' she explains. 'I was only five or six, but once I understood that childhood doesn't last for ever and that my parents wouldn't take care of me for ever, I wanted very badly to champion my own life.'

Uma adds that when she realized her childhood would only be transient, she simply lost interest in it. In the unusual adult world that featured so prominently in her daily life, there seemed to be no place for the girlish delights of fantasy or fairy tales. Furthermore, this sudden comprehension brought with it an unnaturally mature sense of regret, as Uma forced herself to come to terms with the fact that one day she would leave all she knew behind and strike out on her own.

'As soon as I figured that out, it almost became unbearable to me – the comfort of home – because I couldn't have it forever,' she says. 'I could hardly enjoy it.' Until then, 'home' had been the single most important thing in her life, 'and to know that it wasn't going to last . . . I took it really hard'.

*

It is possible that Uma's personal catharsis at such a young age went totally unnoticed by her family. 'My mum, dad and brothers are completely eccentric,' Uma once chuckled. 'In fact, they're not unlike the Munsters.'

Unconventional, profoundly intellectual and about as far from the average Amherst family as could be, the Thurmans set about bringing up their children in their own mirror image. 'I raised them from early on to be independent, to think for themselves and make their own decisions,' Nena recalls. Not a bad thing for any youngster's development, but in this household one wonders how Uma ever made herself heard.

'If you grow up in an intellectually challenging environment, you can feel inadequate if on certain occasions you just don't measure up,' says Uma. 'In my house, my brothers and I were forced to justify everything we said.

'If we made a statement, we had to be able to argue and defend that statement. That type of conditioning can sharpen you intellectually, but it can also make you very insecure. My family could be absolutely merciless when it came to arguments.'

Indeed, her mother readily agrees, 'There were always discussions – and squabbling. Squabbling was encouraged.'

The children were rarely allowed access to television (watching *Dynasty* with Nena was Uma's only luxury in this department), or to hang out with other kids playing time-wasting games. Instead, they were expected to read voraciously and participate in lively debate at the dinner table, normally on fine art, philosophy or religion.

'We were taught to question everything, especially "facts",' says Uma. 'It was always: "Why is it a fact? How did it become a fact?"

'It was a heady environment, but in a positive way. You had to be able to use your mind to get through dinner. Being seven was not an excuse for not being a functioning human mind, with responsibilities and an understanding of oneself as an individual.'

Uma swiftly learned that words were the only way she could defend herself. Not for the Thurmans the rough and tumble of other families' everyday confrontations and concerns.

Unsurprisingly, the rearing of Uma and her brothers to be 'mini adults' and her own precocious rejection of youth made Uma restless and uncomfortable. 'I didn't like the powerlessness of being a child,' she says. 'I wanted bigger problems. Whatever problems I had, I would torture myself with them, so I figured I might as well grab some big ones and get accustomed to them.'

Looking back, Uma feels she forfeited some of the more cheerful aspects of family life and of being young. 'When I compare notes with others, no one quite had an upbringing like mine,' she admits.

Of course, Robert's Buddhism figured prominently in his children's education. In as much as it was a force that had changed his life unequivocally, it infiltrated the rest of the Thurmans' backgrounds immeasurably.

Robert no longer wore the robes of a Tibetan monk, and his hair had grown back.[*] However, while acquaintances knew him as 'Bob', he insisted that his family and intimates used his pseudonym, Tenzin. Later, when his vocation moved him on to Columbia University – where one of his colleagues would describe him as 'spookily saintly' – Uma would have to adjust to students addressing her father by his official title of Jey Tsong Khapa.

Unfortunately, being the daughter of Buddhist parents served to exclude Uma from the close-knit Christian community of Amherst, further setting her apart from her peers. 'As a young girl, Uma found herself wishing that her family was like all the others she knew,' recalls her future religious studies teacher, Sher Sweet. 'She wished they were going to church and attending Sunday school like her neighbours did. Uma didn't want to be seen as odd and this obviously made her uncomfortable.'

Nevertheless, Uma was especially proud of her famous father and his many accomplishments. 'I've always been awestruck that he speaks Tibetan without an American accent,' she says. The early respect fostered in her childhood would ultimately lead to her ongoing support as an adult, and she would later describe him as 'this country's foremost authority on Buddhism'.

Uma's parents could well have instructed their children in the ways of their religion, but partly because they followed the Buddhist belief in reincarnation, and partly because they were such unique, free and

---

[*] Years later, he would recall in an interview with the *New York Times* that Uma commented after seeing a picture of him *circa* 1965, 'Oh, look at Daddy – he looks like Henry Miller in drag!'

unjudgemental personalities, they decided against ramming orthodox instruction down the throats of their offspring.

So instead, Uma and her brothers assimilated the best parts of Buddhist morality while not necessarily subscribing to the religion *per se*. They were encouraged to question authority and to seek their own experiences, even in the deeply personal arena of religion. To this day, each of the Thurman children remains winningly open and philosophical, which must certainly be Robert and Nena's original intention.

'From early on we raised them to see themselves as the extraordinary individuals that they are,' Nena explains. 'There is a verse in the Tao Te Ching that pretty well summarizes how we view our role: parents are like innkeepers at the crossroads, and children are the travellers who use the facilities and move on.'

'They were more like zookeepers,' Uma breezily retorts. 'We were brought up with the understanding that we were not their possessions, just these little animals, these little people, in their keeping!'

Years later, Uma would say she is not a Buddhist; having been in close contact with so many orthodox believers, she is loathe to take the name in vain. However, Buddhism is the religion she is closest to, for obvious reasons. 'I have an intuitive feel for the essentials of Buddhism that has been very helpful to me . . .

'I am not actively religious but I certainly have searched for and struggled to acquire and nurture a centre, a sense of myself: courage and immense curiosity about what comes next.'

Describing herself as a 'cultural intriguist', Uma's own take on the controversial Buddhist subscription to reincarnation is that it's not an issue for her. As she has no sense whatsoever of what or whom she might have been before this life, it is not something she particularly believes or disbelieves. 'It seems as plausible as heaven and hell – I don't dismiss any theory,' she says.

'I don't practise or preach it, but Buddhism has had a major effect on who I am and how I think. What I have learned is that I like all religions, but only parts of them.'

*

Nine years old and struggling to evaluate her femininity in a world dominated by three brothers and umpteen Buddhist monks, Uma expressed herself by playing the piano and burying her nose in any book she could get her hands on.

An early favourite was the *Pippi Longstocking* series, 'because she's the strongest girl in the world . . . There are so few female heroes. She

was the one for me!' It isn't hard to see why the rich orphan of the title should appeal to a child of the Thurman clan: Pippi shuns convention by sleeping with her feet on the pillow and her head under the blankets, and she lives alone with a monkey and a horse. Her mantra of 'I'll come out on top!' stuck in Uma's mind as she vowed to prove herself to the world somehow.

'I was an incredibly trusting, open, intuitive, sensitive nine-year-old,' Uma recalls. 'There was no block between me and the universe.'

Unfortunately, Uma's impressionable nature was to suffer more blows as her unusual features showed no outward signs of balancing themselves, and physically she became ungainly. She confided in her mother when the schoolyard bullying became too much. 'When other kids told me I was ugly my mother would say to me: "What do you care what they think? They're all squares,"' says Uma. 'But I always felt outside and other.'

Although Nena had been a model, she had herself experienced a certain degree of gawkiness in her own adolescence. Confidently she sought to reassure her daughter that looks did not matter in the grand scheme of things: it was the person inside that counted. But this wasn't always easy for the little girl to believe.

'Everyone made such a fuss about my mother; they looked slightly askance at me,' she says. 'I was really wracked with pain. When I looked in the mirror, all I saw were thick lips and a big nose . . . My mother thought I was cute, of course.

'I used to take it very hard when people who knew my mother back in her heyday would come over and look at me and go, "Ohhh!"'

The unkind comparisons reached a head one day when Uma was about ten. One of her mother's friends reached over and tapped the young girl on the shoulder.

'Don't worry, dear,' said the woman conspiratorially. 'You know, you could always get a nose job.'

As an adult, Uma would sigh about this formative experience, 'There's always someone out there to make you feel inadequate if you're listening – and I'm always listening.' As a child, the blow to her confidence was devastating.

Nena was having none of it. 'My mother made a great point of making me not take any of that seriously, [she] showed me that getting by on your looks was going to take you absolutely nowhere and the only thing you could ever count upon was your brain and your wits,' says Uma. As Nena patiently explained, a successful and fulfilled woman should only ever rely on her intelligence, forsaking charm, manipulation and cruelty. 'That was a great gift. She knew from her own experience that I would turn pretty perhaps and was worried it would make me soft.' It was a crucial turning point in the relationship between mother and daughter.

Within the next few years, as her children became more self-sufficient, Nena would ditch her modelling background for good and enrol on a degree in psychotherapy, qualifying and eventually becoming a successful therapist in her forties. 'I admired my mother, not because she was beautiful, but because she's an incredible character,' Uma says. 'Painfully direct and honest. She's a great woman.'

As for Uma, she took note of her mother's wise words and gained a little – just a little – confidence in herself. Enough to progress to the next development, and it was a fairly normal one: boys.

Uma even managed to experience her first kiss around this time: 'It was brief, swift, and then it was done. It was a professional job. I needed to be kissed, and I was kissed.' But mostly she lusted from afar. Uma was yet to grow into her looks, and unhappily this was reflected in the otherwise total disregard from the opposite sex.

'No boy ever liked me,' she laments of this period. 'They always liked other girls. I had mad crushes on boys at ten, twelve and fourteen, which would last for months. I learned that whatever I had going for me, it wasn't looks.'

Despite Nena's reassurances, Uma sought 'perfect beauty' and became fixated with Bond girls and Barbie dolls. 'I wanted to be a Bond girl, I thought they were incredibly powerful,' she says of the former. 'I was awed by their large breasts and amazing bodies, their confidence with their sexuality and their ownership of it.' It was the antithesis of everything her mother fought against – in Uma's own words, an 'anti-feminist projection'.

Covertly, Uma's Barbie dolls became the sexually destructive Bond girls that led such exciting, dangerous lives in the movies and always died horrible deaths. 'I was just obsessed with Barbie dolls as icons, even though their proportions meant that they would never menstruate!' she laughs. 'I played with them for hours and made them into sex slaves. They had boyfriends, and they were addicted to them, and then some other guy would come and lock them in a room.' Unconsciously, Uma was acting out fantasies she thought she would never fulfil as an unattractive female, and also exploring a new facet to her personality, which would one day morph into a certain attraction to 'the wrong kind of guy'.

Interviewed on the subject of her erotic Barbie fantasies in *Esquire* magazine in 1998, Uma vehemently defended her youthful right to experiment. 'I don't see what's wrong with young girls being allowed to fantasize and imagine the great unknown of being a woman through these hyper-dramatic ways,' she said. 'To turn your greatest fear into a mental exercise, whether it be a desire to be overpowered mentally or physically or anything else, it's a way of taking control.'

3

WHO AM I?

'I know adolescence is painful for everyone, but mine was just plain weird. There were non-stop changes of schools, no friends and only acting to hide behind.'

UMA THURMAN

In April 1981, when Uma was eleven, Robert Thurman's work took the Thurmans back to Indian shores. Uma had only been a baby the last time this had happened; at least now she was old enough to preserve some clear memories of this exotic year of her life.

In India Uma encountered many adventures. She met reams of Buddhist dignitaries, artists, writers and poets, all on the search for enlightenment, learned a little of the various native languages, and experienced what she now deems to be among the happiest periods of her childhood. 'It was a wonderful place to be an innocent,' she says.

The move to a school in an altogether different country had a major effect on Uma's development. 'That definitely was challenging for me as a kid,' she admits. 'I was looking for my peer group and acceptance and I was insecure. It's hard when you're new all the time.'

The hardest thing, for all the children in fact, was the expectation that they should just 'fit in' to whichever school was nearest to Robert's placement. It was, however, essentially no different to Uma's education thus far. 'We moved around a lot,' she says of her years in Amherst, 'and even if we stayed in the same place we ended up changing schools a great deal. Apparently moving is one of the five most stressful things in life, but it never seemed that way when I was younger.'

The Thurmans' return to Massachusetts the following year corresponded with an enormous growth spurt for Uma. At the age of twelve, the girl who reacquainted herself with her few friends was barely recognizable at 5 feet 8 inches tall. It was yet another reason to be ostracized.

'I was really obscenely tall compared to my other classmates,' she says. 'So I had a size eight shoe when other kids had a four. I think that probably added to my sense of separation, my lack of co-ordination because my feet were too big, hands too big, head too big, the whole thing.'

As if someone had flipped a switch, Uma continued to shoot up rapidly, until she hit her adult height of just a breath shy of 6 feet, her shoe size similarly expanding to an eleven and her hands likewise outsized. She already considered herself positively ugly and now grew tired of the unflattering remarks she still heard in the playground. With her mother's continuing encouragement, Uma resolved to get by on her wits alone.

'That was how I could make it through the day,' she says. 'Being tough when I was in grade school. There was a point one year that I realized I could act tough because I was tall. And that worked for a while.'

Uma also suffered ridicule because of her attire. The teenage fashion scene in 1980s Amherst was predominantly sporty, and students typically wore popular labels such as Lacoste or Izod. But clothes were of no importance to the unmaterialistic Thurmans, so the gangly girl would turn up to whichever school she had been enrolled at that academic year in hippie-style garb, no doubt handed down from her equally statuesque mother.

'I felt very out of place,' she says. 'The kids couldn't stand me. I always had weird-looking 1970s clothes, and I never really fit into clothes very well; they're either short or long.

'It was very difficult. I failed on a daily basis trying to assimilate.'

Ironically, although Uma hated sartorially resembling Nena a decade ago, she was gradually beginning to mimic her, at least in terms of character. This had as much to do with her towering height as with her mother's loving pep talks.

'When you're tall, you look much older, have a vocabulary and look people in the eye, it's not out of confidence,' Uma says pointedly. 'It's out of simple honesty and directness. It's a challenge, because you're not emotionally capable of dealing with what the world will throw at you just because they think you can take it.'

Falling almost gratefully into the reject crowd, Uma found she could empathize with what she describes as a 'new wave' fringe group, kids who smoked clove cigarettes, listened to progressive rock and hankered after a career in creative design. Awkward and trying to impress in this diverse environment, Uma's personality split in two. On the one hand, she was suddenly overbearing and overzealous, loudly bellowing the wrong lyrics to current chart hits until she drove her friends to distraction. On the other, she became obsessive and distracted, so enthused by the fact that she developed tics when she rode horses that she made up some new quirks of her own.

'I liked the idea of having neuroses, and I was worried about not having any, so I developed a slight obsession with tapping my stick ten times during the ride,' she says. 'I thought I was more interesting if I saw myself as damaged and difficult . . .

'I really wanted to wear glasses. I envied glasses, I envied braces, I envied flaws, all those things that looked like challenges.' It was tough being twelve, and Uma recklessly risked alienating herself from even this new group of outcasts.

*

In September 1982 Uma started seventh grade at Amherst Regional Junior High School. Coming from her background of philosophical intellectualism, Uma found herself excessively bored by the restrictions of structured lessons and her immature classmates.

Making new friends no longer interested her, as there was always enough going on at home to keep her occupied. This year her parents requested that she kindly move out of her bedroom while an entire family of Cambodian refugees moved in. The occurrence was not out of place in the Thurman household.

'When she was a little girl she found it annoying that her parents had Buddhist monks in their house so much of the time,' recalls Sher Sweet. 'She wasn't happy that she and her brothers often had to give up their beds to monks!' This disruption meant Uma spent more time with her siblings, to whom she was devoted. They too adored their strange-looking sister, so preoccupied with life and its many problems.

'I was the only girl, but I was basically one of the guys,' says Uma. 'I felt so atypical anyway.' Playing rough with the boys exposed Uma to more violence than she had ever subjected her Barbie dolls to, and one day Uma proved herself equal in every way.

'This weird Mafia guy backed out of a parking lot and hit my brother,' she recalls, 'and then got out of the car and started shouting at us.

'I got into this guy's face and started shouting at him! My brother was shocked, he had never seen me like that. I was high for hours.'

Despite Uma's brave outburst and her own admission that 'I have three brothers, so I've been thrown through some walls', Uma was not by nature a violent girl and usually adhered to her parents' lesson of talking her way out of scrapes.

She and her three brothers were more likely to be found hooked up to their Atari 2600, playing video games with friends, or with 'boys' toys' typical of the time.

'I do remember playing with our Transformers,' says Steve Gross, a friend of the youngest Thurman boy, Mipam, or Max as he now preferred to be known. 'He had some of the Decepticon planes; Starscream, and Thunder-something. That was fun!' Ben Maraniss, another friend of Uma's brothers while they were growing up, clearly recalls the only girl around being a 'skinny kid' who would carry big bags of groceries home for her family, whose clothes never fit properly, and whose house was always messy.

*

The Thurmans spent the summer of 1983 at their Woodstock retreat. Their house guest during part of their stay was the distinguished actor Richard Gere.

Having initially established himself in theatre, Gere had moved on to films, most notably with the lead in 1980's *American Gigolo*, then starring opposite Debra Winger in *An Officer And A Gentleman*. The success of the latter film the previous year had elevated the charismatic Gere to heartthrob status, so for the thirteen-year-old Uma, his presence must have been something of a treat.

Brought up in a strict Methodist New York family, Gere had indulged his twin passions of philosophy and film at the University of Massachusetts before dropping out to pursue a career in acting. Gere gradually became aware of a hole in his life in the early 1970s.

'When I was about twenty-four, unhappy and discontented, I became focused on Buddhism,' he recalls. 'Back then, the universe made no sense to me. I always wanted to know, who am I?' After some ten years of spiritual study, Gere's path finally crossed with that of Robert Thurman. Both were students of the Dalai Lama.

As the two men conversed deep into the night, Gere impressed upon Thurman the importance of the Tibetan political struggle for liberation from China, something the professor admitted he hadn't really considered before, being more caught up in the complexities of his religion. The two resolved to use their combined celebrity to aid the Tibetans in their plight, and together they set about laying the foundations for what would in 1987 become Tibet House on East 32nd

Street in Manhattan, New York City: a cultural institution dedicated to sustaining Tibetan civilization.

As Thurman and Gere worked together to establish this unique and worthy facility, Uma and her brothers came to know the famous actor intimately. 'Richard was like a big brother to me,' she says.

One day the two were chatting about Uma's ambitions. Comfortable with her new friend, the teenager let slip that she admired his craft and had in fact been thinking of training as an actress herself.

Absolutely horrified, Gere turned to the girl and demanded: 'Why do you want to spoil your life?'

The answer lay both in Uma's blood and in her introversion. 'When I was a kid, it was the only thing that appealed to me. I was painfully shy. I'd find characters and escape into them,' she says of the latter reason.

Uma grew up hearing tales of her maternal grandmother, Elizabeth Farrar, the New York stage actress. 'I guess having had an actress in the family, people used to tease me that I'd become an actress and perhaps that put it in my mind,' she suggests.

And so Uma harboured the romantic secret that she had wanted to act since 'before age was important'. Having received polite applause as a ghost in an elementary school play, it became a distant dream for her future. As she was shunted from one establishment to another, from public school to private, from Massachusetts to Woodstock to India and back again, drama was the extracurricular activity she clung to as one of the few constants in her life.

'I found in acting a place where I could express myself free from my own inhibitions,' she explains. 'For me, the metaphor of emotion and storytelling and theatre, and acting out those things, was a domain in which I could be independent. I loved going to any performance – music, dance – I was just transfixed.'

One thing which particularly appealed was that, despite the historical connection with Farrar and the odd guest appearance by her parents in a documentary, the Thurmans remained largely untouched by the entertainment industry.

'It was unexplored territory, a place in which I found strength and confidence ... In any family different members embody different qualities, a shy child sometimes becomes invisible because they don't want to fight for the same space.' For this shy child, surely suffocating under the strength of her large and dominant family, drama became an arena in which to prove herself. It was a sphere totally disconnected to Buddhism, Tibet, psychology or any of the multiple aspects affecting Uma's daily life, and one that she could claim all for herself.

As would be typical in most families, regardless of their background, Uma's announcement was initially met with derision. 'I think it was something no one thought I would pull off,' she admits, tellingly.

Uma hadn't grown up as a movie buff, and in fact her only memory from early trips to the cinema is sneaking in with some underage friends to see Stanley Kubrick's graphically violent *A Clockwork Orange* before being discovered and unceremoniously kicked out of the theatre. Television was never a mainstay in the Thurman household, so Uma was left to draw her inspiration from the Hollywood greats, names that seemed to have infiltrated American homes on an almost subconscious level. Katharine Hepburn, Bette Davis and Lauren Bacall were her favourites from the silver screen.

'If you go back to the time when women were given less credit and you look at the kind of dames that graced the screen, they were incredibly powerful women,' she enthuses. 'Lightweight women weren't stars back in the day.'

Uma's heroines embodied qualities the teenager admired and hoped one day to possess: 'They were tough; they were intimidating; they were smart; they could turn a phrase; they could carry their sexuality, shamelessly, fearlessly . . .' It seems Uma's private Barbie and Bond-girl fixation had finally found a respectable outlet. 'They could be mean; they were always beautiful.' The would-be actress also admired a more contemporary generation of performers, singling out Meryl Streep and Diane Keaton as special talents.

*

When Uma turned fourteen, her school of the moment was Northfield Mount Hermon School, situated half an hour north of Amherst. She enrolled in ninth grade quietly confident that she had found her niche and was only killing time while she figured out how to break into acting.

Northfield Mount Hermon was a tiny coeducational boarding school, known for its tolerance of nonconformity while preparing its students for college. 'It was, and still is, a progressive college-preparatory boarding school with an emphasis both on diversity and on scholarship assistance to students in need,' says David Rowland, the theatre program director there since 1978. Originally two separate single-sex schools founded by Dwight L. Moody, the institutions combined in 1971 with the aim of providing an excellent secondary education regardless of students' race, religion or financial circumstances. Northfield Mount Hermon's biggest advantage was the small class sizes and relatively large teacher-to-pupil ratio. Also, as Rowland comments, there was no set school dress code, encouraging students to relax outside of the framework of uniformity: 'Kids' clothes tend toward ripped jeans and sweatshirts.' More often than not, the teachers' outfits mirrored this casual attitude too.

The school prided itself on its many sports teams and diverse student clubs, especially those in dance and music. The alumni list is impressive: David D. Hartman (television host and producer), Laura Linney (Oscar-nominated actress) and Tad Mosel (Pulitzer Prize-winning playwright) sit alongside other luminaries in the arts, such as Natalie Cole (Grammy Award-winning vocalist), Will Ackerman (film composer and record-company founder) and Neil Sheehan (Pulitzer Prize-winning author).[*]

It should have been perfect for Uma, with her Buddhist background, who was used to having to fight to be heard over the din of the dinner table. But cooped up in the Moody dormitory, she hated it from the word go. She describes her time there as 'pretty miserable', claiming that the only good thing about it was meeting her best friend, Galaxy. Oddly, this was also the only period of Uma's childhood which she describes as vaguely 'normal'.

Instead of entering the latest in a long line of schools with a fresh start in mind, Uma carried with her the stigma of previous alienation. Physically she still towered over her contemporaries, and socially she found herself at a disadvantage because she wasn't remotely athletic or even 'particularly bright'.

'I was not happy at school,' she recalls. 'I spent a lot of my adolescence in a pretty confused state of mind. My physical appearance made me feel awkward, so there were always these walls I put up. After a while you forget these walls are still there, preventing you from being as open or as secure in your own self as you might want to be.'

Uma swung from being 'too eager to please' to prickly and standoffish, and consequently was no more popular at Northfield Mount Hermon than she had been in any of her other schools. Furthermore, her peculiar hankering after adult concerns and social neuroses left her deeply unhappy within herself. When Uma later looked back on this period, she refers to her state of mind as a fraught 'self-loathing'.

Her religious studies teacher, Sher Sweet, also doubled as Uma's dorm mistress and witnessed her social inhibition. 'Uma was very

---

[*] In the year above Uma was Jamie Walters, an actor who would later make his name in TV's *Beverly Hills 90210* before moving into movies and pop music.

poised and comfortable speaking with adults, and during dorm meetings she wasn't at all hesitant to speak up,' she recalls. 'But some girls felt Uma was arrogant.'

'I spent my youth trying to fit in,' says Uma. 'I longed for approval. Even the kids who rejected me, the minute they were nice I'd put it all behind me. That's how desperate I was.' It was a long way away from the free-spirited ideals of her parents, but now Uma rebelled. To their immense dissatisfaction, she craved a normal name and a typical middle-class American home life.

Despite her denial of her upbringing, one of the few times Uma felt at ease was in Sweet's class. 'This course was a chance for students to learn about the discipline of religious studies and to become aware of the importance of religion in the lives of millions,' explains Sweet.

'Important concepts that were included in the course were: world-view, lifestyle, myths, symbols, rituals. We studied sections of the Bible, and we studied the Holocaust and the struggle for faith by reading Elie Wiesel's book *Night*. Uma was active in class and enjoyed sharing her thoughts. It was clear from an initial encounter with Uma that she was very intelligent. She worked hard and made good grades.

'Uma was interested in learning religious ideas but she wasn't interested in being religious herself.'

At the end of the year, the class was instructed to write an essay entitled 'Who Am I?'. 'Uma found this to be a particularly daunting and intimidating task,' says Sweet. 'She became quite upset and was convinced that she could never write such a paper. But with the support of the dorm faculty, Uma made it through.'

*

Uma's deep-seated unhappiness finally shifted during a fun trip to New York with her best friend during the summer holidays. The months spent away from school also corresponded with another well-timed growth spurt, during which Uma finally grew into her strong features.

'My face became big enough to carry my big nose and my cheekbones changed,' she says. 'I felt more comfortable.' However, after spending the first fourteen years of her life convinced she was hideous, it would take a long time before Uma would ever truly believe a compliment about her appearance, and, according to her drama teacher, David Rowland, she retained an odd obsession about her outsized feet.

Back at Northfield Mount Hermon, Uma's continuing rebellion amusingly dealt the ultimate backhander to her parents' colourful lifestyle as she entered an 'all-American' phase. Tall, pretty and blonde, Uma taunted her mother (who would reproach the Thurman brood for indulging in 'American behaviour') by becoming a cheerleader. '[I did it] just to annoy my parents,' she laughs. 'When I brought pom-poms home, my mother looked as if she was about to faint!'

Only now did the child of Nordic descent and Tibetan influence really understand what it meant to be an American, and she embraced it with open arms. 'I wanted to be part of Americana,' she says. 'My parents were anti-Americana. They were so different I thought I had to work toward assimilating. I was very angry. I was always very angry . . .'

And so Uma shook her pom-poms and marvelled over all-American products like Pop-Tarts and Wonder Bread, much to her parents' disgust. It was a great irony that for this particular teenager, mutiny was all about being as 'normal' as possible, rather than taking drugs, having sex, getting tattoos or shoplifting.

Uma even took her revolt as far as changing her detested name whenever possible, such as for after-school clubs like dance class, where she wasn't already known. 'I hated my name and used to tell people that it was Diana Kelly,' she says. Even for official purposes: 'I cheated and turned my middle name into Karen, which was the closest thing I could get away with.

'It's on my high-school registration: Uma Karen Thurman.'

4

IGNORANCE, BRAVERY AND A SIDE ORDER OF STUPIDITY

'They used to say that talent plus ten cents would get you a cup of coffee. The only difference now is that the price of coffee has risen considerably. What distinguished Uma in my mind was that she combined talent with the willingness to work long and hard to get results.'

DAVID ROWLAND, THEATRE PROGRAM DIRECTOR,
NORTHFIELD MOUNT HERMON SCHOOL

'[Acting] was always a thing that could be mine, rather than the thing that could be far better said by my father.'

UMA THURMAN

Uma's big break came when she was fifteen. It was late spring 1985, and her high-school drama club were putting on a production of Arthur Miller's *The Crucible*.

Miller's 1953 play is set in the Puritan New England town of Salem, Massachusetts, at the time of the 1692 witch trials. The playwright draws on this dark period of American history to make a loosely veiled attack on 1950s McCarthyism, a hysterical modern-day 'witch hunt' that began when Republican Senator Joseph McCarthy charged the State Department with harbouring over 205 Communists.

The character Uma had her heart set upon playing was the finely drawn Abigail Williams, the minister's teenage niece who has an affair with John Proctor, a farmer, husband and father.

'Uma auditioned like any other student for the play,' recalls David Rowland. 'Our auditions are open rather than private, "cold" rather than prepared. Students do some improvisational movement and read various scenes from the play at hand.

'There was a quality of both strength and vulnerability to Uma's audition that really struck me. I also recall thinking that being tall for her age might help her deal with Abigail's feelings of isolation and anger.'

Preparing for her role, Uma was in her element.

'We talked a good deal about the character,' says Rowland, 'the Puritan period, the natural resistance of adolescence to self-righteous adult authority, the juxtaposition of "godly" town and "heathen" forest, the possibility of natural hallucinogens [the fungus ergot] in Tituba's brew which she served to the girls and her affair with Proctor.

'Uma's progress during rehearsals was clear and impressive. She took direction seriously, tried different things, worked outside as well as in rehearsals, and really made Abigail her own. It was a pleasure to watch her improvement.'

One of Rowland's enduring memories is that Uma was so keen to properly explore Abigail's central importance to the play that she actually convinced him to include an extra explicatory scene.

'There is a scene between Abigail and Proctor in the woods that is usually omitted from productions due to the play's overall length,' he explains. 'Our script included this scene as an appendix.

'At one point in the rehearsal process, Uma came to me and asked if we might still include the scene. Although I had not planned to do so, I am perennially a sucker for student motivation. I told her that if she and the student playing Proctor would give me enough afternoon time – over and above our existing schedule of evening rehearsals – I would include the scene.

'Uma talked the other actor into it and worked extremely hard, here as in the other rehearsals, to make the scene work. In the end, it was a very worthwhile addition – largely due to her high level of motivation and effort.'

Uma recalls her confidence during rehearsals: 'When I was on stage I didn't feel any of the inhibitions that every kid tends to feel.' It was a dramatic about-turn for the self-conscious outsider of old.

Her friend Siobhan Reagan remembers her jogging across campus to stay in shape for the part. 'She looked spectacular, with her long hair flying,' she says, 'just like Venus.'

Aside from Uma's pure joy at finally being allowed to prove herself on stage, there was an extra reason for the new spring in her step. The handsome young man playing John Proctor, Cole Bankson, had fallen for her, much to the envy of all her schoolmates. It was also perhaps significant in his willingness to give up his spare time to work on the additional scene.

'[Cole] was very dark with a devastating English accent,' says Reagan, 'Uma was so excited when they started dating. He was her first serious boyfriend.'

Uma's leading man loosely matched her own foreign and educational upbringing, in that he hailed from Barnes, south-west London, and had been educated at Eton before enrolling at Northfield Mount Hermon. Today he recalls of his famous ex-girlfriend, 'We got on pretty well. It's kind of fun to say that I kissed Uma Thurman. I've dined out on one or two more colourful tales of being together at the time! But to be honest, it was simple and innocent.'

On opening night, tensions were high and Uma's heart was full to bursting. Her performance was outstanding, and it was just as well. Unknown to most of the cast and crew, two New York talent scouts had been present in the audience. Blown away by her portrayal of the manipulative Abigail, they approached Uma backstage. There they introduced themselves as two 'people who represent young actors'.

'Go on,' said Uma, flushed with adrenaline, her ears still ringing with applause.

'We think you're great,' they said, 'and if you ever want to come to New York and go to auditions, you should.'

'Sure,' chirruped the uncharacteristically ineloquent Uma, resolving to take up their invitation forthwith.

*

To have been a fly on the wall at the Thurman dinner table that night! There was excitable, headstrong, fifteen-year-old Uma, announcing her imminent departure from school and everything she knew as home in Amherst. To oppose her were her parents, the pair of them intensely academic, but with a combined past that only goes to show that history repeats itself.

Fifteen was the very age at which Nena was talent-spotted in her school playground and had forsaken her studies in Sweden to become a fashion model in England. At sixteen, Robert had been expelled for a high-school prank, then wangled a scholarship to Harvard but later dropped out to become a monk. Even a generation earlier, and most pertinently, both of Robert's parents had dropped out of college in order to pursue his mother's dream of becoming an actress in New York.

Although Nena had recently obtained her degree in psychotherapy and Robert was now a respected professor, given this family track record, how could they possibly persuade their daughter to remain submerged in academia?

The answer was, they couldn't.

Uma's mother, in particular, consulted her closest friends and other parents for advice and was invariably told to keep her young daughter with her at all costs, at least until she could graduate. But Nena had never been interested in cultivating anything but total independence in her children, and so ultimately she found herself incapable of standing in Uma's way.

'Uma always seemed to know what she wanted to do,' she justifies. 'Her sense of destiny was very much in place. I tried to keep her back as long as I could, but when she started to show signs of the family restlessness, I really didn't feel I could say no, because I had done the same thing myself.'

'I couldn't wait to finish school and do something with my life,' remembers Uma. 'That's why I decided not to attend university and become an actress.

'I was confident I could get there, but there are two parts of the journey: why you leave and where you go. I wanted to get out of where I was, so it was more like being pushed from behind than being ambitious in going ahead.' Once she left, Uma knew it would be impossible to turn around and go back.

And so the staff at Northfield Mount Hermon were duly informed that Uma would not be returning in the autumn. She bid fond farewells to her friends Galaxy and Siobhan, and kissed goodbye to Cole, who would graduate and eventually become a musician in Seattle.

'Life is the ultimate university,' she declared to anyone who would listen.

*

Uma arrived in New York in the summer of 1985, finding an apartment in Manhattan with her parents' assistance. She had always loved the annual summer vacations to nearby Woodstock with her parents, usually timed to correspond with a series of her father's lectures.

'The highlight of my growing up was going into the city,' she recalls. 'Manhattan was the home of my dreams. The beautiful campuses my father worked on were like playgrounds.'

Clearly a permanent solo relocation was far removed from a month-long family holiday, but Uma maintains she never thought twice about this astounding move, no matter the complications it would entail.

'Going to New York was something of a blind fury,' she recalls. 'I have this way of visoring myself so that I can simply walk without having to judge the difficulty of the trail, which is a very good way to do some things and not good for others.'

The agents who had brought Uma this far suggested that she enrol in the Professional Children's School on West 60th Street, a foundation which specifically prepares youngsters for the New York stage while providing a balanced education. The staff completely understood and supported their students' necessary absences from school to participate in plays, film and TV work, allowing their more successful charges to continue their studies by correspondence.

Uma demurred, as school was the one thing she had hoped to leave behind, but agreed it was probably for the best. Besides, she was convinced she would already be working full-time as an actress before term was due to start in September.

Uma launched herself onto the audition circuit with gusto – it almost felt like a homecoming, now that she was in control of her destiny.

'It just seemed like give me the pages, put me in the room, and it could happen for me,' she recalls of this magical time. 'I think there was an advantage to being a young teenage actress who was sort of playing hooky from high school.'

Having literally fallen into her career, Uma approached potential job opportunities in a relaxed, happy manner, as opposed to the hungrier desperation of older, more established actors. Rejection for her was an unknown – why should she be hurt by it? It was all so new and she was only just beginning.

Uma says that she dealt with the transition to professional life 'little piece by little piece'. That way it wouldn't seem like such a big deal and nerves wouldn't affect her chances. 'Well, now,' she would tell herself, 'Sure, I'll go to a meeting, and well, I haven't actually done anything, but sure, I'm going to be an actress.'

Whenever she was questioned as to why she had chosen this path, 'Because I feel like it!' would be the naïve response.

*

September rolled around without any definite prospect of work, and Uma started at the Professional Children's High School. She was an unusual student, living alone and washing dishes in Hell's Kitchen to help pay the rent. Her only previous employment had been babysitting the local children in Amherst, so it must have been quite a shock to the system. Soon she was promoted to the position of waitress, but there still wasn't enough money coming in.

Uma consulted her parents. There was a very obvious answer but it was not one that instantly appealed. When Nena was fresh off the boat from Sweden, she had paid her way by modelling, and now that Uma resembled her so closely, it could be a means to an end.

'My mother pointed me in that direction,' says Uma. 'I was surprised because I didn't think I looked anything like the models I had seen.' Having faced many years of derision in the schoolyard, she was amazed to step into an atmosphere of zealous fervour in casting sessions. Using her contacts within the industry, Nena made a few choice introductions and before Uma really knew what was happening, she was signed to the Click agency and being photographed by the likes of Arthur Elgort, Patrick Demarchelier and Sheila Metzner for *Glamour* magazine.

Uma would be the first to admit that, having spent the first fourteen years of her life convinced she was hideous, it was hard to suddenly be the centre of attention in such a positive light. But she was growing up and recognized that the best thing she could gain from her experience, other than an income, was confidence.

'It worked out,' she says simply, 'it got me used to being looked at. I was always shy before that.' Uma was proud nobody could now criticize her for sponging off her parents or living in a dream world. Sure, she was following the dream of becoming an actress, but she was putting herself through drama school by not one but two jobs. And the money was good – 'a fortune', in her own words.

However, Uma was an intelligent girl and no one could convince her that what she was doing was using her brain.

'It was a really uninteresting way to spend time,' she says. 'I didn't like what I saw of modelling. I judge the whole industry as being insignificant. The basic philosophy was along the lines of: "Buy more stuff!" "Don't you want some more stuff?" "It will make you look ten years younger and men will like you!"

'I was never very good at convincing people they needed more stuff.'

Looking back on the period, Click owner Frances Grill comments, 'She was a little aloof. She was a lot more intelligent than most girls her age, she was a loner and mostly hung out with adults. I think she felt modelling was not something someone should take seriously.'

Of course, arriving in New York as a fifteen-year-old innocent and being sent off to all sorts of venues without a chaperone opened Uma up to dangers she had never encountered before. 'I didn't know how risky it was,' she admits. 'I wasn't a woman, I was a kid with stockings on. Ignorance is sometimes an incredible strength . . .'

She has since confessed that she found this period of modelling, studying and auditioning no less than terrifying. 'It was initiation by fire. It was dramatic and difficult.' Over the next three years she would live in twelve apartments and experience countless complications with her landlords and accommodation. 'I had drugs thrown at me and men trying to pick me up on the street. But it was the best thing I've done because there was no one to protect me. I perfected being street-smart very quickly.'

Uma has often alluded to men who 'prey on' young models. While it appears that she escaped from various altercations relatively unscathed, it's easy to see how unpleasant circumstances can arise in the heady world of fashion modelling.

One of Uma's first-ever assignments was with the eminent French photographer Patrick Demarchelier, known in the business as 'The Man Who Loves Women' after a prominent run in the early 1980s capturing the world's most beautiful women for British *Vogue*. Due to an overbooking at the hotel where the shoot took place, Demarchelier and Uma had no choice but to share a bedroom. Street-smart Uma was aghast, despite Demarchelier's protestations that the situation was not a set-up, and slept with one eye open while he spent the night on the sofa. Of course, in this instance, the photographer was entirely blameless and it was only an agent's booking that was at fault, but other scenarios were not always as innocent.[*]

Uma's modelling career continued to prove lucrative, and in 1988 she would even briefly appear on the books of the Elite agency, although by then she would have no real need of the extra income and exposure. She looks back on these days with a trace of sorrow for her lost youth: 'I was an escapee of childhood. There are not that many people that had that type of later-childhood development like I did. I wish I hadn't been so eager to get old, to go.

'I only started acting out of ignorance, bravery and a side order of stupidity. I did a school play and some modelling because I was tall, and based on that I tried to launch a whole career.

'It was crazy.'

*

Sometimes, if the mountain won't come to Muhammad, Muhammad must go to the mountain. After Uma had been settled in Manhattan for a few months, her family relocated permanently to Woodstock, New

---

[*] Uma and Patrick Demarchelier have remained good friends to this day, and Uma still teases him about the supposed 'set-up'.

York. They had missed their only daughter dreadfully, and as Robert recalls, his existence was 'chafing somewhat in the comfortable provinciality of Amherst. It was time to return to my mother city.'

With her family now only two hours' drive away, Uma was greatly heartened, for although she loved the city, she readily admits, 'It can be an exhausting place. It's almost like a purgatory. You have to have a lot of people praying for you to get out . . .' With hundreds of hungry hopefuls competing for relatively few roles, it could be a tough life.

April 1986 came and went, and Uma turned sixteen. She had been self-sufficient for nearly a year. Her modelling began to get her noticed, and finally a part landed on her doorstep.

The combination of dedicated attendance at acting classes and a rough-and-ready street life stood Uma in good stead for her first film audition in the late spring. The psychological thriller *A Rose By Any Other Name* probably looked promising on paper to the wannabe actress, and so she tried out for the vampish lead who manipulates men with her sexuality and cunning.

Uma's crude test performance immediately secured her the role and she joined a predominantly novice cast and crew; it was Peter Ily Hemuer's directorial and screenwriting debut and, like Uma, many others involved were new to the business. The only experienced actor was Paul Richards, and there would also be a notable early appearance by Steve Buscemi, now a master of nervy character roles.

Shot in 16mm, this low-budget flick has a home-movie feel to it. The plot revolves around a curious trio consisting of Laura (Thurman), an old acquaintance named Sid (Paul Dillon) and Laura's middle-aged next-door neighbour William (Richards). The unusual opening scene shows gritty promise as Laura's double life is revealed: she drinks to pass the day and works by night, preying on lonely men whom she seduces, drugs and robs. The intrigue ends there.

While the acting is adequate, the direction lacks focus and pace. Thurman has little to work with (Dillon in particular is very weak), but she begins to shine in her scenes with the veteran Richards. Unfortunately, just as she alludes to the self-denial that underpins her arrogance, the clumsy dialogue and flashback explaining their darkening relationship ruin her good work. The combination of a sorry script, predictable plot and one-dimensional characters quickly equates to tedious trash rather than polished thriller.

After Sid, a shady blast from the past, turns up, Laura's life begins to fall apart, but his motivation is finding Johnny and forming a band – given that the viewer does not know or care about Sid, Johnny *or* the band, this is a flimsy distraction, one that is only tolerable due to Buscemi's gratifying presence on screen.

When the film returns to Laura's plight, it turns out that her mother has been killed and she is being stalked – but suspenseful this is not. Here the bad B-movie takes a rapid turn for the worse, and is crucified with a clumsy ending. Feisty Uma must have despaired at her character's obtuse course of action, not to mention the final fight scene which is laughably lame.

Released in 1987, the film was renamed *Kiss Daddy Goodnight* in a bid to make it sound more juicy, but it remains a terribly uninspiring start to Uma's career.[*]

*

With *Kiss Daddy Goodnight* heading up Uma's otherwise empty CV, she approached an agent with the aim of landing better parts in higher-profile films. She applied to Cary Woods for representation early in 1987.

'My initial reaction was: I'm not interested in meeting some sixteen-year-old model,' Woods recalls, 'but everybody kept telling me she was really special, and she was.

'She was astonishingly poised and confident for her age. The feedback on Uma was always glowing. I don't think there was a time from when she came to town that people didn't consider her something special as an actress.' Drama school fell by the wayside around this time as potential scripts began to arrive on a regular basis. Uma had enough money to live on from her modelling and her acting career took on a life of its own.

The next part Uma read for and accepted was the lead female role in a teen comedy called *Johnny Be Good*. She was to play the supporting 'girlfriend' role of Georgia Elkans, opposite Anthony Michael Hall, former child actor on stage and TV screen.

Johnny Be Good would be directed by Bud Smith, an editor who had enjoyed a previous incarnation as a champion racing driver. His film-editing career had brought him much kudos, including a BAFTA Award for his work on *Flashdance* in 1983. Five years later, he was making his directorial debut with *Johnny Be Good*, a movie featuring Hall and Robert Downey Jr, the latter also famous as a youth and both

---

[*] Recent rumours suggest that around this time Uma also appeared as Courtney Daniels in the teen slasher sequel *Cheerleader Camp II*, but the authors were unable to find any evidence supporting this claim, or even proof that the film exists.

of them recent stalwarts of the popular TV show *Saturday Night Live*.

The plot centres on Johnny Walker (Hall), a hotshot high-school quarterback despite his diminutive height and scrawniness. Spotted by football talent scouts, he receives a string of tempting offers of booze, broads, and various other non-academic inducements to attend their colleges. Johnny's dilemma is whether he should accept one of the many places falling into his lap, or stay within the relative safety of the local state college with his girlfriend. In the end, Johnny makes the right choice, in the process exposing the corrupt nature of American football scholarships.

It was money, it was work, it was experience in front of a camera, but Uma was less than enthusiastic as filming commenced. 'People kept telling me that *Johnny Be Good* would be important for me, and I kept saying, "It's not important,"' she would later recall.

*

If Uma's time spent filming *Johnny Be Good* was unengaging and unfulfilling, her next job would provide a welcome change.

Terry Gilliam, the visually creative wit and the only American among the otherwise thoroughly British *Monty Python* comedy team, had cemented a directing career away from his fellow Pythons with the cult films *Jabberwocky* and *Time Bandits*, each one dividing critics and audiences with Gilliam's unique blend of surreal humour and fantasy. *Brazil*, a nightmarish futuristic satire and his most recent offering, had won prestigious awards yet flopped at the box office, triggering a four-year gap before Gilliam's next project, *The Adventures Of Baron Munchausen*.

Not known for any form of restraint, be it artistic or literary, the director fought against any restrictions in his path. 'The success of the Hollywood marketing machine is to limit what we see,' he once harrumphed. 'Not just to limit what we can see, but also to limit our expectations – to limit what we *want* to see.' *Baron Munchausen* would show Gilliam continuing to test the boundaries of his audience's imagination, although it would be a tough project to make. The director had also co-written the screenplay, which followed the unlikely adventures of an eighteenth-century aristocrat, an odd assortment of henchmen and a little girl in their efforts to save a town under siege from the Turks.

Baron Karl Friedrich Munchausen (a name strikingly similar to that of Uma's own ancestor) was in fact a real German baron who published a volume of tall tales about his exploits as a soldier, hunter and sportsman in 1785. Over the passage of time his stories had been further exaggerated, and his name itself eventually inspired the medical term for an illness associated with telling dangerously convincing falsehoods.*

In the spirit of the Baron himself, Gilliam endeavoured to tell Munchausen's fabulous fables as fact rather than fiction; being swallowed by a whale, flying a hot-air balloon to the moon, and narrowly escaping the Grim Reaper were but three of the many improbable but decidedly majestic escapades during the course of the film.

The commanding British stage actor John Neville took on the mantle of the famed prevaricator alongside an impressive cast that included ex-Python Eric Idle, Charles McKeown, Jonathan Pryce, Oliver Reed and cameos by Robin Williams and Sting. Filming was set to start during the latter half of 1987.

Uma was only seventeen-and-a-half when casting director Margery Simkin brought her talents to Gilliam's attention. He had been searching for someone who resembled Botticelli's Venus for *Baron Munchausen*, and as soon as he laid eyes on Uma, his mind was made up. 'She looks as though she floated down from the clouds,' he has said.

However, for Gilliam, it wasn't just Uma's fresh beauty that so appealed. As her agent, Cary Woods, explains: 'When men fall in love with Uma, her image is 30 per cent of the package. It's the other 70 per cent – something much deeper than her beauty – that sends you off the deep end.'

Originally, Uma was set to make only a brief appearance as the goddess of love, but when Gilliam saw just how closely she resembled the subject of the fifteenth-century painting *The Birth Of Venus*, he extended the role and augmented it with a new one. Uma would play two different parts during the film: Venus, who rises from the sea like Botticelli's heroine, naked and serene; and Rose, a common stagehand who swoons over the Baron while he spins his magical yarns.

*

The shoot for *Baron Munchausen* was acutely problematic. Spreading from Pinewood Studios in England to Cinecittà Studios in Rome and on location in southern Spain for the battle scenes, soon Terry Gilliam's

---

* Munchausen's Syndrome is a condition in which the sufferer intentionally feigns physical or psychological illness for the purpose of gaining attention. It should not be confused with hypochondria – a hypochondriac truly believes he or she is sick.

lack of restraint resulted in the film going grossly over-budget, exceeding it by $45 million.

Studio in-fighting, Gilliam's own admitted depression and the never-ending bills combined to make a marvellous epic, but a phenomenal headache for all concerned. With only two films under her belt, Uma divided her elders with her attitude.

'It was a long and at times stressful shoot,' recalls John Neville, 'and Uma behaved with absolute professionalism. My wife and I were very fond of her. She behaved impeccably to we older folks and exhibited every sign of coming from a wonderful family who gave her an excellent upbringing!'

The leading man may have fallen under her spell, as indeed he does twice over in the film, but the director, whose breath had so been taken away during their first meeting, has conflicting memories of the teenage model. 'She has the ability to get people wound up, slightly wrong-footed,' Gilliam observes, noting how he'd spot her 'cuddled up in a corner like a little girl' between shootings, then an hour later she'd become a 'gorgeous woman', laughing and flirting, and working her feminine wiles at the bar. 'She was freaked out by all the [men] lusting after her, but on one side she liked it,' he says.

Gilliam was party to a telephone conversation between Uma and her mother, during which her mother – appalled at the nudity required in this latest role – pleaded with her to return to high school and resume a 'normal life'. It was most unlike Nena to be so prudish, and without her mother's unconditional backing, the teenager became understandably nervous and even petulant.

It was her first-ever nude scene. As the gown preserving her modesty fell to the floor and an assistant set about strategically arranging Uma's hair, she expressed her concern to her director in no uncertain terms.

'Too late, Uma,' came the terse reply. 'You've got your clothes off. You're a fallen woman.'

Fortunately for Uma, Gilliam softened when he saw her childish look of horror. 'The technicians were all up on the scaffolding with their jaws dropping, so I had her look right into the camera,' he recalls. 'She came through with wonderful innocence and directness.'

Uma, however, speaks of nothing but admiration for her director. 'I was blessed to experience at a young age what it's like to work with a real auteur filmmaker, and that environment was so intoxicating that it really coloured my choices from then on.'

As for her disrobing, she would dismiss any sniggers with a wave of her sizeable porcelain hand. 'I started out sort of healthily indifferent and artistic about it,' she remembers. From the beginning, Uma maintains she was never interested in 'sexploitation' movies, whatever the pay packet, and would only ever strip if it was integral to the plot.

'It's appropriate if the spirit of the entire film is right, [not if] you're doing a movie where you think it would be artistically good to do a scene nude but you feel that it would be exploited by the studio in an unpleasant manner.' Of course, at this early stage in her career, Uma did not have any influence over what ended up on the cutting-room floor and what didn't, but luckily in this instance her momentary exposure is handled with taste.

Although prominent and encompassing two different characters, Uma's part in *Baron Munchausen* was relatively small. Yet she gained much from working with such respected peers and had a few adventures of her own. One that she would draw upon much later was watching the animal handlers resuscitate a panther they had over-tranquillized. Moments after they injected the unfortunate beast with adrenaline, it leapt up as if it had been electrocuted and flew around in circles like a crazed spinning top, the cast and crew diving in all directions for cover.

5

A JAYNE MANSFIELD BODY AND A HORRIFYINGLY GREAT BRAIN

'She had a low opinion of modelling, but how much higher, really, are movies?'

TERRY GILLIAM, DIRECTOR, *THE ADVENTURES OF BARON MUNCHAUSEN*

On 25 March 1988 Uma's second film, *Johnny Be Good*, was released. A potentially interesting peek into the competitive world of US football recruitment involving a good-looking jock, his nutty sidekick and gorgeous girlfriend, unfortunately its tendency towards toilet humour and sexual innuendo did not endear it to critics. The high-school comedy's target audience was tiring of the hackneyed representation of the country's teenagers so common in films of the 1980s, and the crude adolescent jokes throughout, extended striptease sequences and corny ending no longer titillated.

However, many noted that *Johnny Be Good*'s faults did not lie with its youthful cast. Anthony Michael Hall and Robert Downey Jr were promising, the latter particularly good as the lunatic friend.[*]

Interestingly, despite the earlier release of *Kiss Daddy Goodnight*, in which Uma had 'enjoyed' a starring role, the credits on *Johnny Be Good* read 'Introducing Uma Thurman', although she was hardly in the film for the first half-hour and only sporadically thereafter. On the plus side, her acting had visibly improved and she looked perfectly

---

[*] Within four years, Downey Jr would play the lead in *Chaplin*, cementing his career as one of the more interesting actors of his generation, before his drug addiction began to take its toll.

plausible as the cute all-American sports fanatic – which was amusing, given her real-life rebellious cheerleader phase.

Unfortunately for the young actress, just as the movie was one long cliché, so was her part as the sexy girlfriend with an overprotective cop father. One particularly cringeworthy scene involved her massaging Hall's face with her feet while wearing long johns, and would cause her shame for many years to come.

'I used to feel really embarrassed about some work I did in my earlier films,' she later admitted. 'It used to burn inside me but little by little I'm letting go of that . . . One should be grateful for the mistakes as well as for the ones that seem to be successful.'

Fortunately for Uma, very few people went to see the movie, which went to video less than six months later. Within a few weeks of its release, her mind had moved on to other things.

*

Shortly after her eighteenth birthday, Uma was offered a part in *Dangerous Liaisons*. This dream job came almost immediately after her work on *Baron Munchausen* ended, and, in a fortuitous twist of fate, the two movies were set for nigh-on simultaneous release. Both projects were high-profile and intellectual, and, sweeping the respective debacles of *Kiss Daddy Goodnight* and *Johnny Be Good* under the carpet, Uma stood a good chance of bursting onto the cinematic scene with a modicum of credibility.

Dangerous Liaisons originates from the novel *Les Liaisons Dangereuses*, published in 1782 by Pierre Choderlos de Laclos. Conceived by the author as a series of acutely personal letters, the story reveals the clandestine sexual politics of the aristocracy in Baroque France.

The scandalous tale centres on the coyly cynical and competitive relationship between the Marquise de Merteuil and her ex-lover, Vicomte de Valmont. The two regularly indulge in bouts of icily flirtatious repartee, during which they challenge each other to dangerous sexual encounters, using the defenceless and the ignorant as their pawns.

Their latest misadventure begins when Merteuil learns her despised ex-husband is to marry a beautiful convent girl, Cécile de Volanges. Seething, Merteuil launches a cruel plan in which Valmont will deflower the virtuous virgin before her wedding day, thus spoiling the reputation of the bride and the social standing of the groom.

As Cécile is young and simple, her undoing seems to Valmont an unrewarding and wholly untaxing task, and during his conquest he spies a better test of his carnal aptitude: Madame de Tourvel, a God-fearing married woman whose fidelity seems unshakeable. He carelessly dangles this second object of his desires in front of Merteuil while reporting on the first, and, clouded by a twisted sexual jealousy, she counter-challenges him to present written proof of a sexual encounter with Tourvel. His reward will be the ultimate prize: one last glorious night with Merteuil.

The decadent tale of deceit and manipulation had been adapted for the stage in 1984 by the British playwright Christopher Hampton, who deemed it 'one of the most profound analyses ever made of love and sex – and the difference between them'. After a brilliantly successful, award-winning run in London, on Broadway and in Paris, the English director Stephen Frears was enlisted to oversee a cinematic version.

Renowned for his vibrant and provocative low-budget films about society's natural outsiders, Frears's biggest successes to date were *My Beautiful Laundrette* (exploring the relationship between a Pakistani youth and a London street punk) and *Prick Up Your Ears* (a moving and violent biopic of the playwright Joe Orton, whose undisguised homosexuality shocked 1950s society). These two gritty features had been exceptionally well received, won several prestigious awards and made stars of their two principal actors, Daniel Day-Lewis and Gary Oldman respectively.

Dangerous Liaisons was perfect as Frears's next venture. 'It has such a wonderful story,' he says. 'The setting may be just before the French Revolution, but it is very modern in its treatment of romance. People behaving badly is quite familiar.' Used to working in a highly personal, stylized manner, the director asked Hampton to go back to the book itself and adapt it for the screen, a more sensitive method of handling the delicate intricacies of the plot than simply redrafting his stage play.

As Frears turned to the casting of what was already promising to be an exceptional movie, it was clear that his chosen actors would have to be at the top of their field. Although the film was taken from the book and not the play, Frears sensed the theatrical nature of the story called for actors with a stage background and so recruited Glenn Close and John Malkovich.

'It's a part I always wanted to play,' says Close of the scheming Merteuil. 'She's very modern – a highly intelligent woman born in the wrong century. She really has no outlets for her brilliance, except for manipulation.'

John Malkovich was equally delighted with his role as Merteuil's partner in crime, the serial seducer Valmont. 'Valmont is born with so many advantages,' Malkovich enthuses. 'He's intelligent, witty, clever, rich and attractive, yet he devotes himself to destruction.

'All this wit and drive and passion and talent and energy devoted to decadence could have only one result: revolution.'

Michelle Pfeiffer signed up as Madame de Tourvel and Keanu Reeves took on the role of Chevalier Darceny, a music teacher who would fall for Cécile and ultimately cause the downfall of the evil Valmont. That left the part of Cécile, the soon-to-be-corrupted convent girl, for Uma.

For such a prominent part under the care of such an esteemed director, one might expect that the youthful actress would have dropped everything for an audition. But not Uma – unbelievably, she cancelled no less than six meetings with Frears before pulling herself together and getting down to business. This may have been her fourth role, but as witnessed previously on the *Baron Munchausen* set, where she would make tearful calls to her mother one moment and then act the outrageous flirt the next, she still had some growing up to do.

*

Dangerous Liaisons was filmed on location in Paris in May 1988. Frears's previous successes afforded him a relatively lavish budget of $14 million, so the cast were allowed to get into the spirit of their French counterparts in eight different gorgeous chateaux on the city outskirts. A real French count instructed them on eighteenth-century etiquette, and the women were yanked, strapped and fastened into opulent, restrictive, scene-stealing corsets.

There was a certain sense of urgency to the ten-week shoot. This was not the first cinematic version of *Les Liaisons Dangereuses*, previously covered in 1959 under the same name by the French director Roger Vadim. Frears was now facing direct competition from director Milos Forman with yet another interpretation, entitled *Valmont* and starring Colin Firth and Meg Tilly.* The pressure was on to come up with something more brilliant, and if at all possible, sooner than the opposition.

Perhaps because of this need to outshine their rivals, the shoot was a wonderful experience for all concerned. Everyone was absolutely

* A decade later, 1999 would witness yet another version, entitled *Cruel Intentions*, this time featuring heartless high-school students. Then, in 2003, a French-language TV series, also called *Les Liaisons Dangereuses*, would bring the story into the Swinging Sixties.

dedicated to the job in hand, not least the actors. Uma was in her element.

'When I was younger, I always played opposite grown-ups,' she recalled years later. 'I was used to surviving in a different atmosphere. When you're working with people in their thirties, forties and fifties, it's very different from working off a peer.'

With Keanu Reeves her only contemporary on the film, Uma had much to learn from John Malkovich, with whom she shared the majority of her scenes – notably more erotic than anything she had ever attempted before. If Uma had experienced qualms about rising from the sea naked in *The Adventures Of Baron Munchausen*, one wonders how she must have felt when required to rip her blouse asunder and allow the camera to focus on her heaving bosom as Malkovich traced a wicked line of kisses down towards her groin, suggestively explaining as he did so that it was time to 'begin with one or two Latin terms'.

'I was presexual at that time,' Uma admits, 'so everything made me a little uncomfortable.' With just a couple of childish affairs to her name, the eighteen-year-old wasn't far removed from the very character she was portraying, but she was, in her own words, precocious and ready to try anything.

'I tried to play that [sexuality] without necessarily owning it as a woman,' she continues. 'That did slow me down . . .'

Arguably the main reason why the sexually inexperienced actress felt able to submit to such physical exhibitionism was the comfortable relationship she shared with her co-star, John Malkovich. Later, Malkovich (then in the throes of an affair with Michelle Pfeiffer) would highlight his affection for Uma in a zealous interview for *Rolling Stone*, bringing almost as much kudos to her career as any movie ever did. 'She's an extraordinary girl, a particular favourite,' he rhapsodized, declaring her to be a 'natural' despite her relative lack of training, and that every scene they shared was 'effortless'. 'She has this Jayne Mansfield body and a horrifyingly great brain,' he observed in wonder.

The source of Malkovich's great disbelief was Uma's impressionable age. 'I normally don't spend a lot of time talking about the cosmos with eighteen-year-old girls,' he said, elsewhere painting her as 'eighteen going on forty' and the only woman under thirty who didn't bore him the moment she opened her mouth. His descriptions of Uma that didn't relate to the camera were of particular note. Rather worryingly depicting her as 'a very haunted girl, much too bright for her age', he also praised her as 'amazing', 'instinctive' and 'generous'.

If ever it seemed Uma's star was about to explode in the acting universe, it was now. In contrast with the *Baron Munchausen* shoot, on *Dangerous Liaisons* she gained the unquestioning respect of her director and co-stars as she willingly agreed to every request, no matter the content or implication.

This was in direct contrast to her counterpart on and off screen, Keanu Reeves, whose role was cut considerably during the editing of the film. Apparently, when asked by Frears to cry on cue during a scene set at the opera, Reeves was completely incapable, despite his director's frustrated suggestion, 'Can't you think of your mother being dead or something?' His scenes would take several hours to complete, compared to Uma's straightforward 'rehearsed it, did it, shot it' approach – another compliment paid to her by Malkovich.

*

Uma's well-timed assault on the movie-going public began on 21 December 1988, when *Dangerous Liaisons* was released amid much hyperbole. The film of the season, it was splendidly successful, attracting public and critical acclaim and some $33 million in US box-office takings.

As expected, *Dangerous Liaisons* was a visual treat, made possible by James Acheson's intricately lavish costumes, Philippe Rousselot's radiant cinematography, the sumptuous surroundings of the chateaux, and the contrasting looks of the entire cast. Each woman was beautiful in her own individual way: Close with her regal malevolence, Pfeiffer with her luminous purity and Thurman with her voluptuous youth.

Among the men, Reeves just about managed to hold his own, although he would receive some scathing reviews, such as the 'howlingly out of place' epitaph from the *New York Post*. Malkovich, of course, attracted a lot of attention for his portrayal of the treacherous, dastardly Valmont, who reduces women to fluttering moths with his unflinching gaze. Some thought he simply wasn't conventionally attractive enough to seduce his prey so readily, others cited his odd effeminacy in this role, and yet others found his deceitfulness downright sexy.

But the movie unquestionably belongs to Close, with her hilarious series of knowing smiles and rolling eyes, her inner pain, and her amazing ability to switch expressions in a millisecond so that only the audience can read her true thoughts. She also gets all the best lines and spoils Cécile far more than Valmont ever will with a few choice words.

As she had experienced with the casting for this role and for *Baron*

Munchausen, much of the attention paid to Uma's performance focused on the physical love affair she shares with the camera. Hers is a curious, empty-faced beauty that is at once curvaceous and angular, and the pleasing juxtaposition represents an ideal piece of casting, suiting her empty-headed ingénue role down to the ground.

To her credit, however arresting Uma looks, her acting is also excellent. She displays a fabulous sense of comic timing with her gauche reactions, inspiring many laugh-out-loud moments as she faints, bats her eyelashes or says something awfully inappropriate. Importantly, although Cécile completes the cycle of her transformation from naïvete through torment to promiscuity, Uma never loses touch with the girl's essence – her childlike innocence and impressionability – making her performance realistic and thoroughly believable.

Unavoidably, throughout the film Cécile's importance is played down repeatedly by Merteuil and Valmont as an easy conquest, and unfortunately this does serve to highlight the relative triviality of Uma's role. One can't help but wonder how she would have fared in a more complicated and taxing part like that of Madame de Tourvel.

She does, however, appear in several of the best scenes, such as the one featuring the notorious lesson in 'Latin terms' – among the most memorable film footage of that year. Although this sequence is not exactly as erotic as one might imagine, with its mischievous intimation of cunnilingus, the reference is made all the more explicit in the following scene by Valmont piously plucking a hair from his teeth while he stands next to the chaste Madame de Tourvel. It was doubtless quite a daring allusion for a highbrow period drama in 1988.

Dangerous Liaisons was by far the most successful of the two adaptations in production; Frears needn't have worried about Milos Forman's *Valmont*, which limped in at second place the following year. *Dangerous Liaisons* is a richly satisfying film, with Merteuil's mantra 'Win or die', among other subtle messages, flowing seamlessly and cleverly throughout. The ending is surprisingly dark but morally gratifying, as both Valmont and Merteuil's reputations are ruined in their own unique ways.

Reviews for *Dangerous Liaisons* were largely enthusiastic and complimentary. 'Beautifully acted, elegantly phrased, carefully shot [and] directed with a limpidly formalized serenity, it's a handsome and intelligent piece of work,' praised Tom Milne of *MFB*, while Hal Hinson of the *Washington Post* aptly commented, 'The picture exerts an insinuating hold: you feel as if it is being whispered in your ear.' Much was made of the 'delectably naughty' humour to be found within the first half, counterbalancing the less pleasant – but utterly fascinating – menace of the second. Any occasional anachronisms were forgiven in view of the unreservedly absorbing entertainment that the movie delivered.

And of course it didn't harm Uma's career one bit to be forever linked to a film that earned so many plaudits from within the industry the following spring. Awards included Best Adapted Screenplay for Christopher Hampton and Best Supporting Actress for Michelle Pfeiffer at the 1989 BAFTA Awards, and Best Foreign Film at the 1989 French Academy Of Cinema Awards. Out of seven Oscar nominations there were three wins: Christopher Hampton's script, Stuart Craig's art direction and James Acheson's costume design.

Although Close and Malkovich were nominated for Academy Awards, surprisingly neither won an Oscar; Uma for one was stunned, speaking her mind a couple of months afterwards: 'Dangerous Liaisons did not get enough Academy Awards but it just goes to show another example of the Americans' bad taste. I like America, it's fun, but would Europe please ship a little more culture over here?'

6

A KIND OF IT GIRL

'Desperation is the perfume of the young actor. It's so satisfying to have gotten rid of it.'

Less than three months after *Dangerous Liaisons* burst into Christmas cinemas, Uma's other *tour de force* premiered in March 1989. And the public just didn't know what to make of it.

The Adventures Of Baron Munchausen turned out to be one of those films that you either love or hate. Following on from its disastrously out-of-control budget and other issues clouding the filming, the release itself was problematic, with the date and promotion constantly shifting, 'which was a pity,' says Uma, 'because it is an extraordinary movie'.

As the contents of Terry Gilliam's astounding imagination spilled onto the screen, critics were transfixed. The director was never one to be half-hearted about anything and the Baron and his jolly band of adventurers are only the start of what's in store. Everything about this fantastical fairy tale – the sets, the costumes, the music score – is breathtaking, but somehow tarnished. Even the extras seem to have been employed for their quirky features or singular expressions. Perhaps predictably, the whole production resembles a *Monty Python* cartoon brought to life in glorious Technicolor.

John Neville is exceptional in his role as the whimsical Baron, Jonathan Pryce is creepy as the evil civil servant, Eric Idle adds a dash of *Python* to the proceedings, and Robin Williams's disembodied head as the King of the Moon is side-splittingly funny after the visual treat of the Baron's boat landing on the seas of the moon against a darkly twinkling sky.

Uma, of course, has a dual role in the film – as well as the goddess Venus, she also plays Rose, a member of the theatre troupe putting on a play about the supposedly mythical Baron's adventures when who should stroll in but the elderly hero himself. As the stagehand, Uma hams it up a treat; she's as gorgeously gawky as in *Dangerous Liaisons*. But the highlight of the movie for many had to be the pairing of Uma with Oliver Reed.

Playing Venus to Reed's Vulcan, the two are bickering married gods who live on Mount Etna. For some reason, Vulcan is a mad, bad and dangerous Northerner who is slowly but surely boring Venus to death.

Emerging resplendent and ethereal from her clamshell, Venus is briefly naked before she is wrapped in a diaphanous white dress and literally swept off her feet by the lustful Baron, and the couple swirl up in the air for a romantic dance in the clouds. Mindful that the chancing charmer must not steal his missus, Vulcan brands her a floozy, a strumpet and a trollop for her flirtatious behaviour, whereupon, in an echo of Uma's comic turn in *Dangerous Liaisons*, Venus retorts that he's a small-minded petit bourgeois!

Uma's sheer magnetism, her towering nudity and her humorously disdainful performance as Venus seized the attention of viewers all around the world.

'The minute that shell opened and she stepped out, I sat up and said, "Who the fuck is that?" ' recalls director Joel Schumacher, who would work with Uma nearly a decade later.

'Her beauty depends on the angle you're looking from,' adds Terry Gilliam. 'From certain angles it falls apart very quickly, you see the ugly duckling lingering, but from some angles she appears the most stunning thing on the planet.'

This was clearly someone new and special, and those in the industry were beginning to take note. Although *Baron Munchausen*, like *Dangerous Liaisons* before it, was not exactly the right platform for Uma to display her acting skills, it was certainly a showcase for her unconventional allure.

It is interesting to chart the rise of the actress's credit in the billing to the movie: on the original theatrical release she was buried at around the thirteenth name; by the time it went to video she had climbed to top five, thanks to the extra exposure in *Dangerous Liaisons*; and in later reissues she would ascend to the second name in the list.

But that was all in the future. Brimming with eccentric audacity, *Baron Munchausen* wasn't the most comprehensible film to cinema audiences in 1989, and although critics raved about the visual feast, box-office returns did not live up to expectations. Despite BAFTA Awards for Best Costume Design, Best Makeup and Best Production Design, Gilliam's gross over-spend of more than $45 million only recouped somewhere in the region of $8 million on theatrical release.

Fortunately, the film would enjoy a healthy afterlife and cult status when it came out on video, easing the finances a little, and Gilliam would achieve more mainstream accessibility with his next work, 1991's *The Fisher King* – before jumping off the deep end again in 1995 with *12 Monkeys*. As his old *Monty Python* colleague Michael Palin put it, 'Terry will never grow up. He had his chance about twenty years ago and he bungled it.'

*

And so it came to pass that by the spring of 1989, Uma Thurman was a household name. The exposure gained from *Dangerous Liaisons*, closely followed by *Baron Munchausen*, was intense and not something the young actress had expected.

'Things kind of unfolded for me,' she remembers. 'At the beginning, it was like a lark, and then it just continued. It's like being swept up in your own life, being swept along by opportunity, by fluke, by luck, by your own drive, an incredible combination of things.' Whatever their overall views of the two very different pictures, critics were singling Uma out for praise. Her parts may have been relatively small, but her performances were unquestionably striking and it was impossible to watch either film without noticing this bright new talent. Hers was the name of the moment.

Although she must have hoped in her heart of hearts for this degree of success, Uma remained remarkably composed and modest about the praise lavished upon her. 'I always thought it was an exaggeration,' she says of the rave reviews. 'I guiltily accepted whatever compliments were extended my way.' Not really believing her performance was anything special, the experience left Uma a little cold. 'It's weird to be complimented on something you don't think is true . . . even when I got approval as an actress, it felt false. It was cosmetic, not spiritual.'

The 'cosmetic' aspect to which Uma referred was the not-unexpected focus on her looks. 'If people think I'm so beautiful I'll take it as a compliment to my mother,' she initially said of the well-meaning write-ups. 'My looks are not my responsibility. I've looked at myself every day of my life and it's one of the most boring things in the world.'

'It was difficult for me in the early days to hear myself being classified as sensual because I was still a young girl and didn't feel I projected that,' she would later admit. 'People thought I was so sophisticated but really I wasn't at all.'

The emptiness Uma felt when the coverage became predictable and repetitive was doubtless heightened by the main focus of the attention. Although the critics put it slightly more delicately, what the public really seemed interested in was her naked body.

Uma was furious. '*Dangerous Liaisons* is about more than my tits,' she gasped. 'That showing part of the human body would have such an overwhelming effect, and be the cause of such insane media, amazed me. It was shocking to be ripped out of my innocence, and suddenly put up as some kind of hot thing stunned me.'

Uma's upbringing had in no way prepared her for this type of attention, and the experience left her reeling. Considering herself 'presexual' during the shoot of both films, she was still very much a girl, not a woman, and suddenly she had to answer questions – to the newspapers and ultimately to herself and her family – about whether or not she had been exploited.

'I never thought nudity was any big deal,' she says. 'I played characters who are comfortable about nudity and sex – and I thought the same while doing the scenes. I remember being stunned at the reaction after *Dangerous Liaisons* when I bared my breasts . . . it was then I realized sex has such a big impact on screen.'

Cynics might point out that at eighteen, Uma really should have known better and been more worldly-wise, but Uma needed a target for her anger and singled out America, disgusted by the sniggering response in her home country. She was determined to show them to be in the wrong.

'Americans are such puritanical twits!' she raged. 'They can be creeps and perverts and watch peep shows, but don't like looking at nude bodies when it's done in an open way at the cinema.

'I am very proud of *Liaisons* and *Munchausen*, but I don't consider either to be a sex movie. I was never exploited. I will do whatever the hell I want, whenever the hell I want, what I think is appropriate to the piece. And if I don't think it is necessary or appropriate then I won't do it.'

It was going to be very interesting to see what part Uma chose next and how she would deal with any nudity clauses that came her way.

*

Part of Uma's publicity requirements involved a gruelling tour to promote *Dangerous Liaisons* and *Baron Munchausen*. Travelling all across America and as far afield as London, she swiftly realized that she would have to learn a brand-new skill without further delay: that of tackling the endless interviews so that she sounded at least half-interested.

There were no two ways about it – Uma had been brought up in an unusual manner and the teenager could not help but express herself in the way she always had. The Thurman children had always fought to be heard in their haphazard environment and Uma had established her personality with a certain brand of light-hearted, sarcastic wit that didn't always sit well in the American press. In return, she loathed the typical Hollywood attitude she felt forced to assume, labelling it 'fake' and finding it impossible to talk about mindless gumph when her thoughts were on other things.

Unfortunately, she could also come across as flighty and mildly eccentric, and there were publications that would labour the point to her detriment. She suffered particularly at the hands of the journalist conducting an interview in America's *People* magazine. In response to questions she thought to be growing increasingly 'inane', Uma spoke openly and humorously, beginning to take the mickey out of the situation. When the interview was published, her comedy did not translate and instead a portrait was painted of her as a silly little girl, hopelessly naïve and ungrateful.

'You give interviews and the interviewers sit down, chat with you on a human level,' she countered to a different journalist, who was quizzing her on the unfortunate event. 'Then they'll turn around and serpents will be spilling from between their teeth!

'I just can't help it . . . I have to make a joke. Then I get quoted and it looks like I mean it. Well, I guess it gives people something to chew on.'

Uma's negative experience prepared her for the worst, and, although it was not in her nature to come across all sweetness and light just for the sake of it, she realized the merit in adopting a more 'compliant' attitude.

Under the auspices of her new-found fame, Uma continued to answer questions openly and changed the direction of her jokes. As a result, she soon became known as intelligent, thoughtful and mindful of her inexperienced position in comparison to her elders. Interviewers could not help but warm to her frequent self-deprecation – 'I can't help being a real person . . . I've failed miserably at being fake!' – and reported that she was unspoiled by stardom and one of the brightest talents to appear on the scene for a long time.

Uma knew well enough that too much success can drive a person crazy and stated that she was determined to avoid this fate. Level-headed with a dash of quirkiness, she gave a good outward show of not being too desperate to be a movie star.

'There's a certain innocence, despite the wiliness,' said Terry Gilliam of the backwards way Uma seemed to handle the limelight.

Typically for a girl always destined to seek the problems behind the happiness, Uma now ruminated on the dangers of forever being associated with her two largest successes.

'If people are recognizing you,' she said of the autograph hunters, 'that means that what they saw stuck in their minds . . .

'But that is something one did months and months ago. Watching it come out is like watching a dead body float downstream. It's finished.' It was an unusual attitude with which to promote two films that had only just made their mark at the cinemas.

*

Uma hadn't expected to celebrate her nineteenth birthday in the public eye, but she had no choice in the matter. Currently she was the hottest star around, and the papers were full of her exploits, no matter how embarrassing she found it. 'Being nineteen and going on a date with someone and everyone writing about it in this weird, prurient way, that was really hard,' she admits.

The never-ending fascination with a celebrity will forever be intertwined with her love life, just as much as her appearance or her diet. 'Sex turned out to be the currency of the world I was in,' Uma would say years later. 'I'd had sexual experiences – isolated ones – but I still had tremendous crushes, fantasized about Prince Charming.'

At the beginning of 1989, Uma began dating Phil Joanou on a strictly casual basis. A graduate of the University of Southern California Film School, the twenty-seven-year-old director and screenwriter had been Steven Spielberg's protégé. The esteemed director hired Joanou to direct episodes of his TV series *Amazing Stories* in 1986, then encouraged his apprentice as he directed his first feature the following year, the high-school satire *Three O'Clock High*.

Joanou's second big break came in 1988 when the Irish rock band U2 chose him to direct a documentary following them on the American leg of their *Joshua Tree* tour, entitled *U2: Rattle And Hum*. Boldly dynamic and stylishly shot, the film did wonders for the director, earning him critical respect and the group a bestselling soundtrack album.

It was at this juncture that Uma came into Joanou's life, and he was as much a fixture on the cultural scene as she was an 'It' girl. As he prepared to embark on his next feature, the violent Irish-American gangster flick *State Of Grace*, both had to adjust to their fledgling relationship being under the eagle eye of the tabloids.

Phil Joanou was just to Uma's emergent taste: 'tall, dark, damaged and handsome'. His work, always a darkly efficient exercise in extremity and internal conflict, stood testament to his passionate character, and he would later admit, 'My personality is always somewhere in my films. The most often associated words used for my work [are] intense and brooding.' It's not hard to understand why the teaming of this charismatic and artistic young man with the statuesque Uma would cause paparazzi flashbulbs to pop.

But sadly for Joanou, their relationship was shortly to be nipped in the bud. He had recently completed the cast line-up for *State Of Grace* with Sean Penn, Ed Harris and Gary Oldman, who would each go on to make memorably intense performances in the excellent mob film.

Impulsively introducing his girlfriend to the enigmatic Oldman, Joanou had no choice but to step back and let nature take its course. 'It was lightning striking,' Joanou says today, without remorse. 'You know when you've been eclipsed.

'Yes, I was chagrined. But I wasn't devastated. It wasn't like she left me for an asshole!' Two of Oldman's co-stars, Sean Penn and Robin Wright, also met and fell in love during the making of *State Of Grace*, later marrying in 1996. 'There were a lot of fireworks,' Joanou concludes. 'It was a pretty exciting time.'

*

Having decided that being typecast as the naked ingénue was a rut into which she was in grave danger of falling, Uma and her agent searched for a suitable follow-up. She tried out unsuccessfully for a lead role in *The Bonfire Of The Vanities*, the director Brian De Palma turning her down on the grounds that she lacked the necessary comic timing and chemistry with the film's star, Tom Hanks, choosing Melanie Griffith instead.

Uma persevered on the audition circuit and scored two alternative roles within a short time of each other. She signed up for John Boorman's *Where The Heart Is*, followed in a matter of weeks by Philip Kaufman's *Henry & June*. Knowing the rest of the year would be eaten up with heavy filming schedules followed by more promotion, Uma sensibly spent the earlier part of May 1989 living it up at fashionable New York nightspots such as Mars and the Canal Bar.

'Every time before I leave to go to do a movie I lose my mind,' she told journalist Karen Krizanovich, explaining that there was something about going on location and shooting a film that amounted to abandoning herself and her life. 'It's always scary, especially if you're young like I am and constantly in some kind of transition, and having to leave it on hold.'

She sighed. 'It's like, "Oh dear, am I going to go through all this now?"'

*

Uma's next role in *Where The Heart Is* would see her ascend to the giddy heights of second billing. She was to play Daphne, one of three rich kids thrown out of their family home by their father, a wealthy land developer, in a desperate bid to make them more responsible. Handed $750 each as a pay-off, the siblings have no choice but to set up camp in a derelict property called the Dutch House. Angry neighbours and demonstrators have prevented their father from demolishing this odd-looking house, proclaiming it an object of historical beauty; it is the only building left standing on a Brooklyn plot primed for development.

The movie was to be directed by the English filmmaker John Boorman, whose previous film had won respect on the other side of the Atlantic. 'After I made *Hope And Glory* I had the idea of taking another aspect of my own life and exploring it,' he says. 'This was very much about my own kids, their friends and other families.' Boorman wrote the screenplay with his daughter, Telsche, setting the story in London until Disney requested he transported it to New York. 'We did, a little reluctantly, but it was stimulating to do it that way,' he continues.

'*Where The Heart Is* was about the ambiguity between discipline, the values that hold a family together and the notions that can pull it apart . . . Everyone's afraid of the way families are disintegrating now and nobody knows what to do.' Boorman's overall view of the misery and unhappiness of this familial disintegration was that it is inevitable, and he sought to portray an alternative solution.

Although this premise might suggest that *Where The Heart Is* was doomed to be a depressing project from the start, it was in fact a light comedy following the adventures of the three siblings as they struggle to support themselves, find jobs, renovate the Dutch House, take in various disparate and eccentric characters (including a bum called 'Shitty' on account of his unfortunate odour), form a colourful and happy commune and ultimately find their way in an adult world. Dabney Coleman was to star as the wealthy real-estate mogul and put-upon father, Stewart McBain, and his two other children besides

Daphne were Chloe (Suzy Amis) and Jimmy (David Hewlett). Joanna Cassidy and Crispin Glover also featured in a cast of many.

In taking on the role of Daphne, Uma was making a rather strange move. As the story revolves around three young adults and her character in particular starts off as a petulant, airheaded brat, Uma essentially wasn't making much progress from the dire teen vehicle *Johnny Be Good*. But, having failed the 'comedy' screen test for *Bonfire Of The Vanities*, maybe she felt the need to explore this genre further and prove herself an adept comedienne after all.

'Daphne hopelessly over-identifies with everyone from bag ladies to Wall Street brokers,' Uma explained of what attracted her to the part. 'She is a woman of the world, not in a sophisticated way, who is very engaged with other human beings and is always getting sucked into their dances and songs.' In fact, Daphne didn't sound altogether unlike Uma herself: 'She's a very reactive, alive and ferocious character, a contemporary comedienne – which I really wanted to play after spending the last year in the eighteenth century!'

Most likely Uma just wanted to flex her acting muscles and demonstrate she could do more than stand around looking pretty. Within the boundaries of an ensemble she would be allowed to experiment, which was very important for her artistic development. She was also trying out a different outlook on work in general, as she revealed at the time, 'It's better for me to take things bit by bit in a job because it is really against my nature; my nature is to leap wholeheartedly into something and consume the whole shebang and get sick!'

Rehearsals began towards the end of May. Uma was tired after her publicity tour, but settled in well enough on location in Toronto (deemed a friendlier-looking version of Brooklyn) with the aid of her new Siamese cat, Chi-Chi, and her ten-year-old brother Mipam, visiting on an adventure of his own. She amiably described the rest of the cast and crew as 'very nice' and buckled down to a shoot far more straightforward than the histrionics of *Baron Munchausen* or the time pressures of *Dangerous Liaisons*.

*

Uma's performance in *Where The Heart Is* oddly resembles the film itself. Uneven, joyful, silly and experimental, the actress is very effective in portraying an immature idiot, childishly jumping around in her first scene. Daphne is an extremely physical character, echoing Uma's own ease with her immense body: she swings on banisters, lounges on radiators, jumps on cars and shows her knickers in protest before her tired and disgruntled father reaches the end of his tether and the fun really begins.

Like her brother and sister, Daphne is superficial but has good intentions, befriending a homeless man, taking him in and cleaning up his act. This alone allows Uma to develop considerably as an actress. Although there isn't much depth to her alter ego, she continues to exhibit the beginnings of good comic timing, uses her facial expressions effectively and is thoroughly believable as the spoilt artistic dreamer.

But the unavoidable aspect to Daphne is that she allows herself to be painted by her sister – in the nude. The pretext is that Chloe, an aspiring artist-photographer, is compiling a calendar of body art: gorgeous landscapes or icons painted using naked models quite literally as her canvases. Thus Uma would again appear topless in a film several times over – there was no scope for a body double here – and, ironically, in the first instance she is decorated as a goddess along the lines of a classical Venus.

It was hardly an original statement, nor one that would subvert the dreaded typecasting. For a woman who had confessed how 'uptight' she was becoming about exploitation at this age and how the unwanted attention had 'freaked her out', it was a questionable move.

Overall, although a worthy ensemble piece, *Where The Heart Is* was too gentle and slow to be ground-breaking, and barely made a ripple at the box office on its release in February 1990. Peter Martin's swirling orchestral score and Timna Woollard's extraordinary body art went some way towards elevating this sometimes mundane picture onto another level, but ultimately the film was a failure.

Some critics remarked that this was a project that should have been based in England as Boorman originally intended, where the hotchpotch of characters would have seemed more believable, and this is a fair point. It is also very much a 'message' movie, damning late-1980s materialism and extolling the virtues of the family unit, and this jarred with audiences seeking something with a little more bite. The ending in particular is overly twee and neat, Boorman's direction having strayed too far from the promising quirkiness in the beginning and middle of the film.

Uma's reviews were favourable; she does a good job as the giddy but well-meaning Daphne, and shines physically with her extraordinary topless body art. Despite climbing up to second billing, she is often overshadowed in terms of the plot and the development of other characters. Whether or not she was aware of this, it was something that seriously needed to be addressed in her career.

7

TALL, DARK, DAMAGED AND HANDSOME

'I was more fascinated with sadness than I was with joy.'

UMA THURMAN

Chicago-born maverick film director Philip Kaufman started out as an English teacher and had always been an admirer of Henry Miller, but found himself making movies during the 1960s after travelling to California to meet his literary hero. His first two works were satirical comedies. Kaufman then spent the next decade tackling a range of traditional American genres such as westerns and science-fiction, making his mark with films of consistent quality.

Having proved his ability as a director, Kaufman turned his hand to literary adaptations during the 1980s. His first attempt, *The Right Stuff*, was drawn from Tom Wolfe's novel about the foundation of the American space program and the Mercury astronauts. Although it did not fare well commercially, the film picked up four Oscars and has since become a classic. In 1988 he continued his success with *The Unbearable Lightness Of Being*, an art-house film based on Milan Kundera's cult novel starring Daniel Day-Lewis, Juliette Binoche and Lena Olin. The movie, notorious for its explicit yet tasteful love scenes, garnered two Academy Award nominations and proved the perfect forerunner to his next project, *Henry & June*.

Kaufman's lifelong appreciation of Miller finally materialized in a big-screen portrayal of his controversial relationship with another powerful figure in twentieth-century literature, Anaïs Nin. It is important to note that *Henry & June* was never intended as a biopic of

Miller; he provides the catalyst for Nin's own descent into debauchery and the film looks at her resulting conundrum of pain and pleasure. While Kaufman was unable to depict all the developments in the complex association between the lovers, he was a stickler for historical accuracy and the sets of Bohemian Paris during the 1930s are true to the elaborate descriptions in Nin's diaries.

Henry & June opens by adeptly summing up Nin's boredom and frustration with her husband, the straight-laced businessman Hugo Guiller: she complains that he is intimidated by her independence, while Guiller protests that he loves her strength. It is clear from the outset that she is exasperated and eager to expand her horizons, as she cries, 'I need to know people who are alive!'

A struggling author trying to complete a study of D. H. Lawrence, Nin's quest for exotic escapism is fulfilled when she meets the flamboyant American author Henry Miller. The American is staying in Paris while writing his first major work, *Tropic Of Cancer*, a pseudo-biography of his wife June, and Nin is instantly beguiled by the handsome couple. The historical account follows the ensuing emotional roller-coaster ride as their lives become impossibly intertwined.

It was in keeping with the plot that filming *Henry & June* was a family affair: Kaufman shunned Tinseltown in favour of his home base in San Francisco, where he shared screenwriting duties with his wife Rose and production with his son Peter, who bears an unnerving resemblance to Philip. But the director had to choose the actors for his four central characters carefully, as it was imperative to find the right combination to make the film work.

Alec Baldwin (at his peak after *Working Girl* and *Married To The Mob*) as Henry Miller provided a solid box-office attraction, while Maria de Medeiros in her first English-speaking role as Anaïs Nin made a beautiful counterpart, uncannily reminiscent of the real authoress. Richard E. Grant, a gifted young British star who broke through as the pill-popping unemployed actor in 1987's *Withnail And I*, seemed an unusual choice for the part of Guiller, the mild-mannered, sweet husband of Anaïs Nin, but Kaufman was confident that he had found the right person to play the cuckold of the piece.

Finally, for the mysterious June Miller, Kaufman turned to Uma Thurman, ignoring her age and inexperience in leading roles and instead noticing her mesmerizing appearances in *Dangerous Liaisons* and *Baron Munchausen*. Although the film mainly focuses on the quartet, Kevin Spacey was a notable and brilliant addition to the cast, bringing in humour as Miller's unsuccessful friend Richard Osborn.

As the movie was based on the documented relationship between Miller and Nin, the actors had ample material from which to draw inspiration, and over the summer of 1989 the cast embarked on a crash course of Nin's diaries and Miller's writing. Uma devoured Miller's work in her mission to understand June's frustrations and motivation, and for the first time really proved her dedication. 'I felt that Henry boxed her into his projections,' she explains. 'In a lot of what he wrote about her, there was the strange tone of a desperate need to capture her, tie her down to paper . . .

'I believe she had a magic in life that couldn't be described or encapsulated. June needed a great deal. She was an unquenched thirst. She had a great longing and a painful self-reliance. She was a tragic character.' Uma went as far as to say that in her empathy for June, she came to despise Anaïs Nin.

*

With shooting for *Henry & June* set for August, the cast and crew were shaken by the news that Alec Baldwin had withdrawn just a fortnight before cameras were due to start rolling. Unsettled by the prospect of finding an actor strong enough to take over the heavyweight role of Henry Miller at such short notice, Kaufman was relieved when Fred Ward, one of the astronauts from *The Right Stuff*, agreed despite the limited preparation time.

With just one week's rehearsal for even the most demanding scenes, the actors were forced to become rapidly acquainted, in the hope of producing the desired sizzling chemistry. According to Richard E. Grant's memoirs, *With Nails*, Ward was self-contained and monosyllabic (presumably preoccupied with brushing up on his character), de Medeiros was delightful and easy-going with a good sense of humour, and Spacey, a great comic and mimic, kept the cast entertained. With regard to Thurman, Grant noted how she seemed adept and in control, but, more poetically, he described her physical transformation from unassuming and unmade-up during rehearsals to the bewitching beauty of June Miller she became when cameras rolled.

But appearances can be deceptive: Thurman, like Grant, was a relative novice. Breaking the ice by talking about their less noteworthy films (*Johnny Be Good* and *Killing Dad* respectively), the pair discovered a mutual anxiety: perfecting their accents. The well-spoken Brit, born and brought up in Swaziland, was particularly nervous about adopting an American accent, not least because he was surrounded by natives, while Uma required help altering her dialect to that of a native of the Bronx.

Cindia Huppeler, a graduate from the drama division of New York's eminent Juilliard School, had turned her attentions to coaching, namely voice work. Brought to the set of *Henry & June* predominantly to work with Uma, she was also a godsend to Grant.

Thurman and Huppeler discussed the physical differences between the actress and her character, right down to the way they would breathe. 'Uma is a complete delight to work with because she's so open and keen on learning,' praises Huppeler. 'She's really quite chameleon-like.' This was the first time the women worked together, but they formed a lasting relationship, both professionally and personally. Huppeler and her husband would join Thurman's circle of close friends, and when their son Edgar was born six years later, Uma became his godmother.

While the cast became acquainted, Philip Kaufman began to quietly pull out his hair. The delay caused by Alec Baldwin's untimely exit led to much stress and anxiety over location organization and spiralling costs. When filming finally got underway in September 1989 at the ancient Épinay studios and in replica Nin households in the Parisian suburbs, the stifling heat was just one of the problems. Kaufman battled against the language barrier and encountered numerous clashes with the art department over the authenticity of accessories, until shooting had fallen well behind before it had even started.

The ongoing ramifications of the setback brought fresh challenges throughout production. For instance, when the elaborate re-creation of the bacchanalian street carnival was pushed back to October, not only did it entail re-securing permission to cordon off the streets, but the 350 naked extras were colder and less co-operative than they would have been in August. As Grant recalled in his diary, 'For the first time, Phil is visibly and audibly freaked.'

The strained atmosphere meant a simple gripe could rapidly escalate to a full-scale argument, and one subject that made everyone a little jumpy was the issue of nudity. Kaufman was determined to adhere to Nin's explicit and controversial recollections of her sexual adventure, an objective of which the cast were painfully aware. Grant had signed a contract agreeing to full-frontal shots if required, Ward too was prepared to grin and bare all, while de Medeiros amused everyone in anticipating her imminent exposure, excitedly declaring: 'I get to fuck everyone in this picture!'

Thurman, however, who had so far stripped for most of her pictures, was distinctly concerned that she was being typecast as a sex object. Although she had accepted a script that clearly required abundant flashes of flesh, and had previously stated she was comfortable with nudity if it was artistic and required for the role, Uma suddenly refused even to bare her breasts.

Given the succession of trials put in Kaufman's path, this last-minute change of heart was not well received. 'Philip Kaufman and I didn't get along,' explains Uma, 'and I'd never not gotten along with a director . . . It was the first time I'd ever tried to refuse direction.'

In fact, they clashed at every turn. 'He wanted more sexuality, beyond what was written on the page,' she continues. 'I wasn't really prudish where I felt it was merited artistically, but I fought him about a lot of things . . . I think he found me to be a neurotic little frightening kid. It was an initiation for me, because I had to take the beating and try to persevere.'

The teenager stood her ground and in the end felt satisfied that her scenes were as she had envisaged, a body double having absolved her of any responsibility for some of the more exotic proceedings.

It soon became apparent that the reason for Uma's reticence had more to do with her being in a serious relationship than concerns about pigeonholing. She was preserving her modesty for the sake of her beau. It was a hush-hush affair about which the cast and crew were supposed to be in the dark, but Uma found it increasingly hard to contain her secret and dropped heavy hints in conversation that she was desperate to spill the beans.

'Since I fell in love, I'm finding this stuff really hard to do,' she blurted out one day. She was supposed to be lusting after Fred Ward, a man old enough to be her father and unattractively shaved bald on top to achieve the Miller 'pudding bowl' hairstyle, but it was clear that what she really wanted was to get her hands on her mystery man.

The gentleman in question was none other than Gary Oldman, the same actor with whom sparks had flown the spring before. In an uncanny twist of fate, Uma's role in *Dangerous Liaisons*, another film about infidelity, was originally played on stage by Lesley Manville – none other than the soon-to-be ex-Mrs Oldman.

Oldman's courtship of Thurman was complicated to say the least, but then so was his past.

*

Gary Oldman is one of Britain's greatest actors. Accomplished and versatile, he is a veritable chameleon, adept at all genres. But ultimately Oldman remains unrivalled as the archetypal villain: evil, perverted and often borderline psychotic.

Born on 21 March 1958 in New Cross, South London, Leonard Gary Oldman was raised in a drab working-class area and attended a brutal boys' school. His formative years were dominated by his father, an abusive alcoholic, but when Gary was just seven years old, his father left his mother for a younger woman and cut all contact with the family. His sisters had married and left home; so he was brought up by his mother, but was more often home alone.

Bored and rebellious at school, Oldman voraciously busied himself with various hobbies, including boxing, classical music, reading and literature. Aged sixteen, he dropped out of education and found a job as a sales clerk in a sports shop.

After watching a film starring Malcolm McDowell, Oldman decided to become an actor, but his application to the Royal Academy of Dramatic Art was turned down. Instead, the tenacious young lad trained at the Greenwich Young People's Theatre, where the director, Roger Williams, started tutoring him privately. Oldman received a scholarship to the Rose Bruford College of Speech and Drama, where he completed a BA in Theatre Arts in 1979.

During his twenties, Oldman undertook prominent roles in numerous plays throughout Europe and South America and won several awards for best newcomer. But his cinematic breakthrough came in 1986, when he played Sex Pistols frontman Sid Vicious in Alex Cox's disturbing docudrama *Sid And Nancy*. Determined to accurately portray the tragic punk rocker and his relationship with Nancy Spungen, Oldman visited Vicious's mother, taught himself to play Fender bass and lost 30 pounds in order to resemble Vicious, with his gaunt heroin-addicted frame. Although Oldman was at one stage hospitalized for physical exhaustion, his hard work paid dividends: the film was a success and his utterly absorbing performance was singled out for particular praise.

His next project was an equally striking portrayal of Joe Orton in the biopic *Prick Up Your Ears*, adapted by Alan Bennett and directed by Stephen Frears (who had boosted Thurman's career with *Dangerous Liaisons*). Oldman was sexy, dangerous and utterly compelling as the vibrant and flirtatious playwright, flaunting his homosexuality in the face of 1950s society until his violent bludgeoning to death by his long-term lover, Kenneth Halliwell, played by Alfred Molina. Boasting a stellar cast, *Prick Up Your Ears* became cult viewing upon its release and earned Oldman a BAFTA Best Actor nomination.

During this hectic work schedule, Oldman had fallen in love with a British actress named Lesley Manville. The couple married and had a son, Alfie, in 1988, but Oldman found it hard to sustain normal family life as he was constantly jetting off to America, where he was now getting noticed.

Surprisingly, the quintessential Brit felt immediately at home on the other side of the pond. 'I don't miss much about Britain,' said Oldman. 'I don't know whether I ever felt it was really home to me. Once I moved to America, I found it natural to say words like sweater, elevator and sneakers rather than jumper, lift or trainers.'

As it happened, Uma found the difference between American and British men refreshing. 'A British man is far more accepting of being in touch with his feminine side,' she explained. 'Maybe the British aren't as homophobic as the Americans, who are very afraid of expressing the feminine in themselves.'

By the time Oldman met Thurman in 1989, he had separated from Manville, who had custody of their son, and so was free to pursue a romance. However, mindful of the adverse effects of his own father's desertion, Oldman attempted to visit Alfie regularly. The mutual attraction intensified over the summer, and in the autumn he took a few days out of filming *State Of Grace* in New York to visit Uma on the set of *Henry & June*, slightly blowing their cover of secrecy. When Uma finished work on *Henry & June* in November, she was able to spend all her time with her new lover.

Part of the key to Oldman's brilliance is the all-encompassing devotion he pours into any given project. Dating back to his childhood, when he became completely fixated by each new hobby, Oldman has always been obsessive about his passions and his developing desire for Uma was no different. When the pair were together they were literally inseparable, and for her part, Uma was giddy with emotion as she considered this her first real experience of love.

But it was his tireless dedication to his vocation that really drove Oldman – sometimes to the detriment of his physical and mental well-being, notably with the dramatic hospitalization after *Sid And Nancy*. The actor was aware that his all-consuming approach was often unhealthy. 'My acting was based on fear and neurosis,' he acknowledged. 'I would use the work as a stick to beat myself with, constantly researching parts, becoming very book-bound. I really gave myself a hard time over it, in the belief that if I was remotely good at the end of it, it was worth all the pain and anguish and shit I'd been through.'

While Oldman was becoming increasingly conscious of his harmful habits, it seemed inevitable that Uma would be attracted to the wrong kind of guy, as she bore out her teenage fantasies of tragic destiny. 'I was more fascinated with sadness than I was with joy,' she reflects. 'I thought that was deeper and more interesting. I was drawn to what was dark in myself, to darker, more complicated, damaged people.'

Uma's family were aware of this tendency and nicknamed her Florence, as in Nightingale, 'because I was always attaching myself to sick and diseased people and trying to help them'. Even more of a concern, though, was the nagging suspicion that Oldman had inherited his father's fondness for alcohol, but for the time being both parties were blissfully in love.

The biggest problem they had was co-ordinating their schedules. As soon as Oldman had finished work on *State Of Grace*, he started on an art-house two-hander, *Rosencrantz And Guildenstern Are Dead* with Tim Roth, directed by Tom Stoppard. While Oldman was working on cult pictures, Uma's fifth film, the bland *Where The Heart Is*, was released with little impact. Although she turned twenty in April 1990, Uma continued to act like a teenager in love, and insisted that the affair was kept a secret – nigh-on impossible, given the fickle, gossipy nature of the showbusiness world.

*

In September 1990 Philip Kaufman's eagerly anticipated *Henry & June* was premiered at the Venice Film Festival, followed by theatrical release the next month.

Many critics mistakenly expected 'The Henry Miller Story' and so were disappointed with the concentration on Anaïs Nin's love affairs. As a consequence, the reviews were generally poor, with complaints focusing on the film's lack of direction and self-indulgence. To be fair, the script is flawed, practical questions are left unanswered, and jumps in chronology sometimes result in confusion, but any failings in the plot are more than made up for by the spectacular re-creation of Bohemian Paris, sensuous cinematography and magnificent performances. Guy-Claude François was responsible for the production design, Philippe Rousselot justly received an Oscar nomination for the photography, and Philip Kaufman can take credit for the perfect casting.

Ultimately it is Anaïs Nin's story, and de Medeiros is utterly bewitching, providing a solid anchor from which the supporting cast can derive strength. She expertly captures Nin's concurrent innocence and eroticism, her delicate childlike beauty belied by mischievous eyes and a wicked smile. Ward portrays Miller as brutish, boorish and passionate, yet he infuses the character with enough intrigue and excitement to remain appealing.

Thurman's performance in particular was noted as one of the highlights of the piece; it showed tremendous improvement in her ability. Uma truly embodies June – she starts the film as dominant, alluring, smouldering and worldly-wise, but as she loses control of the situation she initiated, she collapses and is exposed for the tragic figure she is.

Having poured her heart and soul into the role, more than ever before Uma had to learn a valuable lesson about rising above the reviews. 'You put a tremendous amount of energy and love into a project, and it just evaporates,' she says. 'You have to absorb a lot of praise and criticism and rejection and separation. It teaches you a lot about letting go and getting your ego out of it, because it's not about you.'

Comments that the films drags in places are justified, but the slow pace helps build tension and there are some lovely comedic moments to retain the audience's interest: Guiller's wide-eyed reaction to the brothel; Nin and her two lovers in bed together reading; Miller tweaking Nin's nipples while Guiller strums his guitar; and any scene involving Osborn (Spacey).

But it was the frank sexual content that caused the greatest uproar. The Motion Picture Association of America created a new rating of NC-17 (No Children Under 17) for *Henry & June*. Certainly by today's standards the film is erotic rather than explicit, but the ample displays of flesh, evocative moaning and gratuitous rump shots warranted an X rating, which would have prevented the film from being shown in many parts of America. The new classification was intended to set this genre apart from pornography, pinpointing works as 'art films'. 'It was all to do with one scene of two prostitutes in a brothel and a Japanese etching, which children can see at the Met or in *National Geographic*,' explained Uma, unfazed by the commotion.

Although *Henry & June* only took $11 million at the box office, it was a worthy – if notorious – addition to Uma's growing CV.

8

NO MAN'S LAND

'I've always been too sophisticated to play the young characters and too young to play the others. Stuck in no man's land.'

UMA THURMAN

Uma may not – for once – have appeared naked in *Henry & June*, but a large proportion of her audience were not to know that, unaware as they were of the technicalities of employing a body double. More favourable reviewers compared her luminosity to the likes of Lauren Bacall and Marlene Dietrich. Grubbier tabloid accounts were more unsettling. Here was a gorgeous young Hollywood actress who seemed happy to expose herself in each and every film, and regularly indulged in explicit sex scenes with both men and women: what could be better?

The gross misunderstanding sickened Uma. She had completely failed in her attempt, however half-hearted, to avoid becoming known as a sex symbol, and any onscreen shenanigans were the last thing she wanted anyone to focus on in the light of her intense relationship with her new lover. The situation was to get worse before it got better.

Even though Uma no longer lived with her parents, they suffered an unwelcome deluge of phone calls from stalker-like fans trying to track her down, eventually forcing them to unlist their number. 'Weird people have fallen in love with her image,' said her father, frustrated at his helplessness in the situation. 'One guy from Brooklyn kept writing letters for a year. We kept ignoring them and let them pile up.

'Finally he sent a switchblade with a note that said, "Is this what you want me to do? Kill myself?"'

It was all too much for Uma. Nothing could have prepared her for the seedier side of celebrity. Any views she had previously expressed on nudity and its rightful place in films were now eclipsed by the horrifying reactions she received in the gutter press, in her publicity and in her daily sack of uncensored fan mail.

Over the next few years, Uma's sex-symbol status was further cemented in other media, including a series of increasingly sordid pop songs: 'Uma' by Majesty Crush, 'Uma Fourteen Times' by Zoinks and 'Ben Sherman' by Heavenly, in which an unthinking boyfriend 'says he'd like to fuck Uma Thurman / I don't think he'll get too far'.

It is important to remember that it wasn't so many years ago that Uma had experienced serious hang-ups about her looks. Her self-confidence had always been fragile and now, at the other end of the scale, she was crippled with insecurity. She laid low with Gary Oldman in England, turning down role after role that poured into her agent's office.

'I grew up with a negative image of my appearance and then had to deal with an insane amount of attention to my looks and that was quite disorienting,' she says. 'It made me want to withdraw completely.

'I was shy about my body and the last thing someone who feels awkward needs is to have people writing about them as a sexual object.

'I curled up in a hole for a long time. I consistently turned things down that were by-products of that sex thing. I wasn't able or interested in fulfilling that.' In time, Uma would learn to overcome the daily intrusion into her life with a characteristic dollop of cynicism. For now, she dressed in baggy clothes, continued to turn down parts with any sexual content whatsoever, and hid away from the media.

'I preferred not to work if I was going to be pigeonholed as the sexual flavour of the month,' she explains. 'I had too much respect for acting.'

*

Media unpleasantries aside, Uma had found happiness with Gary Oldman. As his friend Jeroen Krabbé observes, 'Gary *always* falls in love and he *always* wants to marry', and so Uma indulged the volatile actor's romantic tendencies in a quiet civil ceremony in October 1990.

From the outset, the marriage was a curious one. Thurman had repeated the cycle of the women in her family marrying foreign men many years older than themselves after a relatively short courtship. But Oldman, charming and charismatic despite his underlying problems and personal history, was a hard man to refuse, and by all accounts, twenty-year-old Uma was completely swept off her feet.

'I believed that I was more adult than I was at the time,' she reflects. 'He was my first true love and I had no prior experience of what was expected.

'When we married, I thought, "Now we'll settle down and have a family." ' Technically, Uma was now stepmother to Oldman's son Alfie, but as he was in Manville's custody and the atmosphere between Manville and Oldman was not always harmonious, it is uncertain how much of a relationship she managed to form with the toddler.

*

Uma had taken her time before choosing her next project, nervous of accepting anything that would entail physical exposure. 'Let's just say I've been through a lot of high-stress jobs recently and I was looking for a gentle way to get back into things,' she admitted at the time. It was only the security of newlywed life in England, and the very respectable role on offer of Maid Marian in John Irvin's version of the Robin Hood legend, that changed her mind.

Irvin started out making documentaries during the 1970s, but gained a reputation as a stalwart director with masterpieces such as Fred Astaire's final film *Ghost Story* (1981), Harold Pinter's romantic comedy *Turtle Diary* (1985) and the Vietnam War drama *Hamburger Hill* (1987). His adaptation of *Robin Hood* was intended as a gritty, British tale, set against the Norman–Saxon clashes of the twelfth century. The plot is based on the traditional story, but the retelling adds a few important twists and fresh dynamics to breathe life into an old saga.

Robert Hode is a Saxon nobleman who offends Sir Miles Folcanet, a ruling Norman, and is consequently outlawed along with his friend Will Redding when he refuses to accept his punishment. Changing their names to Robin Hood and Will Scarlett, the duo are welcomed into an unruly gang as a result of Robin's skill at archery. Gaining respect among their fellow fugitives, they lead an attack on Folcanet's party while out riding one day. Humiliated, Folcanet is so determined to defeat Hood that he offers a handsome reward for his capture, and then raises taxes to anger the public enough to turn him in. The greedy Normans can be seen as a thinly veiled stab at the Tory government of the time.

In this version, Hood's famed tactic of 'robbing the rich to give to the poor' is in fact only a counter-measure to pacify the masses; he is portrayed as less of a thief, more of a resistance fighter. In the meantime, Folcanet's unwilling fiancée, Maid Marian, dresses as a boy and joins Robin's merry men. Trust becomes a complicated issue and allegiances are tested as Marian's actions inadvertently lead to Robin's capture by the Normans. Needless to say, in the spirit of a happy ending, the gang rally round and free the people's hero, who in turn rescues the helpless maiden, falls in love with her and reconciles the Norman and Saxon rulers to boot.

Unfortunately, just as Irvin decided to rework the Errol Flynn classic, so too did Hollywood director Kevin Reynolds. The competition was far more serious than it had been with *Dangerous Liaisons* and *Valmont*. For his big-budget blockbuster *Robin Hood: Prince Of Thieves*, Reynolds enlisted Kevin Costner in the title role, just a year after Costner's smash hit *Dances With Wolves*. Furthermore, Reynolds secured tremendous supporting actors such as Morgan Freeman, Christian Slater, Alan Rickman, Sean Connery and Brian Blessed for a massive swashbuckling adventure.

John Irvin, on the other hand, aimed for a more realistic version, and worked with casting agent Susie Figgis to put together a well-rounded professional ensemble. The lead was undertaken by Irish actor Patrick Bergin (*Mountains Of The Moon*), pitted against Jürgen Prochnow (*A Dry White Season*), Edward Fox (*The Dresser*) and Jeroen Krabbé (*Kafka*). Undertaking the role of Maid Marian's uncle and Robin Hood's friend, Krabbé was appearing in his second film with John Irvin after *Turtle Diary*.

'I love him, I think he's a wonderful director,' enthuses Krabbé. 'He is very laid-back with a great sense of humour. He influences actors and you feel he knows about the craft of acting – when it's all right, he will let you continue, and he'll help you when things go astray or wrong.'

Irvin's flair for diplomacy was called on almost immediately as the production quickly ran into problems. With shooting set for November and December of 1990 near Chester on the border of Wales, the most obvious and pressing challenge came from Mother Nature.

'I remember it was cold, rainy and very muddy,' laughs Krabbé, 'it was miserable! We were on a very tight schedule, and not only did we have to reckon with the weather, but at that time of year it doesn't get light until ten or eleven in the morning and it gets dark at about three or four in the afternoon, so we really had to fight against the light all the time.'

On top of the discernible trials of winter, Irvin's lead actor fell foul of the bitter temperatures. 'Patrick went to hospital for about a week,' continues Krabbé, 'so the whole schedule had to be turned upside down. Everything was stressful as we were trying to shoot around him for a while, but John was easy-going about the whole thing. Sometimes he would say, "I don't know what to do because we have to film without Patrick and we don't have enough to do today, so let's get it done quickly and go for a drink!" '

Although Irvin made light of the situation, the impact of altering the shooting schedule affected everyone.

*

In spite of, or perhaps because of, the challenging circumstances, the cast and crew of *Robin Hood* rallied together and enjoyed a lively sociable life during filming. There were two notable exceptions to this revelry: Patrick Bergin and Uma Thurman. While Bergin can be excused due to ill health for some of the time, the truth of the matter was that both actors adopted an unattractive aloof attitude.

Jeroen Krabbé kept a diary during the shoot and on looking back at his notes realizes that he was distinctly unimpressed with the young actress. 'She was at the beginning of her career and behaved like a Hollywood spoilt brat, both she and Patrick were quite snotty about things. We were all stuck together in an awful castle, and they were both acting as if they were on a Hollywood set, which one should never do.

'I wrote in my diary: "Patrick and Uma pretend something there isn't, like big American stars who come late on the set, are not interested in their colleagues and not very nice towards us. They play Hollywood on a non-Hollywood set."

'I have seen that attitude in young Hollywood stars – men and women, they're all the same – they are very self-centred and unco-operative. They don't play with you, they play on their own in a role.'

During one particular scene, Uma had to speak her lines to the camera while Krabbé responded out of shot. When it came to Krabbé's turn to be filmed, she was supposed to be on call to feed him his cues off camera, but had disappeared to her dressing room to change as she was otherwise finished for the day. When she returned, she agreed to read her lines but was bored and distracted, which infuriated Krabbé.

'Could you *please* give me your lines without smoking your cigarette and chewing gum, because I can't concentrate!' he snapped.

'Oh, yeah, OK, I can do that,' she responded sullenly, as if it was a waste of her time.

Krabbé found Uma's apathy harder to stomach than her egotism, and could not abide her disinterest in the film. 'Another time we had four days off, I think because of Patrick's illness, and when we came back on set she didn't know her lines,' he recalls. 'You don't want to get into an argument with people you only vaguely know, especially on a set with so many people around, but I couldn't stand it that after four days she still didn't know her lines. I was really furious.'

Krabbé understandably lost his temper and confronted her. 'After that moment she completely turned around and was nice to me, maybe because I scared her and stood up to her!'

Uma's lack of dedication to *Robin Hood* was in complete contrast to her deep personal involvement with *Henry & June*. This time, not only was it a supporting role in what she considered to be a lightweight project, but her mind was elsewhere due to her recent nuptials with Gary Oldman. That she was wholly wrapped up in her husband was no excuse for her amateur attitude and, not for the first time, her immaturity became apparent to her colleagues.

'The first time I met Uma was at the hotel where we were staying,' says Krabbé. 'She was with Gary and very much in love; they were kissing and hugging and fondling each other all the time. One of the actors shouted, "Why don't you go to your room, it's just upstairs!"

'I only saw them together over dinner and then they rushed straight off to their room. Gary was madly in love with her – but then he's always madly in love!

'Gary was not around much,' he continues more seriously, 'as he was having difficulties with his ex-wife and was not able to see his child. He was very stressed about that.'

*

Filming *Robin Hood* was a strained affair from beginning to end, due to adverse weather conditions, ill health, delays and perceived lack of commitment from certain actors. But nagging at the back of everyone's mind was the threat of the competition.

'There was talk about it almost every day on the set,' says Krabbé, 'but I thought we had a very good cast and a wonderful script, so we would survive. They said ours would be better because we were nearer to the original story, and I remember it was beautifully shot. But we had to be the first one to come out, so everything was rushed because of that.'

Irvin's tale was pushed through at breakneck speed and released on 17 May in England, beating the opposition by a month. However, Reynolds's film premiered in America on 14 June with a worldwide release to follow. As the star-studded spectacle naturally attracted promotion prior to the event, it essentially rendered Irvin's early release useless. Furthermore, Reynolds's movie took $86 million at the box office, making it one of the top-grossing films of 1991, while Irvin's film missed its intended theatrical release in America and went straight to television.

Reviews of both films were in fact equally mixed. Some critics loved the accessible Hollywood extravaganza, while others found it overwhelmingly cheesy and preferred the darker British drama. The dank weather gives the English countryside a very gloomy feel in Irvin's production, yet the stately photography prevents it being too depressing. The director adds humour to lift the mood, although it is not always successful and was often criticized, particularly the smutty innuendo between Robin and Marian which crosses over into embarrassing *James Bond*-style smarminess. That Robin is so gullible as to believe Marian's flimsy disguise as a boy seems unlikely and weakens the plot, but equally there is a hint that he has seen through it, which is confusing. Either way, there is certainly little sexual tension between the key characters, presumably not least due to Uma's wandering attention.

Although Krabbé is proficient as Daguerre, torn between friends, family and politics, and Fox and Nuttall contribute fine cameos, many of the revamped characters don't work. Bergin in particular makes Robin Hood appear naïve, unpredictable and disorganized. Prochnow infuses Folcanet with a suitably evil quality, although his over-the-top accent and camp death scene are a little grating.

Uma wanted to make Marian feisty and liberate her from the conventional damsel-in-distress stereotype. As in *Where The Heart Is*, she ably portrays a stroppy brat used to getting her own way, but in *Robin Hood* sometimes she simply appears aloof. Given Krabbé's recollections of the shoot, perhaps this was more coincidence than fine acting.

While it remains an enjoyable romp through olde-worlde forests, ultimately *Robin Hood* suffers from trying to bridge too many genres, ineptly combining heavy political allegory, thought-provoking drama and misguided farce.

*

Still on the hunt for work that would pay well but not prove too physically revealing – or even, dare one suggest, too taxing during that first flourish of love between the newlyweds – Uma bounced straight into her next film without a break, around the same time that she turned twenty-one. Her choice of director was odd, but proved that any relationship is best dissolved amicably.

Phil Joanou was obviously a well-trusted mutual friend of the Thurman-Oldmans, and in the spring of 1991 he cast Uma as Diana Baylor in his new movie, *Final Analysis*. When asked how he approached each project, Joanou's response was: 'Stay as objective as you can, while at the same time trying to stay focused on your personal vision for a film and not to become dissuaded by those around you who may derail you from that vision.' It is hard not to ponder how 'objective' this director may have felt with an old flame on the set.

For Uma, *Final Analysis* was not just a reunion with her ex; she was also going to star opposite a friend more long-standing than any romantic association. At last Richard Gere's star had collided with her own, and she was going to work with the very person in whom she had first confided her ambition to act. Although Uma's role was decidedly third fiddle to Gere (hot from the success of 1990's *Pretty Woman* with Julia Roberts) and sultry sex symbol Kim Basinger, who would take the larger female part in this movie, she must have felt comfortable, proud of her achievements and excited to work with such an influential family friend.

And so it was within this close-knit environment that filming commenced in Los Angeles. With the tagline 'Hot-blooded passion. Cold-blooded murder', *Final Analysis* was Joanou's shot at recreating Hitchcockian suspense. The story was an old-fashioned intrigue in three distinct parts, mixing romance with courtroom drama and murder.

In the film, Isaac (Gere), a psychiatrist who just wants to 'be surprised', is treating a young woman, Diana (Thurman), who seems to have obsessive-compulsive traits triggered by buried traumatic memories. In the first of many rather nonsensical plot developments, Diana suggests Isaac should speak to her elder sister, Heather (Basinger), about the violent history they have shared. Naturally, as soon as Isaac lays eyes on Heather, a spark ignites and the two dive into bed at the next available opportunity.

Heather, however, has problems of her own. Not only is she married to a sadistic mobster called Jimmy (played by Julia Roberts's brother, Eric), but she also suffers from pathological intoxication – which means she is unaccountable for her actions after even a small amount of alcohol. Nonetheless, Isaac falls in love with her during their secret affair, and on learning about her tyrannical husband he asks her to seek a divorce. One night, Jimmy's regular bout of abuse is met with an outburst from Heather, who is under the influence, and the marital spat ends in his murder.

The middle section of the film then centres on the homicide case, during which Isaac is requested to testify in his professional capacity. As events unfurl, Isaac realizes that his lover is not all she seems and begins to suspect he may have been set up by Heather and Diana from the very beginning to help them dispose of Jimmy and avoid jail. The conclusion is a lengthy chase scene, during which Isaac battles for his life and attempts to outwit the two sisters.

Although *Final Analysis* would both begin and end on an extreme close-up of Uma's face, the role of Diana was minimal and the actress's involvement on set could not have taken more than a couple of weeks. All the same, it was not long before the Hollywood rumour mill ground into action, and Uma was accused of dating Richard Gere, mainly because they were spotted having coffee together in a restaurant. It didn't register with the tabloids that Uma was the wife of Gary Oldman, that Gere was married to supermodel Cindy Crawford, or that the pair were old family friends: they were obviously having a torrid affair.

It was the first time Uma had been romantically linked with a co-star, and it certainly wouldn't be the last, but for her the very idea was laughable. It was hard enough getting to grips with him in character: 'Because I do know him so well, it was bizarre, almost surreal, to work with Richard as an actress,' she says.

Besides, Gere's own views on the opposite sex may not have appealed and his interviews have often hinted he might not be an 'easy' date: 'I'll never understand women,' he remarked to *Woman's Day* in 2000. 'In general, I think they are needy and vulnerable. They are more emotional and want to be seen for who they are. It's more mechanical for men – if you've got a problem, let's fix it.' If women 'in general' resembled the female characters in *Final Analysis*, he would have had a point.

*

Final Analysis was released in February 1992. It should have been a hit, given Joanou's famously polished direction and the box-office pull of Gere opposite Basinger, but it wasn't. In fact, it failed dismally.

It has to be said that, fashion atrocities of the late 1980s aside, *Final Analysis* looks and sounds great, thanks to Dean Tavoularis's extravagant art direction, Jordan Cronenweth's tense photography and George Fenton's well-meaning musical score. Gere and Basinger themselves were proven A-list heavyweights and the whole premise set against the *film noir* backdrop has much potential.

But for a thriller, right from the outset the story is unavoidably lame, lacking any real suspense or intrigue. Plot twist after plot twist becomes more outlandish, red herrings outnumber the cast, and even within the film itself the characters admit it's not normal practice for a shrink to break doctor–patient confidentiality with a patient's relative, let alone sleep with her. Consequently the critics were left uncertain as to whether this was a homage or instead a parody of the genre: 'Nothing rings very true in this slick, vacuous Hitchcockian thriller,' lamented *Newsday*, one of many publications to slam the film.

The two main stars buckle under the storyline early on, sinking into a murky sea of indifference. Gere's psychiatrist is an especially wet fish, and Basinger – supposed to be the 'butterfly' to Uma's sisterly 'caterpillar' – can barely be seen beneath her voluminous clouds of puffy blonde frizz and enormous shoulder pads, let alone vamp it up sufficiently. With an almost complete lack of any onscreen chemistry between the leads, the audience's interest in this unlikely, odd connection wanes rapidly.

Clocking in at over two hours, the film is way too long and drawn out, and could have benefited from some heavy editing. Points are laboured until they bleed, in particular the courtroom obsession with pathological intoxication; the viewer soon tires of hearing endless repetition of this term and its very obvious implications. Unfortunately, subtlety is not the name of this game. The climactic closing scenes set in a lighthouse, in a nod to Hitchcock's far superior *Vertigo*, are visually arresting but seem utterly unconnected to anything that has gone before.

Perhaps unexpectedly, any scenes that were open for stealing belonged entirely to the two supporting actors, Roberts and Thurman. Eric Roberts is genuinely menacing, his presence somehow commanding the viewer's attention far more than Gere. And as for Thurman, almost every reviewer agreed she is criminally underused.

Uma brings a nervy edginess to the troubled Heather, the catalyst that sparks off the story. She handles her character's real and supposed neuroses subtly yet effectively, adding depth as the viewer notices first her affection for Isaac, then her jealousy of her controlling sister, and she even brings a dash of deadpan humour to proceedings. Particularly amusing is her early monologue about a gun being a penis and the bullets being the semen, as she hints at the sisters' underlying plan to her unsuspecting analyst.

Oddly, the two sisters don't appear on screen together until just shy of one-and-a-half hours into the film. Although this may have been intentional, it doesn't work at all, as the lack of contact between them is glaringly obvious and in itself misleading: the conniving sisters would be a lot more convincing if they could at least establish a relationship with one another.

Unfortunately, when their scenes do eventually coincide, Uma completely and unintentionally overshadows Basinger. Diana is supposed to be her big sister's stooge, but comes out of the equation so much fresher than the rather tired Basinger. When Diana 'morphs' into her sister, complete with hair extensions and Ray-Bans, there is a glimmer of insight into this frankly more interesting sibling, and the final shot in which her expression changes suddenly from laughing naïvety to pure evil is inspired.

Luckily for her, Uma emerged from the murk that was *Final Analysis* the only name left undamaged by the proceedings. The talented Phil Joanou headed back to the world of TV, which in itself was a terrific waste, and Gere and Basinger both had to wait several years before better roles came along. But critics noted that Uma had showed herself to be a solid, promising character actress who should have been used to much better effect, but was sadly squashed by the two bigger names. An appealing element of danger and madness had now been added to her repertoire, but the question was, what would she do with it?

Perhaps because her love life was so all-consuming, Uma's career choices since her marriage had been questionable. *Robin Hood* was unavoidably bland and she was utterly stifled in *Final Analysis*. For the sake of her career, she needed a meaty lead role to get to grips with, but, at twenty-one, could she actually hold a movie on her own?

9

THE END OF THE CRAZY LOVE AFFAIR

'I love him dearly, although he is a nutcase, a wonderful nutcase!'

JEROEN KRABBÉ, FRIEND OF GARY OLDMAN

'An older, very witty woman once said to me that most women don't even count their marriages before the age of twenty-one.'

UMA THURMAN

Given that she had just played an obsessive-compulsive herself, one wonders at what stage Uma realized life with Gary Oldman wasn't destined to be easy.

For his efforts Oldman had acquired numerous acting accolades, but he was increasingly more distracted by an altogether different pursuit. As a fifteen-year-old, Oldman had started drinking regularly due to peer pressure. It was as much a part of working-class South London pub culture to drink 'light ale' and 'keg' as it was to prop up the bar, put the world to rights and play endless rounds of darts.

'The truth is, I hated it,' he recalls with a heavy sense of irony. 'I never even liked beer. But I'd do it and just make myself incredibly ill, because it was like my graduation. It was a case of, "Now I've reached fifteen, I get to graduate to a pub."'

It wasn't long before Oldman realized he had inherited his father's addiction to alcohol, but he didn't see any point in changing his ways. In fact, as neurotic as he became about his career as an actor, Oldman was equally compulsive about his drinking and almost celebrated his alcoholism. Rather than let it affect his performances, he insisted that he was a better performer inebriated than most actors were sober. As his work didn't suffer, nobody thought to raise it as a problem.

It helped that Oldman managed to avoid disgracing himself in public; his reclusive drinking became one of the best-kept secrets in the business. This took the form of lengthy binges when he would lock himself in a hotel room for whole weekends and emerge without any recollection of the previous forty-eight hours. Tragically, in 1984, after just a few brief moments of contact, Oldman's estranged father died aged sixty-two from complications linked to alcoholism, but even that wasn't enough to shake his son's addiction.

*

Over the summer of 1991, the shine rubbed off the tempestuous romance between Uma and her wild-card husband. Uma had thought she could put up with the parties, the countless late nights and unpredictable mood changes, but when Oldman was arrested for drink-driving in Los Angeles one night and thrown into jail until his release on bail the next morning, it was the beginning of the end.

One could argue it was the company he was keeping: Oldman's passenger was his good friend, the actor Kiefer Sutherland. Having established something of a laddish reputation by mixing with unsuitable friends ('My best friend Robert Downey Jr succumbed to drugs – that was like a warning to me,' he says), Sutherland had recently split with Julia Roberts. It was a huge embarrassment as the pair were just days away from walking down the aisle, so Oldman decided it was time to cheer his friend up.

Going on a bender wasn't the problem; it was the fact that they got into a car afterwards. While Oldman was charged with drink-driving and punished with a six-month driving ban and community service, Sutherland faced the degradation of clearing up litter along the highway near his Santa Monica home.

One wonders which was worse for Uma: the shock and the shame of her husband being publicly branded a drunk and a danger to society, or the unbelievable fact that, for Oldman, the wake-up call that he could have killed someone had such a limited impact. Instead of giving up or even tempering the demon drink, he simply vowed never again to drive while under the influence, and continued along his excessive, self-destructive path. (To put it into perspective, the actor has since admitted to regularly putting away two bottles of vodka a day at this time and had recently blown £18,000 in one weekend on alcohol just for himself.)

As Oldman would soon discover, once labelled a drunk-driver, the reputation stuck. 'I got arrested more than a decade ago, but people can write about it and it sounds as if it happened last week,' he lamented in 2001. 'I try hard to ignore it and accept that it goes with the job.'

For a few weeks, nothing changed in the Thurman-Oldman household. 'I'd get out of bed, crawl across the floor and throw up in the shower,' he admitted. 'I wouldn't do that to an enemy, so why did I put myself through it?'

*

The following months were the most difficult of Uma's life.

Back when she had started work on *Robin Hood*, Oldman had seized upon the idea of starring opposite his wife on the big screen. He excitedly described the ambitious biopic of Welsh poet Dylan Thomas to his friend Jeroen Krabbé.

'He told me that he wanted to make a movie with Uma on the last months or half-year of Dylan Thomas's life,' Krabbé recalls, 'so he was setting that up and wasn't around much.'

The movie amounted to the love child the couple never had. Oldman spent much of 1991 feverishly preparing for the role, and shooting was scheduled to start in Wales in August 1991, somehow fitting in around his current job as the lead in *Bram Stoker's Dracula* in Culver City, Los Angeles, during the latter half of the year.

Mysteriously, just eight days into the Dylan Thomas project, filming ground to a halt and the movie was shelved for good. It was reported – but never confirmed – that Oldman was close to a nervous breakdown. He and Uma vanished from the set, never to return. 'It was unfortunate he never succeeded, because he might have been wonderful in that role,' remarks Krabbé fondly.

Not only did the biopic collapse – so too did the Thurman–Oldman union.

Oldman rebounded manically and predictably back to his other film, dealing with upset the best way he knew how: by burying his head in his work. During the filming of *Dracula* he consoled himself by crying on the shoulder of Richard E. Grant, the couple's mutual friend and his current co-star, telling him, 'Maybe I'm gonna be one of those people who gets married a lotta times,' and joking, 'A shrink can identify your grief but they can't fix your life . . .'

The unhappy shoot was plagued with Oldman-related problems until it wrapped the following January. Other than his obvious distress at his marriage breaking up (he said he needed to be 'scraped off the floor'), he suffered an allergic reaction to his foam-rubber make-up, and argued with both his esteemed director, Francis Ford Coppola, and his leading lady, Winona Ryder. The latter was particularly upset when tabloid headlines began to emerge along the lines of 'Wild Man Oldman Abandons Uma Thurman And Seen Choosing Music In Tower Records With Winona Ryder', although this latest rumour seemed to have more to do with promotion for the movie than the truth.

*

For Uma, the end of 1991 and her marriage to Gary Oldman passed in a blur. She has never spoken publicly about exactly what was the final straw, although clearly his stormy nature and excessive drinking were contributing factors to the breakdown of their marriage after just eleven months.

It is known she spent an extended period with her close family, trying to come to terms with what this meant for her on both personal and professional levels. For a while, both she and Oldman had a pact never to discuss their failed marriage, although time, incessant media prodding and an unforeseen quote in the press would remove the gag, at least for the injured party.

'Gary will always be crazy,' one of his well-meaning 'friends' told an interviewer when news of their pending divorce was announced. 'It takes a special kind of woman to put up with him.'

The implication that Uma wasn't 'special' stung, and soon she was dismissing the brief union as nothing more than a childish fling – although she was always careful to imply she had also been at fault for acting on an immature romantic impulse. 'Gary was my first love,' she said. 'It was an infantile gesture to marry my first boyfriend, which he basically was. It was a mistake . . . a crazy love affair which needed to end.'

Feeling less generous on another occasion, and generally getting fed up of the speculation, she offered: 'Teenage weddings are in the category of things that don't count . . . It wasn't a real marriage from the first day. It was one of those rash decisions that adolescents make and then regret almost instantly.'

For his part, Oldman only once griped in print. No doubt sickened by the ongoing stereotype of himself as the drunken hell-raiser and of Uma as the much younger innocent, he retorted, 'You try living with an angel!' – bringing to mind the actress's onscreen incarnation as Venus.

It would be a long time before Uma spoke about the subject again, certainly not until after the divorce was finalized in 1992. She has remarked that coming to terms with such an important loss can take as long to get over as it did to fall into the relationship in the first place, which would suggest at least a couple of years passed before the wounds were healed enough for her to discuss the subject openly.

When she eventually did so, it was an older, wiser woman speaking. The actress had shrewdly realized that, in crude terms, when it came to her career, her personal life was a commodity, so she had to evoke painful subjects without giving too much away. Following Oldman's shame after his arrest, she knew she would always have the public's sympathy vote, so her words were carefully chosen only ever to hint at the truth behind the break-up and always to show the experience as a personal learning curve, which of course, it was.

First, she always placed events firmly in the past: '[My marriage] has no relation to the present. It's like a black-and-white movie and the subtitles are in a language I don't remember how to speak.' Although setting it aside in this way, she by no means dodged responsibility for its failure.

'It's complicated,' she would continue, 'but basically I had a delusion that I was more adult than I was, that I was responsible for all kinds of things that I wasn't . . . I didn't have enough experience to realize that relationships can be so dysfunctional.'

Only ever vaguely alluding to her ex-husband's alcoholism, Uma said, 'Gary had his problems then,' before speaking in more general terms about people who refuse to be helped: 'You realize that you're not gonna save anybody's day. They might like their unhappy circumstances, and ultimately resent you for thinking you're going to offer them something else.'

Finally, to show she was completely recovered, Uma would always conclude the subject on a positive note, saying, 'Even if it's painful, ultimately you may find it was an inoculation against something else. And you can, in hindsight, be grateful.'

Of course, one of the most striking things about Uma's personal development started when she was very young: the ability to view life as transient. 'Most of us want to cling to the familiar and the safe,' says Phil Joanou. 'But [Uma's] very aware of the temporary nature of most things in life.' Indeed, the actress's sorrow at the discovery her parents wouldn't always be there for her at the age of five or six now translated into a calm acceptance of fate.

'I believe you learn as much as you can from every relationship,' she said. 'Most aren't meant to last a lifetime and you keep on looking . . .

'The divorce from Gary Oldman was very extreme and difficult, but when I look back at an extraordinarily colourful chapter, there is no mark on me from it . . . I think resilience is one of the most important qualities a person can have.

'I found out a lot, though. And I loved him so much. It was an amazing initiation into adulthood.'

And so Oldman drifted off into a complicated personal wilderness of his own making: a two-year broken engagement to Italian actress and model Isabella Rossellini, and a third marriage to American photographer Donya Fiorentino, which collapsed amid allegations of abuse after three years and two more sons. He eventually tackled his alcoholism in rehab when he realized he couldn't remember the entire shoot for *The Scarlet Letter*. Professionally, his career went from strength to strength with stellar performances in Tony Scott's *True Romance*, Luc Besson's *Léon* (retitled *The Professional* in America) and Ridley Scott's *Hannibal*, among many others. His 1997 directorial debut, *Nil By Mouth*, was an unflinching, semi-autobiographical examination of a dysfunctional working-class family and was instantly hailed as a critical masterpiece.

'We're good friends now and I've nothing but good wishes for him,' says Uma, forever loyal about his particular brand of genius. 'He's a fine actor. Anything he plays, he'll play with ridiculous, manic professionalism and excellence.'

Her parting shot gave as much insight into their volatile personal life as anything ever would.

*

Back in September 1991, the show quite literally had to go on. Just days after splitting from Gary Oldman, a hollow-eyed Uma busied herself with her next film. Having submitted to third billing for her last picture, *Final Analysis*, she now had a starring role in the true sense of the words and she was determined to do it justice.

Uma was to play Helena Robertson in *Jennifer 8*. Unusually in terms of contemporary cinema fare, the heroine would be disabled, in this case blind.

The picture was a thriller about a burned-out detective's obsession with a serial killer who targets blind girls – 'Jennifer' being the Jane Doe-like code name assigned to the case. Having witnessed his last assassination, Helena looks likely to become the eighth victim on the killer's list. Facing resistance from within the police force as he reopens the case, the detective, John Berlin, finds himself increasingly attracted to Helena, who closely resembles his dead wife. He vows to protect her life, whatever the cost to his own.

Jennifer 8 was written and directed by Bruce Robinson. A former actor, the Englishman's screenwriting talents were demonstrated in his award-winning script for 1984's *The Killing Fields*. He followed this with exceptional turns as a director on two satires starring Richard E. Grant: *Withnail And I* in 1987 and *How To Get Ahead In Advertising* in

1989. *Jennifer 8* was to be Robinson's third directorial foray, and his first in the serial-killer genre.

Relocating from Wimbledon, south-west London, to Gore Vidal's villa on Outpost Drive, Los Angeles, Robinson was delighted when *Jennifer 8* was granted a generous budget from Paramount Pictures. Over the summer he recruited Uma as Helena, Andy Garcia as John Berlin and Lance Henricksen as Berlin's brother-in-law and fellow detective. John Malkovich, from the heady days of *Dangerous Liaisons*, would feature in a small but potent cameo as a fey interrogator with a nasty head cold.

Before filming commenced at North Shore Studios in Vancouver that October, Thurman and Garcia arrived at Robinson's villa for rehearsals in mid-September. For Garcia, it was business as usual, as the actor had allowed himself to be somewhat typecast over the last decade. 'I spent seven years without working, so if they're making cop movies, I'll play cops,' he said by way of excuse. 'I got two kids to bring up.'

But in the bizarre revolving world of Uma, rehearsals at Robinson's home coincided with Richard E. Grant visiting his old friend and colleague; the unexpected meeting must have been awkward to say the least, considering that Grant had been comforting a frazzled Gary Oldman on the set of *Dracula*. It was not a fortuitous start, and unfortunately the making of *Jennifer 8* was doomed for yet more disaster.

*

A new group of executives at Paramount had inherited *Jennifer 8* from a previous management, and from the very beginning the shoot and subsequent editing process formed a hostile battleground, or, as Bruce Robinson put it, 'a first-rate, Class A nightmare'. Having handed over a $25 million budget to a British director – who, although undeniably proven and respected within his field, had yet to oversee a real Hollywood blockbuster – the producers were on Robinson's case from the outset.

The disputes started early on when the suits from Paramount descended on the film set, where the director was busy presiding over some dramatic chase scenes. Working closely with his cinematographer, Conrad Hall, Robinson was attempting to make the atmosphere on screen mirror the claustrophobic darkness of the twofold subject matter (the hunt for the killer and Helena's blindness), using various exploratory lighting techniques for different effects. Much of the film employs two extreme weather conditions alternately – deep snow for an oppressingly harsh brightness and incessant rain for dense depression – to excellent effect. To heighten the tension further and concurrently reflect the experience of the killer's blind victims, many scenes were shot in the dark with just the detectives' flashlights as illumination. It was a bold move, but not one which should have sounded alarm bells, considering the ground-breaking visual impact of films such as Ridley Scott's perennially rain-drenched *Blade Runner* or John Carpenter's snowy and intensely claustrophobic remake of *The Thing*, both from 1982.

Yet Robinson recalls that the executives suddenly became very nervous. 'These guys are scratching their asses in their Gucci shoes, saying, "What was that? It's all black and dark!" They freaked out,' he says.

As Uma rightly recalls, 'If films didn't cost, this wouldn't be an issue. When there's $25 million lying around, it's trouble.' So Paramount began to fret that Robinson was frittering their money away on a shadowy turkey that no one would pay to see, and when the shoot spilled seventeen days over schedule, things got very nasty. Although the screen stars were safe due to their high profiles and contracts, soon the main crew members found their very jobs under threat.

'They tried to fire everyone at one point or another,' says Garcia, referring to Paramount's attempts to remove Robinson and Hall from the project. The actor – on whose name the success of the movie largely hung – took it upon himself to campaign on the director's behalf. 'The only reason I didn't get fired was Andy,' Robinson agrees.

Uma too wished to protect the integrity of the film and joined forces with her co-star. 'We were fiercely loyal,' she recalls. 'We weathered it that way. It's hard to make a film when there's a dispute about the movie itself.' Further quarrels would continue long after the actors had moved on to their next projects, as the original cut of *Jennifer 8* was trimmed by some fifteen minutes when test audiences deemed it far too long.

The director would become very vocal in his disappointment with Paramount, speaking in a BBC interview about his anger at the enforced change of climax and the huge amount of scenes – mainly featuring the enigmatic John Malkovich – that sadly ended up on the cutting-room floor.

*

Jennifer 8 was released on 6 November 1992 in America in a somewhat low-key fashion. Ludicrously, it was suggested that audiences avoided the film because they incorrectly assumed it to be a sequel, and they hadn't seen *Jennifer 1*, *Jennifer 2* and so on. In Britain and throughout much of Europe, the film went straight to video.

It received praise from many critics because, despite its faults, it was a worthy attempt at a different slant on the archetypal serial-killer flick, which would normally focus mostly on violence. Conrad Hall's cinematography and Bruce Robinson's adamance had paid off in full as many reviewers were affected by the film's atmospheric stillness, its dark sense of menace and foreboding, and the bleak oppression of the weather. As the director rightly claimed, 'No one can say this is not a brilliantly photographed film.'

Furthermore, the characters were interesting, the plot was tense and intriguing, the downbeat, melancholic approach was new, and all of the cast put in sterling performances. But there was no escaping the fact that this was a severely uneven piece of work.

Most likely because of the pressured shoot and the severe cuts, after an excellent beginning *Jennifer 8* seems to lose its sense of direction in the middle section, where parts become slow and inexplicably drawn out. Worst of all, the ending is rushed: everything seems forced, very little is explained, and consequences are not explored. The inappropriate presence of an obviously tacked-on retrospective voiceover attempting to smooth over the rough edges does not help. It really does feel like the people behind this film simply ran out of the time necessary to do a good story justice.

Jennifer 8 also suffered from the same grating implausibility in its basic premise as *Final Analysis*. Where the plot of the latter crossed the doctor–patient boundary, here it was highly unlikely that a professional cop would have a fling with the sole witness and suspected next victim in an open murder case, regardless of her resemblance to his dead wife.

Once again, it has to be said that Uma's performance is excellent. Dressed in baggy clothes and bereft of any make-up or accessories, here she displays for the first time on screen her extraordinary ability to appear beautiful, ugly, or completely blend into her surroundings at the drop of a hat. She portrays Helena as distant and otherworldly, which works well given her blindness and the circumstances which caused her affliction. For the character of Helena required the actress not only to portray sightlessness, but also to play a woman who was blinded at the age of fourteen in a car accident that wiped out her entire family. Because the tragedy occurred at such a crucial stage in her development, she never properly finished puberty (nor, presumably, had a mother figure to guide her into adulthood), so she almost doesn't know how to be a woman, making her doubly disabled.

This unexpected depth is depicted sensitively by Uma during a party scene in which she finds herself utterly lost. Left standing among strangers who don't realize that she is blind, Helena's nerves shatter one by one and, unable to express the pain she is experiencing in this public place, she breaks down.

Uma's performance is equally mesmerizing when she is stalked. The scene in which Helena strips and takes a bath, all the time watched by the killer, who is present in the room from the outset, stands as being genuinely frightening. Having by now totally rejected any nudity clauses in her contracts, the obvious body double does not detract from the close-ups on Uma's face as Helena first relaxes, then slowly begins to suspect something is terribly wrong. Her growing terror in her vulnerable state is thoroughly convincing and uncomfortable to watch as her eyes literally shoot everywhere uncontrollably.

As a blind woman and therefore without using her eyes, Uma also manages to convey Helena's thoughts and feelings when she is alone on screen by the flickering expressions on her face and her hunted body language. She is also accomplished at not completely focusing or slightly crossing her eyes, which is creepy in itself. Her performance is subtle and not at all clichéd, which would have been all too easy a trap to fall into with *Jennifer 8*, and she thoroughly deserved the accolades afforded her and the director at the Cognac Festival du Film Policier in 1993.

10

EVEN FILM STARS GET THE BLUES

'I didn't feel light for a while. The girlish laughter had gone.'

UMA THURMAN

After Uma's twenty-second birthday in April 1992, she stood at a crossroads. Looking back on this unhappy period today, she admits that she was confused and unsatisfied, lacking direction both in her career and her personal life.

Professionally, although consistent, she had so far failed to live up to the high expectations resulting from her explosive beginnings on *Dangerous Liaisons* and *The Adventures Of Baron Munchausen*. She was clearly a strong and talented actress and had showed as much in almost every movie, but her choices of material were often poor or misguided.

The worst effect resulting from Uma's constant shift in genres was an almost total antithesis of typecasting, as she herself acknowledges: 'My attempt not to be cast in a Hollywood niche definitely started hurting. It hit my ability to get good work. I never seemed an obvious choice for anything.'

Behind the scenes, Uma had obviously been through a lot more than her peers, the initial joy and then very public anguish of her failed marriage providing her with an understandable excuse if her work was sometimes off kilter or unfocused. Terry Gilliam recalls his surprise to see her at a party held for *Bram Stoker's Dracula*, a bash at which her ex was also present. Her former director noticed a great change in the actress's demeanour – '[She] had somehow aged overnight, lost her youth' – and wondered why she seemed so 'drawn to difficult people'.

Uma hated people knowing about her private life: 'I would go to any lengths to keep it secret. I became neurotic.'

It was obvious that something had to give; after a stressful year, Uma was spent. 'The film business can turn you into an infant,' she says. 'You become addicted to the telephone and talking to your agent all the time . . .

'I needed to take a break; I didn't want the memories of my early twenties to be in a trailer, eating catered food.' So, following in her parents' footsteps, Uma announced she would be taking some much-needed time off and went travelling.

She relished the freedom. 'I was totally independent – just getting up, leaving everybody behind and flying off from one day to the next without stopping,' she says.

Rediscovering the youth buried under the wreckage of her marriage to a much older man, Uma revisited her childhood haunts, returning to India. As an adult, she now noticed far more the plight of the sick, the hungry and the homeless, and somehow the horror of it all turned into an inspiration to go on fighting.

'There were people with their noses falling off from leprosy,' she says, 'but I didn't scream and go running off to Bloomingdale's.' Slowly but surely, Uma regained her sense of perspective.

During this pilgrimage, Uma examined her motives to stay in the film industry. A niggling feeling had wormed its way to the forefront of her mind: she had whimsically decided on an acting career as a teenager, and her desire to succeed and assert her independence might now be standing in the way of her happiness as a grown woman. In dropping out of school she had inadvertently closed too many doors – maybe she *should* please her parents and return to her education?

'I thrashed out whether I should go to college,' Uma remembers. 'The decision of a sixteen-year-old person is a lark, not a mature person's all-things-taken-into-consideration epiphany.'

After much soul-searching, Uma found a deep-rooted passion remained for acting that was not to be easily shaken off. She no longer needed the money, but Uma still craved the challenge, the excitement and the risk.

'In the end, I decided to stick with it,' she says.

*

The Uma who returned from her voyage of self-discovery was virtually unrecognizable. Pensive, unmade-up and often dressed in neutral, sexless clothes, she was surrounded in a swirling, hazy cloud from her endless chain-smoking. Sick of the constant criticism of her work, Uma had done a lot of growing up and was determined that people should take her as they found her.

Her burning ambition was the first thing that struck those who met her during this period: a steely determination to face the stalemate in her career head-on. When questioned about her personal shortcomings, Uma wouldn't hesitate. 'I don't think I'm terribly diplomatic,' she said. 'I notice many more times when I've been short with people than when I've been empathetic. I think, "Why did I have to say that to that person?" '

Resolutely arriving at her agent's office, Uma was relieved to find that work was still there if she wanted it, although the available options might not be as obvious as for other more typecast actresses. Perhaps because she now recognized the need to test herself rigorously to make her career work for her and fill the void that remained after Oldman's departure, she accepted two very different roles at the same time.

The first was the part of Glory in *Mad Dog And Glory*, a high-profile 'girlfriend' part in a romantic gangster comedy, placing her opposite a big name: Robert De Niro. This would fulfil the necessary box-office demands as well as require her to prove herself opposite a major star.

The second couldn't have been more different: Uma would star as Sissy Hankshaw in Gus Van Sant's forthcoming *Only Cowgirls Get The Blues*, which would allow her to stretch her ability to its limit in a potentially ground-breaking movie.

With two such exciting projects lined up, the recovering divorcée even allowed herself to relax and enjoy a few casual dates in the late spring of 1992. Uma found to her irritation that many men did not approach her, either viewing her as untouchable due to her iconic image, too complicated after her divorce, or simply too experienced, as she explains, 'You're just not helpless any more, so there's a whole section of men that don't take a shot because you're too much trouble.'

Still, a beautiful young film star will inevitably attract attention, and Uma found herself briefly hooking up with John Cusack. A fellow actor, he understood the limitations of Uma's career and was closer to her own age, at just four years her senior. Born into a theatrical family, Cusack had also broken into movies in his teens, and his dark good looks, solid performances and versatility had carved out a reliable niche in the Hollywood machine. Having recently starred as a con artist in Stephen Frears's 1990 film *The Grifters*, and in *Shadows And*

Fog with John Malkovich the following year, he and Uma had several mutual friends.

But Thurman wasn't interested in getting into anything serious, and for a while Cusack provided her with no-strings entertainment. 'I was still pretty much single and getting over Gary,' she says. 'My ambition was just to be free and young. Whether or not I dated, I needed a lot of space around me.'

It was perhaps fortunate that Uma did not become involved, as during this period her mother was diagnosed with Guillain-Barré Syndrome and was hospitalized in intensive care.

GBS is an acute autoimmune disease of the peripheral nerves, which causes the nerves in the arms and legs to become inflamed and stop working. Affecting only one or two people in every 100,000, the rare condition is thought to be triggered by a throat or intestinal infection, influenza or stress. Initially manifesting itself in a tingling or numb sensation in the fingers and toes and a progressive inability of movement, it can be extremely painful, leaving the victim weak and suffering from loss of feeling in the limbs. There is a very real risk in some cases of complete paralysis, which if it spreads to the chest and freezes the respiratory muscles leaves the patient dependent on a ventilator and feeding tube. But for those 80 per cent of cases making a full recovery, a hospital stay of more than three months is necessary.

It was a horribly frightening period for Nena and all of Uma's family, but with time and care she returned to good health.

*

During the summer of 1992, Uma started work on her next project, *Mad Dog And Glory*.

Martin Scorsese is one of the most prominent filmmakers of the post-war era, redefining modern cinema during the 1970s and 1980s with classics such as *Taxi Driver*, *Raging Bull*, *The Color Of Money* and *Goodfellas*. It was his life's ambition to film a biopic of Jesus and in 1983 he began work on *The Last Temptation Of Christ*. When the project's funding collapsed, he was forced to take on other work to raise the required cash.

The success of *The Color Of Money* finally enabled him to finish *The Last Temptation Of Christ*, but in order to secure Universal Pictures' backing, Scorsese signed a contract agreeing to produce one movie a year during the early 1990s. The first was *Cape Fear*, swiftly followed by *Mad Dog And Glory*.

Keen to give the second commercial venture a different feel,

Scorsese chose protégé John McNaughton as director. The veteran filmmaker had supported McNaughton's disturbingly violent debut, *Henry, Portrait Of A Serial Killer*, the previous year and now offered him the chance to break into mainstream movies.

McNaughton was fascinated with crime and criminals, and *Mad Dog And Glory* was the perfect project for him. 'Mad Dog' is the ironic nickname given to Wayne Dobie, the most mild-mannered police photographer in Chicago, known for never having used his gun. Walking in on a robbery at a convenience store, Dobie is forced to take action and saves the life of the feisty shop owner. The victim turns out to be local mobster Frank Milo, who is disgruntled that he owes his life to a cop.

Nonetheless, Milo is indebted and invites Dobie to his club. Dobie, equally uncomfortable at fraternizing with the enemy, believes that to be the end of the matter – until the next morning, when a young lady named Glory lands on his doorstep. It turns out that she is a gift, an accessory for his apartment on loan for a week. Dobie refuses the kind offer, but Glory insists on staying, explaining that she is working for Milo to pay off her brother's debt.

As the two awkwardly muddle through the week, they play straight into Milo's hands by falling in love. Milo is willing to sell Glory to pay off her debt, but Dobie can't raise enough cash. Instead, he musters the strength of character to battle it out.

McNaughton, along with producers Martin Scorsese and Steve Jones, supervised the casting over the summer of 1991, and predictably they organized a read-through with Robert De Niro, one of the most respected actors of his generation who had repeatedly and successfully worked with Scorsese for almost two decades. What was unusual was that De Niro performed the screenplay twice in succession, trying both the leads to see which he preferred.

'I was leaning towards Wayne but I wanted to get some input on it,' explains De Niro. 'Everyone seemed to feel that Wayne was the better part for me to do. Frank Milo is a great part. He's ironic, he's a comedian, there was a lot of fun stuff. But I've done that before, so it was actually better for me to do Wayne.'

Some critics suggested that De Niro could have done the role in his sleep, but as producer Steve Jones comments, 'Wayne's sort of a homebody, a nerdy kind of guy. For Bob, who's often the crazy man, it was much more of an acting role.'

In preparation for this different part, De Niro spent some time on the beat with New York detectives, attending the scene of a homicide in the Bronx and a murder-suicide in Queens. According to the professionals he was shadowing, the actor did not shy away from the incidents, adopting a hands-on approach.

When De Niro opted not to play the role of Frank Milo, he made an odd suggestion that Bill Murray should play the gang boss. One of the original *Saturday Night Live* cast during the 1970s, Murray naturally graduated to mainstream comedy movies, culminating in 1984's smash hit *Ghostbusters*. In a sudden about-face, Murray tried his hand at literary drama in an adaptation of Somerset Maugham's *The Razor's Edge*, but the unsuspecting public seemed uncomfortable with his change of image and the film flopped. Following this humiliation, Murray took a few years out in self-imposed exile and only gradually returned to films in the late 1980s. The meaty role of comic baddie Frank Milo therefore appealed as a way to reprise his tried-and-tested funnyman role, while branching out into new genres.

'The first time you hear the idea of Bill Murray as this mobster, it doesn't sound so great,' admits McNaughton. 'Then you go, "Well, wait a minute, he'd be great." He's really rather amazing to see with his hair slicked back, in an Italian suit.' The leading men were backed up by reliable character actors David Caruso and Mike Starr, which left only the alluring part of Glory to cast.

Uma was resolute in her determination to rebuild her career after a run of mediocre films and, although she was once again cast because of her looks, jumped at the chance to star opposite the brilliant Robert De Niro. 'She's like Garbo,' McNaughton says. 'Feature for feature it shouldn't work, but put them all together, and you get this incredible face.'

Uma didn't like the way her character could be portrayed as a helpless victim, but she acknowledged that abuse happens and resolved to tell Glory's story without resorting to being the prey. 'She is an indentured servant, an unsophisticated, working-class South Side Chicago girl desperately trying to get some control over her life,' explains Uma. 'That's her plight, but she's not a wimp.' Uma had learned a lot from squaring up to her director on the set of *Henry & June* and drew on her confidence and conviction to play the character as she saw fit.

*

Filming for *Mad Dog And Glory* commenced in the summer of 1992 and went relatively smoothly. The biggest issue encountered was the love scenes between Mad Dog and Glory.

De Niro had rarely been required for major romancing on screen. Contrary to his moniker, Dobie is shy and unconfident, on top of which he is firmly against any relationship with Milo's 'property'; conversely, it is Glory's job to entertain Dobie's every whim. This makes a promising scenario and the first sex scene is as realistic as it is clumsy.

'That was one of my favourite scenes when it was written and it was pretty well realized too,' said De Niro. 'I've done love scenes in other films which were maybe a little more pretentious, but I thought this was a good love scene . . . They are very hard to do, they're very awkward.' Like many actors, De Niro found it difficult to evoke intimacy while the rest of the crew ogled from the sidelines, but here his self-consciousness actually helped. Uma, however, was weary of her sex-object image and was apparently miserable about being treated like a piece of meat on the set.

Physicality aside, her co-star proved the perfect acting foil for Uma, despite his reputation for being demanding. His self-confessed combination of 'anarchy and discipline' at work was of invaluable assistance to the uneasy divorcée in her early twenties. 'His approach was irreverent and playful. He had an intense, focused, lively, interactive energy,' she says. 'He gave everything to me as a performer, shouted at me off-camera till he was hoarse to get me into the emotional state that the scene required and that I was struggling to get to. He was an absolutely pure and pristine professional, an actor who demands total concentration on the work.'

Interestingly, De Niro's rapport with younger female actresses had always been that of quietly controlling tutor. Cathy Moriarty, who worked with him on *Raging Bull*, was one such innocent novice. 'The way the movie was shot I wasn't able to create my own character,' she explains. 'I was playing what Robert De Niro saw through his eyes . . . Learning acting from a genius like De Niro is like getting singing lessons from Pavarotti.' Although Uma was no beginner, she too absorbed all the advice and wisdom De Niro was offering.

Mad Dog And Glory was released at the beginning of March 1993 in America to mixed reviews and poor box-office takings. Unfortunately, as the crux of the plot is a man treating a woman as a commodity to sell, it felt tired – Scorsese and McNaughton had jumped on the bandwagon too late. In 1990 Richard Gere bought prostitute Julia Roberts for a week before setting her free in *Pretty Woman*, while two years later Nicolas Cage lost his wife Sarah Jessica Parker for a weekend in a poker game in *Honeymoon In Vegas*. *Billy Bathgate* (1991) told the tale of a gangster's moll falling in love with her temporary keeper and had an equally heavyweight cast, including Dustin Hoffman, Bruce Willis and Nicole Kidman.

Worst of all, 1993 also saw the release of the long-awaited *Indecent Proposal*, in which Robert Redford pays $1 million for a night with Demi Moore, which turned out to be one of the top-grossing films of the year. *Mad Dog And Glory* didn't stand a chance, although the screenwriter defended the originality of his version, saying that it was inspired by a real story.

Overall it is a good film, with a smart script combining comedy, action and drama in an accessible fashion, well acted by a stellar cast. Although hardly ground-breaking or edge-of-the-seat material, it is not disappointing, as *Variety* summarized: 'A pleasurably offbeat picture that manages the rare trick of being both charming and edgy.'

While De Niro endured a lot of criticism for acting in 'quickie' lightweight films to fund his property purchases, Uma shone opposite the veteran and truly showed her ability when given the chance. As Glory she is refreshingly down-to-earth, and her portrayal of a woman frustrated at being trapped yet honour-bound to pay off her brother's debt is touching. Although *Mad Dog And Glory* won no awards and didn't really aid the careers of De Niro or Murray, it certainly boosted Uma Thurman as an actress.

*

Robert De Niro is a powerful Method actor with an extensive CV encompassing landmark films such as *Mean Streets*, *Taxi Driver*, *The Deer Hunter*, *Raging Bull*, *The Untouchables* and *Goodfellas*. Yet beneath his glittering professional career lies an abnormally complicated personal life, primarily caused by his inability to commit to a monogamous relationship.

During his marriage to Diahnne Abbott (during which he adopted her daughter Drina), De Niro fathered a son, Raphael, but husband and wife curiously maintained separate lives and homes. Simultaneously, De Niro conducted an ongoing romance with Doris 'Toukie' Smith, with whom he tried but failed to have a baby. After divorcing Abbott, De Niro pursued a series of high-profile affairs with the likes of Helena Lisandrello, Gillian De Terville, Whitney Houston and Naomi Campbell. All the while he continued to see Toukie, who tragically suffered a miscarriage, and the two finally split due to a paternity suit from Lisandrello.

The ladies' man was simultaneously dating the fiercely possessive Campbell and resolving the messy Lisandrello affair when he first met Thurman on *Mad Dog And Glory*.

It appears that Uma, like many young actresses before her, fell for the mature charms of De Niro, at once inspired by and in awe of his magnitude. A relationship seemed almost inevitable given De Niro's propensity for affairs with younger women, but perhaps it is more important to note once again Uma's gravitational pull to volatile 'bad boy' types touched with pure genius.

While De Niro's acting prowess cannot be denied, he is also renowned for public outbursts. When harangued by the press for spreading himself too thinly during the early 1990s, De Niro repeatedly exploded at trusted interviewers and was accused more than once of assaulting photographers who got too close to him.

With her recent and newsworthy divorce in mind, Uma was careful to keep her association with De Niro both quiet and casual. The nomadic life of a working actor (not to mention De Niro's wandering eye) helped to enforce the nonchalant approach: the couple only dated when they both happened to be in the same place at the same time, rather than passionately chasing each other around the world.

Furthermore, they toyed with the press, occasionally admitting to being an item and then laughing it off as a joke. 'I'd love to make another movie with him,' Uma elaborated, 'but it's not like a social arrangement for either of us. It's our work. I hope some agent puts that on their list of things to do – a good movie for us!' While the focus of this comment was on De Niro as an actor, Uma also hinted that they enjoyed each other's company whenever possible.

Uma was an unusual choice for De Niro. He rarely dated white women and she was a couple of inches taller than him, although in fact he was unfazed by her height. 'Robert De Niro, who's shorter than me, loved it [that I'm tall],' she giggled. 'I think he wanted me to wear heels.'

During this happy, carefree time in her twenty-third year, Uma finally learnt to drive. She usually travelled on the subway, citing it as a 'busload of reality', but thoroughly enjoyed the freedom of a car when she passed her test. August 1993 also signalled a landmark for De Niro as he turned fifty – the age gap was more than double that between Thurman and Oldman. With a guest list resembling a *Who's Who* of New York, including Thurman, Smith, Abbott and his children, he revelled in his surprise party. Realizing that he had reached a turning point, he branched out into directing and producing, notably with *A Bronx Tale*, the acclaimed film released later that same year.

Unfortunately, De Niro's time of change also spelt the end for his fling with Uma and the pair stopped their relaxed dalliance amicably in 1994. A few years later, Uma inexplicably felt obliged to deny the two-year-old affair, stating to *Vanity Fair*: 'We became friends, though contrary to rumour never an item.'

Young, free and single, Uma returned to the dating scene refreshed and invigorated. Stopping one day at a cash machine, she was accosted by a good-looking young man, who fell over himself in his enthusiasm, praising her work and saying he was also an actor. Assuming he was a fan, Uma politely brushed his attentions aside.

'I tried to sound smart to impress her. But she just gave me a filthy look and swept off with another bloke,' said Ethan Hawke later, with a wry smile.

11

A HITCHHIKER'S GUIDE TO DISASTER

'What do you believe in?'
'Ha ha, ho ho and hee hee.'

SISSY AND THE CHINK, *EVEN*
COWGIRLS GET THE BLUES

After *Mad Dog And Glory* wrapped, Uma's schedule led her straight into *Even Cowgirls Gets The Blues*, potentially the biggest role of her career.

Certainly the most colourful character Uma had worked with since Terry Gilliam, the openly gay Gus Van Sant specialized in avant-garde and experimental dramas. When the wind blew his way, the director was capable of pleasing both an unconventional cult following and a mainstream audience with his quirky visual flourishes, vibrant humour and an innovative way with actors.

Having developed a keen fascination with people existing on the margins of society – junkies, disturbed geniuses and disaffected teenagers – Van Sant's first release was 1985's *Mala Noche*, which was critically if not commercially successful. This promising debut was followed by the excellent *Drugstore Cowboy* in 1989, the story of a gang of drug addicts who rob pharmacies to support their habit, which provided Van Sant's true breakthrough. *My Own Private Idaho* in 1991 traced the exploits of two male prostitutes (beautifully played by River Phoenix and Keanu Reeves); exploring the director's favourite themes of alienation, unrequited love, betrayal and the meaning of family, *Idaho* brought him immense prestige.

Searching for a suitable vehicle to expound his singular style, Van Sant seized upon Tom Robbins's bestseller *Even Cowgirls Get The Blues*, a virtuoso piece of American counterculture in which the heroine, Sissy Hankshaw, follows a Jack Kerouac-inspired trek across the country, hitchhiking her way to adventure with the aid of her oversized thumbs. Van Sant had first read the novel shortly after its publication in 1976. 'I really liked it and it was something I'd wanted to film ever since, though I had no way to really do it,' he recalls. Flushed with the success of his last two films, Van Sant sought out the author and requested his permission to adapt Sissy Hankshaw's odyssey for film. 'I was absolutely delighted,' says Robbins, 'because I had seen *Drugstore Cowboy* and realized that this man is a real artist.'

Casting for *Even Cowgirls Get The Blues* began as early as September 1991, when Van Sant revisited his beloved former stars, recruiting Keanu Reeves and River Phoenix for small roles and River's sister Rain in the larger part of Sissy's gay lover. Finding his Sissy was a different task altogether, until the director became bewitched by one Uma Thurman.

'She was very exotic, a kind of self-taught girl,' he recalls of their meeting. 'Sissy is described in various ways, and one of the ways to go was a presence that Uma had. Uma is somewhat otherworldly, a kind of divine presence.' Uma signed up on the spot, having read and adored Robbins's novel as a teenager.

She and director Gus Van Sant were joined on set by a large, eclectic cast including John Hurt, Noriyuki 'Pat' Morita, Lorraine Bracco, Angie Dickinson, Heather Graham, Roseanne Barr, Crispin Glover, Keanu Reeves, and Rain Phoenix in her first major film role as an adult actress. The movie was also littered with cameos, including Rain's brother River in an uncredited part as a heavily disguised birdwatcher and the Beat author William S. Burroughs, appearing as himself.

It was nice to work with familiar faces again, although *Cowgirls* was a far cry from Uma's last work with Reeves and Glover: costume drama and domestic farce had made way for offbeat lesbian-feminist exploratory cinema.

In *Even Cowgirls Get The Blues*, after a spell of teenage modelling for feminine hygiene products, Sissy Hankshaw (Thurman) becomes the self-proclaimed greatest hitchhiker in the world. She was born with abnormally large thumbs, which she counts as a blessing because they never fail to stop cars. Seeking adventure, Sissy hooks up with her old 'agent', a transvestite known only as The Countess (Hurt). Sissy is still a virgin at the age of twenty-nine, and after an unsuccessful bid to improve her sex life, during which she meets asthmatic artist Julian (Reeves), The Countess sends her off to his cattle-ranch-cum-women's-health-farm, the Rubber Rose, to film one last commercial. The advert is to be set against a background of the last surviving flock of American whooping cranes, during their mating season.

But the Rubber Rose is in the process of being taken over by a gang of lesbian and feminist cowgirls led by Bonanza Jellybean (Phoenix). Jellybean has had a crush on Sissy since seeing a picture of her in a magazine, and her free-spirited enthusiasm for life soon wins Sissy's undying love and lust. Jellybean also introduces Sissy to The Chink (Morita), a mysterious wise man living on a cliff overlooking the ranch whose philosophy is embodied by the mantra 'Ha ha, ho ho, hee hee'. To his delight, both Jellybean and Sissy engage in sexual intercourse with him.

Meanwhile, as the mutiny at the ranch approaches its climax and the cowgirls drug the whooping cranes and hold them hostage, Sissy's loyalty is torn between The Countess, Jellybean and The Chink. As armed federal agents descend upon the ranch to try and save the birds from extinction, the showdown reaches epic proportions and a life will be lost.

It was an ambitious project, but Van Sant had his largest budget to date (a comparatively meagre $8.5 million) and everyone seemed committed to their highly unusual characters.

At first Uma was particularly inspired by Sissy, whose path to the ranch had been far from smooth. She and Van Sant had long talks about exactly how to portray the character around whom events seem to occur without really affecting her. In Robbins's book, Sissy, the perennial hitchhiker, is convinced that she can alter reality by her perception of motion, so it was a conscious decision between director and actress to play Sissy as very still, as if always in a trance.

'She is always observing, a witness to her own story,' says the actress. 'She's not a reactive, interactive, average human being like you and me but has a very Zen perspective, reflecting Tom Robbins's multicultural worldview.'

Therefore, even before shooting commenced, Uma was presented with an immediate dilemma. As everything happens *around* Sissy and she merely watches over events with a benign indifference, Uma felt she had nowhere to go with her character, a considerable problem for an actress who badly needed to prove herself on screen.

It almost seemed unworkable.

'I was stuck with an untranslatable thing as the core of my character,' she says. 'And I had to develop it . . .

'There are many scenes when I don't speak. It's difficult to make a film where the central character is not active.' One thing Uma decided she could do in her 'mute' scenes was to make the most of her reactionary shots and give away clues to Sissy's character with her expressions and body language. It was something she had developed beyond the normal range of an actor in the part of *Jennifer 8*, and here it might just save her skin.

'I think of Sissy as being supremely simple, completely reflective and dreamlike in her own space,' she continues. 'At the same time she's a goofy, comic character with big thumbs.'

Ah yes, the thumbs. A freak of nature, Sissy's thumbs are twice the length of normal digits, are super-supple and basically represent phalluses – part of the reason she is so attractive to the cowgirls. That they get stiff and sore if Sissy ceases hitchhiking for too long and that one of them continues to move after it is severed are metaphors perhaps best left unexplored. The symbolism goes deeper than the obvious level, though, as they allow Sissy to hitchhike wherever she wants in the country, signifying liberation as well as individuality and nonconformity.

And so for the duration, Uma was fitted with two long prosthetic thumbs and had to learn to use them as if they were naturally part of her body – no easy task. Remarkably, over the course of the shoot she became quite attached to them, though not in a literal sense.

'I had a dream in which my great thumbs were mine!' she laughs. 'I woke up and felt the phantom limbs. As if I had them. I felt for them and grieved their loss.'

'It's not penis envy, it's freedom envy!'

Finally, Uma seemed to strike a balance between Sissy's problematic passivity, her physical restrictions (thanks to the props department) and her own intense motivation to develop the character further. It was just what Van Sant had hoped for.

'With her energy, her looks, her adventurousness, Uma becomes Sissy Hankshaw for me,' he said towards the end of the shoot. 'The character at this point is an amalgamation of Uma herself and a fictitious character. I think Uma's more in touch with the intellectual building of character than I am.'

Working off Uma, the rest of the cast eventually settled and found their own way in the muddle of characters and cameos.

'I've wanted to be more communicative so that I'm not simply Miss Aggressive to Sissy's Miss Passive, even though it is that way with regards to the dialogue,' said Rain Phoenix of her quest to bring a rather sweet love affair to life. 'As far as how we relate when we're sleeping under the stars, it isn't like I jump on top of Sissy and start going at it; it's more that I look for her approval in the way I behave.'

Nevertheless, Uma's transformation was beyond some of the cast and Keanu Reeves for one would later admit that he was terrified of her as her 'character was so powerful'.

*

Even Cowgirls Get The Blues received its world premiere in September 1993 at the Toronto Film Festival. As Roger Ebert, one of the critics in the audience, recalls, 'I remember the hush that descended upon the theatre during the screening; it was not so much an absence of noise as the palpable presence of stunned silence.'

Set to open shortly thereafter, the film was pulled by its distributor for a crisis meeting, followed by intensive re-edits. With the movie deemed preposterously inaccessible and incoherent, Van Sant hastily buckled down to the task of avoiding a complete box-office turkey. But just the following month, tragedy hit when River Phoenix died outside Johnny Depp's Viper Room nightclub in Los Angeles on Hallowe'en. Overdosing on a mixture of cocaine, heroin and other drugs, the twenty-three-year-old actor passed away in the company of his sister Rain, his brother Joaquin, and his girlfriend.

Van Sant was distraught. Close to River and his whole family, he now witnessed his previous picture, *My Own Private Idaho*, being used both in eulogies to the actor's enormous talent and being indirectly blamed for his death, for it was during production of that film that Phoenix became addicted to drugs. The director isolated himself with *Even Cowgirls Get The Blues*, pouring his energies into righting that wrong while simultaneously releasing two albums and publishing a novel, *Pink*, a thinly veiled exploration of his grief.

In his attempts to add coherency to *Cowgirls*, Van Sant cut the ending (in which the audience would have discovered Sissy's pregnancy after her encounter with The Chink) and the majority of Sissy's romances with both The Chink and Julian. An extended narration by Tom Robbins was dubbed on to help explain proceedings. Van Sant also added a dedication to the credits, reading simply 'For River', although even that move would later be criticized for forever linking the deceased actor with a film which, among other things, celebrates drug-taking.

Cowgirls was finally released on 20 May 1994, but sadly all of Van Sant's efforts seemed to have been in vain. The freak show paraded across the screen alienated all but a very few of its audience, even provoking raised eyebrows from parts of the gay community.

It is true that homosexuality is fairly rammed down the viewer's throat in this film. John Hurt is overbearingly camp, nothing is remotely subtle about the cowgirls, and the 'dirty pussy attack' as they stage a mutiny at the ranch can be seen as either uproariously funny or sickeningly offensive. Watching Uma pleasure herself with her outsized thumbs didn't make easy viewing for the more prudish viewers either.

Most of the negative criticism focused on the disjointed and surreal nature of the movie – the long period spent re-editing didn't appear to have made any significant dent in the absurdity and there was a severe lack of momentum. Nothing made sense and everything was too out of focus and pretentious for the viewer to care about the characters. Many of the actors were panned for either overacting or not acting at all, with wooden or bland performances at best.

Sissy's giant thumbs unsurprisingly copped a lot of flak, as no matter how hard the prosthetics and make-up departments worked, they still looked unbelievably fake. No one knew how to translate the unspecified meaning of this film – was it a ruthless, hilarious satire of the 1970s hippie and feminist movements, or did it extol those very values at the highest level?

In the States, the *Village Voice* attacked its director, saying, 'Van Sant deranges the novel's eccentricities with his own' and proclaiming it otherwise 'increasingly dull'. *Variety* called it 'at best amusing; at worst, uninvolving, often confusing and sometimes a little boring'. Overseas, *Cowgirls* fared no better, slated as 'a mess' by both the *Guardian* and the *Independent*, an 'epic whimsy' by the *Financial Times*, and 'an embarrassing miscalculation' by *Time Out*.

There are actually some good points to the film. The evocative soundtrack by k. d. lang hints at greater depths than are evident on screen, and the romance between Sissy and Jellybean comes across as the only sincere part of the movie. Interspersed with the unintelligible dialogue are moments of genuine humour, and the silly situations such as Sissy's modelling and hitchhiking could produce a smirk from a viewer whose head isn't buried in his hands by this point.

Incredibly, Uma again emerged from the whole sorry mess relatively unscathed. While her gormless yet serene Sissy irritated some, many praised her for drawing the best she could out of a vastly underwritten part. Her blissful stillness provides an anchor for the rest of the film's crazed meanderings and her innate joy and wonder at life in general breathes much-needed life into her floundering surroundings.

The terrible reception *Cowgirls* endured from so many reviewers and audiences unfortunately doomed what was supposed to be Uma's defining moment to be her most underrated role to date. Far from running screaming and blameless though, Uma answered her critics without flinching. Although admitting that 'the script never really worked', she stood by her choice and her director. 'It was just one of those things that was really ambitious, an adventure into [an] unpaved area, one of those chances I take.' When asked years later if she would repeat the experience given its reception, she said generously that she would, 'because there were some interesting elements and subtexts to that film which for one reason or another weren't recognized'.

Gus Van Sant, although knocked severely off kilter, recovered his otherwise excellent track record with 1995's *To Die For*, taking Nicole Kidman to another level as an actress, before winning mainstream acceptance and a Best Director Oscar nomination with *Good Will Hunting* in 1997.

But recovery takes time and effort, as directors and actors alike well know. Uma may have survived the experience on a personal level, but her career was still in dire jeopardy. The flow of good scripts into her agent's office dwindled, then spluttered to a stop.

12

THE MIA MOVIE

'It is a completely abnormal existence. You live a life of extreme fantasy: everyone thinks you're beautiful, brilliant . . . then the next day you're ugly, you're not talented and you're gone. It's so ruthless.'

RICHARD E. GRANT, ACTOR, HENRY & JUNE

After an inauspicious start, Uma's career had peaked early with *Dangerous Liaisons* and *Henry & June*, and by 1993 she found herself struggling to regain some of her former kudos. She was seriously in need of a boost, but neither starring opposite Robert De Niro nor going out on a limb with the artistic *Even Cowgirls Get The Blues* had provided the answer.

'Every time you haven't worked in a while and you do a bomb, it's like pouring cold water on yourself,' she sighed, unsure of when her next break was going to materialize. No one ever expected that it would come in the guise of Quentin Tarantino.

Tarantino's rise from film-obsessed freak in Tennessee to Hollywood cult writer and director is legendary and reinforces the American mantra that, with conviction, anything is achievable. He grew up watching all genres of movies (not least hardcore foreign-language action films) and Jean-Luc Godard, the figurehead of the post-war French New Wave, was one of his idols.[*]

Upon leaving school, it was natural for Tarantino to take a job in a video store, and it was here, rather than at film school, that he learnt his trade. He began writing scripts in his spare time, often

---

[*] Tarantino later took his production company's name, A Band Apart, from Godard's 1964 film *Bande À Part*.

collaborating with his shop colleague, Roger Avary. By his early twenties, Tarantino had finished the screenplay for *True Romance* (which sold for an impressive $50,000) and the first draft of *Reservoir Dogs*.

The latter movie was to be Tarantino's directorial debut. It describes the preparations and aftermath of an ill-fated heist, slowly unfolding what went wrong. It caught the attention of Harvey Keitel, and, aided by considerable hype about the script within the industry, *Reservoir Dogs* went into production. The film boasted an impressive cast, led by Keitel and also including Steve Buscemi, Tim Roth, Michael Madsen and Chris Penn. Its release in 1992 was awaited with keen interest. The slick dialogue, Scorsese-influenced camerawork, black comedy and shocking violence instantly propelled *Reservoir Dogs* to the height of cool. Suddenly everyone was singing 'Stuck In The Middle With You', talking about Mr Pink, dissecting the ear-slicing scene and raving about Quentin Tarantino.

As is the fickle way of the press, while they loved the new geek-turned-director and heralded his style as the way forward for cinema, they were also waiting for him to fall, convinced that he would simply be a one-hit wonder. Like Thurman, Tarantino was anxious to get the next film right.

Danny DeVito and his production partner, Stacey Sher, saw potential in the vibrant young director even before he filmed *Reservoir Dogs*, and the eager duo offered him a $1 million deal with their company, Jersey Films, for his next picture on the strength of his reputation alone. The distribution was initially taken on by TriStar, but they pulled out when they realized it would be controversial, explicit, drug-fuelled and violent – had they not seen *Reservoir Dogs*?

Possessing a stronger constitution, the Weinstein brothers stepped in and Miramax co-financed the project for a little over $8 million. This was an about-turn for Harvey Weinstein, who had previously pulled out of *True Romance*, but after the success of *Reservoir Dogs* he was pleased to announce that he was now 'in the Quentin Tarantino business'. Even more ironic is the fact that Miramax were shortly after taken over by Disney – it's unlikely that Tarantino ever thought he'd be linked to children's films.

Basing himself in Amsterdam while promoting *Reservoir Dogs*, Tarantino set to work on the script in the city's numerous hashish and coffee shops. 'The starting-off point for the piece was the idea of doing a crime film anthology,' he explains. Inspired by the seminal pulp magazine *Black Mask*, he soon realized that he was sitting on a wealth of material.

'It would be really neat to have three separate stories, but have the same three characters floating in and out,' Tarantino continues, extending the idea of the film *Black Sabbath* from 1963, in which Boris Karloff links a trio of chilling horror stories.

As with *True Romance*, Tarantino wanted to incorporate some of Roger Avary's work, and so he bought and adapted his friend's short film script called *Pandemonium Reigns*. While Tarantino wanted full credit for the writing, Avary stood fast and refused – a wise move as it turned out.

Originally entitled *Black Mask*, Tarantino's composition was renamed *Pulp Fiction* to literally spell out the film's objective – material with little depth or designed to shock. Predictably, it contained an excessive amount of violence and drug use (specifically referencing the hash bars of Amsterdam), but DeVito remained positive. 'When I read it, I was laughing my head off, thinking, "Either this is brilliant, or I'm the sickest man you ever met in your life!"' Tarantino adds, 'If you say you don't like violence in movies, it's like saying you don't like slapstick comedy or dance sequences in movies.'

In *Pulp Fiction*, two small-time thieves, Honey Bunny and Pumpkin, begin the chaos as they spontaneously decide to hold up a restaurant. Meanwhile, two philosophical heavies, Vincent and Jules, pick up a mysterious briefcase for their boss, Marsellus Wallace, Vincent has to escort and entertain his boss's cocaine-addicted wife, Mia, on a date, and a has-been boxer, Butch Coolidge, defies Marsellus's orders to throw his last match and goes on the run.

*

Capitalizing on his current popularity, Tarantino had always intended to have a high-profile ensemble cast for *Pulp Fiction* and found himself in the enviable position of being able to turn down A-list celebrities in order to get the right actors. Many parts were written with specific individuals in mind, such as Jules for Samuel L. Jackson and a returning role for Harvey Keitel (aka Mr White) as The Wolf, but the most predestined parts were Pumpkin and Honey Bunny.

'I'd seen Tim Roth and Amanda Plummer together once in real life and was struck by their look, their energy and their size,' says the director. 'Everything about them just made them a great couple, so I wrote the characters. I knew they would be so terrific together; all I had to do was write characters that could let them go to town.'

Alongside Honey Bunny, the addition of Mia Wallace as a major player was a huge step for Tarantino; *Reservoir Dogs* had contained no significant female roles. 'He usually bases his characters on people he has met, characters he has "danced with" in his own life,' explains Thurman. 'But he told me that Mia was not based on any woman he'd known. She was perhaps a breakthrough for him because he wrote her entirely from his imagination.'

As Mia evolved during the writing, Tarantino had no actress in mind for the part and many auditioned for the demanding wife of Marsellus Wallace. Isabella Rossellini didn't meet the requirements, likewise Holly Hunter, Meg Ryan, Brigitte Nielsen, Meg Tilly and Rosanna Arquette, the latter instead securing the part of Jody.

Uma's agent had actually put her forward for the role of Honey Bunny, but when the director met her at the Ivy restaurant, he knew he had found his Mia. She was in awe of Tarantino as a director and did not know what to expect of their encounter.

'I was just overwhelmed by his incredible energy and personableness and enthusiasm, and our first dinner together was like a dinner of two close friends,' says Uma. 'It was really wild.'

During the evening, Uma's initial qualms about the foul language and excessive violence were allayed. 'I realized he was an artist who was using violence and profanity in a painterly way, not a brutal, ghoulish one, like the bold colours of the pulp fiction of the 1930s, so people could experience it but not have to confront it,' she says.

After a positive meeting, the pair made plans to see each other over the weekend, but Uma contracted conjunctivitis from her hotel swimming pool and holed up in her room. Apparently she was too embarrassed to call the director, but fortunately his typically persistent nature prompted him to keep phoning until she answered.

By this time, Uma had got cold feet about the project and needed some persuasion. 'I was really shy about doing it,' she recalls. 'I was really nervous and I was in a weird place in my life . . .

'He convinced me, he made me feel fearless again. He restored a kind of unselfconsciousness that had just simply been overshadowed by other experiences.'

Most importantly, Uma found the easy connection she experienced at their first meeting continued into rehearsals and on set. This was something about which she felt strongly, because she was very conscious that she drew inspiration from those she worked with, particularly directors. 'I'm a very bad actress when I'm not interested enough in what I'm doing,' she admits. 'I like stuff that may be a little messy, different, problematic. That's much more attractive than something I can walk through.

'Quentin and I had a remarkably creative relationship. It was the first time I had worked with someone who was roughly my own age.

It was definitely fun.' Actress and director worked from the original script that Tarantino had written and developed the character together, building on his original ideas.

'He told me to pretend I was in "the Mia movie",' she elaborates. 'He said that I should pretend the whole movie was about Mia and not to worry to explain everything because the rest of the movie had already done that. Mia is a failed actress, the wife of a low-rent gangster, a former heroin addict who still does coke. I think she's quite happy in her marriage and does a lot of shopping and talks to people and tries to stay away from heroin and is a little nervous when she has to get inoculated.'

The final detail was Mia's look. The classic sleek black bob is said to have been Uma's idea, but an informed film aficionado will point out that it is identical to that of Catalaine Knell. A powerful producer at CineTel in the early 1990s, Knell was a mutual friend and colleague of both Tarantino and Tony Scott, and the latter had already used a similar wig on Brigitte Nielsen for *Beverly Hills Cop II* in 1987.

Uma was pleased with Mia's style, particularly the black three-quarter-length trousers and white shirt. 'When we found that outfit, she was just over the moon,' remembers Tarantino. 'She was like, "I am going to look cooler in this movie than I've ever looked in any movie I've ever done!"'* The actress was also in good physical shape at this time, not least due to her unusual eating habits: 'I go in and out of diets. When I was making *Pulp Fiction*, it was all brown rice.'

*

Tarantino now moved on to casting the male leads in *Pulp Fiction*. Jules was written for Samuel L. Jackson and he loved it from the start. 'I read it straight through, which normally I don't do,' says Jackson. 'And then I took a breath and I read it again, which I never do, just to make sure it was true. It was the best script I'd ever read!'

Unfortunately, when he was called in for an audition, Jackson simply read the part aloud, as he assumed he already had the role. His unbearably understated performance placed doubt in Tarantino's mind and immediately opened the door to the competition. Rather than walking away with a part in the second Quentin Tarantino film, Jackson (*Jungle Fever*, *Jurassic Park*) was embarrassingly required to take a screen test.

---

* Amusingly, her painted talons would start a trend and launch Chanel's first cult nail-polish shade, Rouge Noir.

'This other actor and I had to show up on a Sunday in L.A. and audition for the film again,' he says. 'Meanwhile, I did all the stuff I was supposed to do, figured out how I wanted to be and how I wanted to approach it and the rest is history . . . but I almost didn't get it.'

Along with Uma's distinctive wig, Jackson's hair stands out as one of the most memorable props. 'I love afros,' says Tarantino. 'I talked to Sam about Jules having an afro and he was up for it. Because the make-up woman didn't know the difference, she brought back some afros and the jheri-curl wig. Sam put it on and it was perfect. It *was* Jules.'

Casting Jules's partner proved equally problematic. Michael Madsen, Mr Blonde from *Reservoir Dogs*, was originally offered the part of Vincent Vega, but he turned it down, bizarrely opting instead for a supporting role in Kevin Costner's epic western *Wyatt Earp*. Tarantino toyed with the idea of Daniel Day-Lewis before making his most controversial choice yet: that of *Saturday Night Fever* star John Travolta.

'It was an amazing script,' recalls Travolta. 'Beyond clever, it was alive and unique and real. I thought I'd love to play this character, but there was no way in hell they were going to let me.' Travolta may have had a glittering career once upon a time, but in the early 1990s it was just a distant memory. Like Uma, he was in need of a miracle.

Taught to dance by his mother, Travolta was signed up as a chorus boy at the age of sixteen. From there the leaps to Broadway and Hollywood posed no problem and before long he had become a household name and 1970s icon. In 1977 he hit the big time, starring as the original white-suited, hip-grinding disco king in *Saturday Night Fever*, followed by his tight-black-leather-clad performance in *Grease*.

Just as the world became his oyster, Travolta's personal life took a tumble: first his membership of the controversial Church of Scientology caused a stir, then his girlfriend, actress Diana Hyland, eighteen years his senior, died of cancer, followed by his mother just eighteen months later. After backing out of first *An Officer And A Gentleman*, a role written with him in mind that eventually went to Richard Gere, and then *Splash* due to bad advice, he became increasingly unpopular in the industry. From there he virtually became a recluse, appearing in a series of lightweight films simply to survive, notably the *Look Who's Talking* trilogy.

Tarantino had been a staunch devotee of Travolta since *Blow Out* in 1981, managing to overlook his lamer efforts thereafter. He initially contacted the actor with a view to casting him in a future project that was under development, entitled *From Dusk Till Dawn*. But when they met, Madsen had just turned down the role of Vincent Vega, and now

Tarantino offered it to his hero. It was not the meagre wage of $150,000 that nearly caused him to say no – due to his religion, Travolta wrestled with both the violence and narcotics, notably his character's own killings and drug use. But, like Thurman, he was eventually persuaded by the relentlessly persistent director.

While Tarantino may have been confident about the casting, the producers and distributors were distinctly unimpressed.

'In some ways, it would have been easier casting an unknown than Travolta, because John has a lot of baggage with him,' says Tarantino. 'When I mentioned his name to people they were like, "What?"' As Travolta recalls, 'He had to do some fast talking to get me in. Basically, he told the producers he wouldn't do the movie unless I was part of it.'

The other male lead was that of the boxer with a heart. Harvey Keitel told his friend Bruce Willis that Quentin Tarantino was preparing for his second film, and, having loved *Reservoir Dogs*, Willis got hold of the script, read it and promptly offered himself up for the role. Keitel arranged an introduction and the two men went for a walk on the beach to discuss their ideas. Once assigned the role of Butch, Willis even shifted the production schedules on two of his other films to secure the part.

With Ving Rhames (*Dave*) on board for the powerful role of Marsellus Wallace, and Eric Stoltz (*Mask*) opposite Arquette as Lance the drug dealer, Christopher Walken from *True Romance* was brought in for the bit part of Captain Koons. 'I'd love to do a character with a wife, a nice little house, a couple of kids, a dog, maybe a bit of singing, and no guns and no killing, but nobody offers me those kind of parts,' laughs Walken.

*

Not unexpectedly, such a rich cast made for some major headaches, as producer Lawrence Bender explains: 'One of the major difficulties with *Pulp Fiction* was getting twelve major actors in one spot at the same time. For instance, one actor got a part he really wanted to do and we had to change thirty actors' schedules while we were in production.'

Filming finally got underway in September 1993 and wrapped a few months later. As with the familiar faces in the cast, Tarantino preferred to work with trusted crew members, many of whom came with him from *Reservoir Dogs*.

The director was convinced that the key to a successful movie was a family atmosphere on set and so organized various team-bonding sessions. 'We'd have dinner gatherings,' recalls Samuel L. Jackson. 'He'd have a big dancing night where everybody goes dancing together. Every week he has a big screening of some B-movie he's chosen.' Stoltz amusingly sums up the unorthodox director's approach: 'Working with Quentin as a director is like being with Steve McQueen on speed.'

Uma thrived in the relaxed environment and felt she came alive working with a director who was a peer and really understood her.

'Quentin's at a similar place in life to me,' she said at the time. 'He doesn't isolate the actors at all. He loves them and engages them in the process while keeping his own mind. He's effusive and excited and passionate, from a sincere place, about his work.'

Undoubtedly referring back to *Henry & June*, she said, 'Sometimes great things come out of unpleasantness and suffering, but this came out of joy. Pure joy. Every day we'd have some new adventure, some new mountain to climb, and we'd just climb it together and it was great.'

With the cast and crew happy, Tarantino's major difficulty was trying to avoid an escalating budget. Having secured many big-name actors for relatively low wages, he constantly battled to keep overheads down as his eye for detail pushed set and production costs through the roof. One such item was the portrait of Mia hanging in her modern apartment.

Although the painting is only viewed for a few moments, Tarantino paid artist Steve Martinez $1,500 for the work. The only stipulation that the director made was that Uma should be curled up on a couch with bare feet.

'She's real gangly and double-jointed,' says Martinez. 'She does things most people can't, and this turns into wonderful poses.' Both artist and director were fascinated by her oversized hands and feet and wanted to make them a feature, but Uma was only able to attend one of the two promised sittings and so Martinez had to draw them from memory.

'She's got this kind of praying-mantis body language. And Steve captured that really well in the painting,' enthuses Tarantino, who included a shot of the finished piece in the film.

This obsession with Uma's extremities was not surprising coming from Tarantino, who has a well-documented foot fetish, with virtually all his female characters appearing barefoot. In *Pulp Fiction* this is given particular importance: in one scene Vincent Vega and Jules debate the intimacy and significance of foot massages because Marsellus once threw a guy out of a fourth-floor window for massaging Mia's feet.

'I think with a non-blood-related, non-eunuch member of the

opposite sex, foot massages are definitely raising the stakes slightly,' offers Uma. 'It's the pleasure zone.' Much fuss is made of Uma's feet in the role of Mia Wallace: she wears three-quarter-length trousers to accentuate them, is often seen barefoot and takes her shoes off for the dance sequence at Jack Rabbit Slim's Diner.

The whole scene in the 1950s-themed restaurant was expected to be one of the biggest expenses, with a starting budget of $500,000. Tarantino knew exactly how he wanted the place to look but found it hard to verbalize and so instructed set designer Sandy Reynolds-Wasco to watch Howard Hawks's *Red Line 7000* from 1965 and Norman Taurog's Elvis Presley vehicle *Speedway* from 1968, both of which featured kitsch club scenes, for inspiration. The flimsy yet aesthetically pleasing set was eventually constructed for just $150,000.

Yet the stunning scenery was surpassed by Uma and Travolta's fancy footwork in what has since become a legendary dance scene. Borrowing heavily from Anna Karina's star turn to the jukebox in Jean-Luc Godard's *Bande À Part*, Tarantino devised a 'dance-off' competition, which Mia demands she and Vincent must not just enter but win.[*]

Despite his background, Travolta insisted on strong direction to get the scene exactly the way Tarantino wanted. 'I told him that I could do anything with my body, but he'd have to guide me,' recalls Travolta. 'He did two things that are typical of him. He showed me a dance in a Godard film, then he himself got up and did this terrific, tight-fisted little dance.'

Tarantino's twist gave Travolta a general idea of what was expected, but the actor pointed out, with all due respect, that he grew up in the 1960s and knew that there were also other popular steps such as the swim, the hitchhiker and the cowboy. 'I asked him if I could have a couple of days to teach those to Uma,' recalls Travolta.

'When it came to doing the scene, we were just completely immersed in the magic of the material for twelve hours and then for another twelve hours the next day.' With the aid of instructor Paul Lester, the pair choreographed a combination of all the popular steps to Chuck Berry's 'You Never Can Tell'.

'The dance scene was so camp. I just couldn't pass it up,' laughs Uma. 'To dance with Travolta was like doing a western with John

---

[*] Godard's classic scene has often been replicated, also notably in Rainer Werner Fassbinder's *Rio Das Mortes* (1971) and Hal Hartley's *Simple Men* (1992).

Wayne. You'd happily play some bar-room slut just for the opportunity.'

Tarantino was understandably thrilled with the final sequence. 'When he's in that booth with Uma, he's not John Travolta, he's Vincent Vega,' says the director. 'But when he steps up to dance, it's like, "Wow! That's John Travolta!"'

*

Tarantino often favours a bathroom setting in his films. 'It's small, it's private, and you have a mirror in front of you. What more could you want?' he justifies. On the contrary, there is a brilliant scene in the very crowded and public ladies' room at Jack Rabbit Slim's where Mia comes up from doing a line of coke, beautifully played by Thurman.

Another of *Pulp Fiction*'s most memorable moments again involves Thurman and Travolta, when Mia mistakenly snorts Vincent's heroin, thinking it's cocaine, and overdoses. The director recruited his old friend Craig Hammand to explain what a heroin overdose would be like to the actors. Hammand met Thurman and Travolta at a Thai restaurant, where he explained, 'When you OD on heroin, if you snort, it's like bad nose drops – you bleed from your nose.'

Panic-stricken that he is about to be held responsible for his boss's wife's death, Vincent rushes Mia to the house of his dealer Lance (Stoltz), where he has to inject adrenaline directly into her heart. 'The hypodermic scene was a bit difficult because I am unconscious and they [Stoltz and Travolta] are carrying me,' Thurman recalls.

'They never dropped me but it's tough to stay unconscious, defenceless, with jokey buddies around. They'd keep tickling me or something and I'd never know when it was coming, lying there with my eyes closed!'

Thurman backed up the information Hammand had provided with further medical research, and then suddenly she remembered the unusual incident that had occurred when filming *The Adventures Of Baron Munchausen*. Tarantino's script called for her to arise from the drug-induced coma in a zombie-like trance, but she recalled the electrifying response of the over-tranquillized panther when brought round with adrenaline. She suggested to the director that she could affect a similarly startled response.

'At first, Quentin wasn't too into this idea,' she explains, 'and he said, "Well, just show it to me."'

'So they carried me into the rehearsal hall at Jersey Films, and John punched an imaginary needle through my chest, and I just flew across the room like the Tasmanian Devil, just like it is in the movie! I scraped my knees up and I think I cracked Rosanna Arquette in the chin with my knee. When I did that, they all just scattered.'

Tarantino was impressed and kept in the change. Interestingly, the majority of filming for the scene was done in one long take, but the moment Vincent pierces Mia's heart with the needle was actually reversed for the camera.

'We started filming with the needle in her chest and then pulled the needle out,' explains Stoltz. 'Then they ran the film backward to get the effect of us thrusting it into her chest.' Finally, Mia leaves Lance's house looking like death warmed up, as she literally was.

Filming on *Pulp Fiction* wrapped in November 1993, and Tarantino spent the next few months editing the film. Sadly, one of the scenes to be axed was an extended getting-to-know-you interrogation of Vincent by Mia, although it has since shown up on the special-edition release.

During this period, Tarantino added one of the film's most distinguishing features: the music. A few sexy golden oldies, including Dusty Springfield's 'Son Of A Preacher Man' and Al Green's 'Let's Stay Together', Urge Overkill's version of 'Girl You'll Be A Woman Soon' and the unmistakeable opening riff made the accompanying soundtrack an absolute must-have.

While some of the music was chosen in post-production, certain songs, such as 'Son Of A Preacher Man', were crucial to a scene staying in the film. Either way, Tarantino was particular about the music creating the right feel and preferred to pick meaningful tracks himself rather than have a score specially written for the film.

*

Pulp Fiction was previewed at Cannes in May 1994. It was the acid test of whether Tarantino would be more than a one-hit wonder. He was up against strong competition for the illustrious Palme D'Or award: Krzysztof Kieslowski's entry was the superb final part of his acclaimed trilogy, *Three Colours: Red*. Kieslowski also announced his retirement, thus virtually ensuring the award would be handed to him on a silver platter.

Although Tarantino experienced his first taste of 'rock-star' fame as he was mobbed by the crowds, he accepted Kieslowski's prior claim. No one was more shocked when jury chairman Clint Eastwood announced the Palme D'Or winner was *Pulp Fiction*.

'That's a big shield,' beamed the victorious director. 'When people are throwing bricks at me because my films are violent, the Palme win is something that says: "You're misunderstanding me. I'm not just about that." '

They waited a further six months for general release, as Travolta succinctly told Harvey Weinstein of Miramax, 'You can't fuck around with this movie. You do not release this in the summer. The hardest group to get is the intellectual group. Give them the respect of loving this movie as an art film, and you'll get a big commercial success out of it.'

Other than a sneak preview at Nottingham's Shots In The Dark crime-film festival in June, *Pulp Fiction* was not unleashed on the masses until the autumn. Opening at the New York Film Festival on 23 September 1994, the first screening was interrupted as a diabetic member of the orchestra collapsed during the shocking needle-in-the-heart scene – whether it was a genuine physical reaction to an outrageous piece of cinema or a canny PR plant, the incident caused a suitable furore and the film's hype reached fever pitch.

It was at that same premiere that Uma once again bumped into the young actor Ethan Hawke, who was standing next to her agent.

'I've got to get out of here,' sighed Uma. 'I can't take any more. I'll meet you somewhere else – I'm going.'

Hawke rolled his eyes as if to say, 'Oh my God, here's another crazy actress'. But Uma neither noticed nor cared. At the time she had no recollection of her first meeting with Hawke, who would later remind her of her haughty brush-off.

Whether the incident at the premiere was propaganda or not, *Pulp Fiction* was a stroke of genius in the realm of ground-breaking modern films, even if most of it was lifted from elsewhere. 'I steal from every movie made, all right? I love it,' boasts Tarantino. 'If my work has anything, it's because I'm taking this from this and that from that and mixing them together and tumbling them around . . . Great artists steal – they don't do homages!'

Uma, like everyone around her, was simply stunned by his encyclopaedic knowledge. 'I've never met anyone like Quentin – he's beyond a geek,' she says affectionately. 'He practically knows every actor who ever got lit on screen, even people who had walk-ons and extra parts. And he knows all the directors, all the movies, particularly all the rough stuff – every grindhouse movie, every exploitation movie, every B-movie, every television series that was ever done.'

The lack of originality – using well-versed pulp themes and blatantly copying scenes from a disparate range of films – did not seem to matter in the least. It was the smart script, innovative story-telling and gripping visuals that captured people's imaginations.

In fact, there has been much debate as to what *Pulp Fiction* is actually about, with many reviewers getting bogged down in side issues such as the contents of the briefcase. More importantly, the film has become an acknowledged essay on the 'psychology of cool', posing the challenging question of how far people will go to be hip. Mia takes it to the extreme and almost dies as a result; Jules and Vincent wear the clothes, talk the talk and feel threatened when forced to dress like dorks; after his enlightenment Jules realizes that actions speak louder than words; and Butch and Marsellus reach their own conclusions about image and reality after their hideous humiliation. It is interesting to note Tarantino's own appearance on screen as Jimmie, a former hitman who ran with Vincent before finding his peace in domesticity.

Moral messages aside – for the film is littered with religious connotations, such as Lance dressed as Jesus, resurrecting Mia from the dead, Jules's preaching from the Bible and his epiphany – the unique style that Tarantino carves out for himself is itself a lesson in cool. His constant changes of pace make *Pulp Fiction* truly deserving of the clichéd description 'roller-coaster ride', while the unusual twists and turns in the plot retain the viewer's interest.

Tarantino had already proved his gift for smooth dialogue in *Reservoir Dogs*, but here he takes it to a new level, where wonderfully real conversations can either divulge character history and advance the plot, or merely provide amusement with inane banter.

The greatest aspect of *Pulp Fiction*, however, is its complex and enthralling structure, affording many levels of enjoyment and new discoveries on every viewing. It proved popular at Cannes, but would the critics agree?

Variety hailed it as 'A spectacularly entertaining piece of pop culture', and the *New Yorker*'s resident film critic, David Denby, heartily agreed: 'A very funky, American pop masterpiece, improbable, uproarious, with bright colours and danger and blood right on the surface.'

On the other side of the pond, Q magazine's Sue Elliott echoed the praise: 'The entire cast inhabits Tarantino's wacky little world to perfection, and there are signs that the young genius is fast developing his own desperate, frazzled visual style to match his subject matter.' But the British broadsheet relics found it all too intimidating: Hugo Davenport from the *Daily Telegraph* slammed it as 'souped-up trailer park trash', while the *Sunday Times*'s Gilbert Adair attacked the director: 'I have no hesitation in writing Tarantino off as Hollywood's sleaziest filmmaker.'

*

Of course, reviews are only one measure of success, and financial return undoubtedly counts for more at the end of the day. Adhering to the small budget of $8 million, *Pulp Fiction* has to date made more than $100 million in America alone.

Industry accolades poured in, with the film, cast and crew sweeping the boards at the L.A. Film Critics' Association and the New York Film Critics Circle. The Golden Globes brought a host of nominations, but only Tarantino won with Best Screenplay. Notably, while Avary stood his ground and is credited as a screenwriter on the film, he was excluded from wins of this category at the Golden Globes, BAFTAs and numerous smaller awards. Uma was shortlisted for her supporting role at the Globes, BAFTAs and Screen Actors Guild Awards, but failed to pick up any trophies.

The biggest night, as always, was the Academy Awards and *Pulp Fiction* was nominated for seven Oscars: Best Picture, Best Director (Tarantino), Best Actor (Travolta), Best Supporting Actor (Jackson), Best Supporting Actress (Thurman), Best Original Screenplay (Tarantino and Avary) and Best Editing (Sally Menke).

The chief rival that year was the heart-warming epic *Forrest Gump*, directed by Robert Zemeckis. An immensely popular movie starring Tom Hanks (on a roll after *Sleepless In Seattle* and *Philadelphia* the previous year), *Forrest Gump* would attract votes from the older, more conservative Academy members, who found *Pulp Fiction's* exuberance frightening. Still, there was everything to play for on the night. Uma arrived excitedly on 27 March 1995, looking ravishing in a floor-length lilac-chiffon Prada dress and accompanied by her father.

Sadly, and as predicted, the innovative film lost out to *Forrest Gump* in most categories (Best Actor, Editing, Director and Picture), with Martin Landau in *Ed Wood* beating Jackson (who was clearly seen ungraciously mouthing '*Shit!*' at the announcement) and Uma being beaten by Dianne Wiest in *Bullets Over Broadway*. The saving grace was Tarantino and Avary's win for Original Screenplay.

Miramax hosted a post-Oscars bash at Chasen's, where Uma mingled with the likes of Christopher Walken, Hugh Grant, Gabriel Byrne, Ellen Barkin, Jodie Foster, Jessica Lange and George Clooney, not to mention her old flame Robert De Niro.

*

Awards aside, perhaps the greatest achievement *Pulp Fiction* can lay claim to is resurrecting and redefining the careers of all those involved.

Bruce Willis was certainly an A-list actor at the time, but he had made his fortune as a burly action hero, chiefly due to the phenomenal success of the *Die Hard* series. Tarantino afforded him the opportunity to demonstrate a wider range of emotions and prove his credibility as an actor. Following *Pulp Fiction*, Willis was able to break the mould with projects like *Twelve Monkeys* and *The Sixth Sense*.

Likewise, the director raised Samuel L. Jackson from the regular drug-addict and character-actor supporting roles he had grown used to throughout the 1980s and set him up to be one of the leading actors of the 1990s, with diverse roles in *The Long Kiss Goodnight*, *The Negotiator* and *Jackie Brown*.

Undeniably the actor to have benefited most from *Pulp Fiction* is John Travolta. 'I wanted to play a different kind of character,' said Travolta, explaining that he was keen to shed his pretty-boy, clean-cut image. 'Vincent is 20 pounds fatter than I am now, has long straggly hair and a big gold hoop earring. He has to shoot a man in the head, inject heroin, and do all kinds of things.

'I think [*Pulp Fiction*] is perhaps the best moment of my professional life since I got to play Tony Manero [in *Saturday Night Fever*]. And it's happened because Quentin believed in me.' Indeed, Travolta's asking price suddenly soared to $10 million, almost doubling again over the next two years, and he starred in a variety of box-office hits such as *Get Shorty*, *Phenomenon* and *Face/Off*.

Thurman, too, received a welcome boost to her flagging career, although she failed to capitalize on it to quite the same extent as her male co-stars. Far from being in the same league as Travolta, she was now commanding $1 million per film.

There were rumours that she actually gained something more meaningful out of the experience, namely a romantic relationship with the director.

Uma denied the gossip, saying, 'If he weren't my great friend, I'm sure I'd be banging down his door like the rest of female-kind.' It is important to note a few details about their relationship, though: the pair formed an instant and lasting connection; Tarantino liked to surround himself with familiar actors and crew for each new project; and the director had fully immersed himself in his new-found world of fame and fortune (some say to the extent of cutting out his old life completely).

Travolta sums it up well: 'Quentin is captivated and fascinated by Uma. There's something exotic and unusual, maybe even unique about her. She sparks something in him, and he sparks something in her, too.

'You have to remember that in terms of talent, Uma is way up there.'

13

THE ENJOYMENT OF BUSTLE

'I always avoid Hollywood if I can, because I don't share the ideals and motives of the average Hollywood person.'

UMA THURMAN

In the wake of Uma's most significant role to date as Mia Wallace in *Pulp Fiction*, she faced the decision of where next to channel her energies.

Although of course her talent had been a huge part of it, Uma's work in that film hadn't only been about stretching her acting abilities beyond the norm. Mia had also made her an icon.

Mia alone had fronted most of the advertising for *Pulp Fiction*, and it was Uma's angular face plastered on posters, magazine advertisements and video covers that would lure yet more viewers into watching the film. The smouldering image staring down from a thousand billboards of the dangerous vamp with her sleek black bob had changed the public's perception of Uma forever.

Ironically, the actress was practically transported back to the days of *Baron Munchausen* when the vision of her as Venus had been the most memorable thing about the movie. Who knew – or cared – about Uma's versatility as an actress? She was cool, she was hip and she would go down in history with the Garbos and the Dietrichs for her attitude alone.

If Uma had been one of those Hollywood acolytes whose whole existence is to front magazine covers and wear the latest trends while attending a glut of award ceremonies and A-list extravaganzas, she could have capitalized on her fifteen minutes of global fame. But Uma being Uma, even her new status had to be analysed and recognized for the transient falsehood it probably was.

'I try to be able to enjoy it, to not take it too seriously, to appreciate the good aspects but not be deluded by their importance,' she says of her fame. And certainly Uma has never been renowned for engaging in many of the sparkling by-products celebrity can bring. Although not reclusive, Uma has admitted that she actually *tries* to be enigmatic, knowing that it will prolong the interest in her and therefore her career.

'I've had a lot of time to study what it feels like to be a person in my position,' she continues, explaining that she is aware everyone has to 'pay a price' for personal success and happiness. 'It has an interesting effect on your life. You have to consider: do you approve of what you're doing? Do you approve of it enough that you want to hear about it for the rest of your days?'

Many other actresses in Uma's position would just grab the limelight and run, accepting high-profile roles the minute they became available and squeezing the very last drop out of their momentary fame. Evidently Uma saw things in a calmer, more rounded way, preparing to accept the consequences in an unaffected, open manner. It was a credit to her Buddhist-influenced upbringing that her inner peace and honest acknowledgement of her mistakes and shortcomings stood her in good stead at this point. Astutely, Uma fully understood that although Mia had raised her to the highest position she could hope to reach in the current Hollywood hierarchy, her problems might only just be beginning.

'Everyone says the worst times are on the first few rungs of the ladder, when the sharks are really nipping at your heels, as you are scrabbling aboard the boat,' she shrugs. 'I think it is worse at my level. You always have to land on your feet.

'The higher the stakes, the scarier it is.' Uma realizes her motivations are deeper than a basic need for the public's approval and support, and is grateful for her shakier moments, because they have taught her what is really important.

She has likened her need to constantly test herself to a gambling addiction. 'The thrill of surviving, to do what you want, against all the odds is truly like an adrenaline shot . . . You always have that feeling: "Oh my goodness, suppose I never work again?" '

Uma has also pointed the finger of blame at the lack of challenging, Mia-type roles available for a woman of her age, stature and appearance. Miramax co-chairman Harvey Weinstein delights in recounting how the actress refused a role that would have paid her

$2 million because it involved little more than providing eye candy while other characters admirably tested their individual mettles around her. 'Young people admire her guts and integrity,' he says, 'she isn't your usual blind-ambition type.'

Uma herself agrees, 'Most films these days are men's stories. Women are for add-on romance . . . I'd rather have a less flashy part in a piece that could be excellent.' So, rebounding off the set of *Pulp Fiction*, she signed up for something completely different yet ostensibly low-key, affording her the time to ponder where next to take her career.

*

Uma arrived on the set of *A Month By The Lake* during the summer of 1994. *Pulp Fiction* had not yet been put on general worldwide release, but industry rumblings already indicated it was going to be a Very Important Film indeed.

The character of Miss Beaumont in *A Month By The Lake* afforded Uma a little light escapism before the publicity for *Pulp Fiction* exploded, under the familiar good-humoured guidance of John Irvin, her director on *Robin Hood*. Although she had a relatively small role, she would be working with an exquisitely accomplished cast including Vanessa Redgrave, Edward Fox, Alida Valli and Alessandro Gassman.

Adapted from the novel by H. E. Bates, the romantic comedy is set shortly before the eruption of World War II against the breathtaking beauty of Lake Como in Italy. Following the death of her father, the middle-aged Miss Bentley (Redgrave) decides to visit the lake on a much-needed holiday. There she falls for the vulnerable charms of the only other Brit among a set of brash Americans, Major Wilshaw (Fox).

Unfortunately, the tentative romance seems to be nipped in the bud as the Major's sleeping libido is awakened by the arrival of a young American, Miss Beaumont (Thurman). Expelled from a Swiss finishing school, she has taken on an unfulfilling position as a nanny. Bored out of her mind, she toys with the Major's affections, shamelessly leading him on. In the meantime, Miss Bentley pretends to flirt with a handsome Italian youth in an attempt to make the Major jealous and win back his attentions.

'It's a small movie, it's a nice part, she's kind of obnoxious but somewhat unknowingly,' said Uma at the time. 'I feel it's a good role for me.'

'Miss Beaumont has contempt for all the attention she gets, which is something I can relate to.' Spoiled and petulant, Miss Beaumont wasn't a million miles from Mia in her self-absorption and elevated status, but the similarities stopped right there.

Happily, filming took place in the warmth of the Italian sun, on location at Lake Como. Things were made even more pleasant for Uma with the arrival of Cindia Huppeler, her acting coach and close friend, who helped Uma with the subtle inflections of an upper-class accent, in keeping with the period of the movie.

For Uma, the shoot was relaxing, fun, not overly taxing – and it afforded her the opportunity to extinguish an area of her repertoire for the last time.

'I did my last ingénue part ever in *A Month By The Lake*,' she says. 'I enjoyed the hell out of it, because I knew I was doing my last. I loved that movie so much. It was like I had perfected "ingénue" for myself.' And so Uma bade farewell to the role she had explored in varying degrees and different epochs in films like *Dangerous Liaisons* and *Where The Heart Is*.

*

A Month By The Lake emerged quietly the following summer. It made ripples at the box office rather than the tidal waves of *Pulp Fiction*.

The picture couldn't be faulted for its photography: veteran Italian cinematographer Pasqualino De Santis perfectly captures the tranquillity and beauty of the area with his shots of the lake, the countryside and the architecture. Sadly, though, many critics simply weren't interested in a light 'middle-aged' romance, so it was on a bad footing from the start.

Although the characters are plausible within their setting – Redgrave's Miss Bentley is dizzy and attractive, Fox's Major Wilshaw alternates between vulnerable, bumbling old gent and pompous, stiff-upper-lipped fool, Thurman's Miss Beaumont is brashly bitchy – the film seems over-edited in the first half. This leaves the audience a little cold as neither Miss Bentley nor the Major appears sufficiently endearing in their individual awkwardness to fully capture the imagination. Meanwhile, Miss Beaumont has so little screen time that the viewer is left puzzled about her motivations, if any, for causing such trouble between her elders, and Thurman struggles to make any impression at all.

In the second half things begin to make a little more sense, with help from some more comical scenes. Thurman, who beforehand had no real depth of character, gets into her stride as the audience learns more about Miss Beaumont, going as far as possible within the boundaries of her role as the forthright and derisive American.

Uncomfortably, one thing pointed out by quite a few reviewers was that, at twenty-four, Uma looked a darned sight older than the teenager her circumstances (being expelled from boarding school) would suggest. She makes up the difference with amusing and exaggerated mannerisms, her performance subtly hinting once again that she could be well suited to comedy. Indeed, she received praise for this from within the ranks, with Cindia Huppeler commenting, 'Uma gives such a large, animated performance for the screen. Most don't dare go that far.' Similarly, Redgrave generously told the *Los Angeles Times* that Thurman was 'special – a fantastically good actress as well as being very beautiful. She has a marvellously individual sense of character and comedy.'

Ultimately, it seemed that sumptuous surroundings, sympathetic direction and a stellar cast could not prevent the overriding feeling that nothing really happens in *A Month By The Lake*. Thrills and spills aplenty there are not, prompting *Variety* to comment, 'This isn't exactly a vacation to remember.' *Empire* was a little kinder in its précis, 'If you like your love affairs autumnal, and can overlook the rather pat, obvious ending, this whimsical little fairy tale will engage well enough.'

In fact, the omnipresent use of the word 'little' in the reviews aptly summarized the film as a whole. Sweet, charming, but not particularly engaging, it neither stretched Uma nor did her any harm – just what she needed as she took a step back to survey her career.

*

After *A Month By The Lake*, Uma, still determined to take everything in her stride, purposely took some time off work to devote herself to what she called 'real life'.

'I like working when I'm working, but I could live without it,' she said in 1995. 'It's more honest to think that you don't know what lies ahead. I'm free – that's enough right now.'

Uma had always led an itinerant lifestyle, right from her childhood stretching from Amherst to Woodstock and India and beyond, then her teenage years in New York, living in around a dozen different apartments before 'settling' with Gary Oldman in both London and the States.

After the divorce, Uma would rent a big loft space in New York and keep her furnishings sparse, never knowing when wanderlust might strike again. She admitted at this time, 'I'm still nomadic, constantly shedding skin and home and trying over.' Despite this transient nature, Uma did seem to have found her spiritual home in New York and never moved too far from its centre. She especially loved having the nuclear family of her parents and brothers re-created in the Big Apple.

'It's good to have them close by,' she said, relishing the opportunity to spend some quality time with the Thurmans during her break. 'I've missed their zany approach to life. Working non-stop can make you forget how to have fun.

'In a big family, there's a wonderful pack feeling, and that's something I've always had – the enjoyment of bustle.'

In the decade since she had moved away from Amherst, Uma's brothers had each carved himself a niche within the entertainment industry. Ganden, the eldest, had a foot in many doors. A computer whizz and self-described 'carpetbagger on the infobahn', whatever that may be, he would also go on to become a director at Tibet House and a production assistant on the 1997 film *Julian Po*, about an unassuming bookkeeper bringing excitement to a small town by announcing that he's about to commit suicide.[*]

Dechen, meanwhile, balanced a promising career as an actor with directing, channelling his energies towards off-Broadway theatres. Mipam, the youngest brother who had long since abandoned the alias of 'Max', had clearly inherited the genes that produced Uma's traffic-stopping good looks. Six foot four, blond and slim, the Columbia undergraduate would go on to become a successful model in advertising campaigns for Donna Karan and Bill Blass.

Her three siblings were Uma's best friends: 'We fight, but we're really close,' she says.

*

During her time off, Uma indulged in her favourite hobby, reading. Wherever she lived, books lined the walls, and Uma devoured them voraciously.

Describing herself as 'a literature buff – working at it always', Uma could often be found with her nose deep in Jane Austen, and she especially loved poetry: e. e. cummings ('my first passion'), Anna Akhmatova, William Wordsworth and Amherst's own Emily Dickinson were among her favourites. More modern reads would include Frank McCourt's *Angela's Ashes* and *The Private Life of Chairman Mao: The Memoirs of Mao's Personal Physician*. Uma's preferred background music while curled up with a book was equally varied, spanning the Beatles, Bach, Joni Mitchell, Bob Dylan and Van Morrison.

---

[*] This film was also released as *The Tears Of Julian Po* and would feature a small cameo from Nena Thurman as 'Sarah's mother', as well as an unspecified contribution from Uma.

An animal lover at heart despite her hectic lifestyle, Uma always had a pet to keep her company. When her beloved Siamese cat Chi Chi died at the grand old age of twenty-one, Uma consoled herself with the acquisition of a large and boisterous purple-tongued chow called Muffy. Naturally, any member of the Thurman clan needed an appropriately erudite name, and the dog was originally christened Senge Mukha by Uma's father, meaning 'golden-flower mountain lion' in Tibetan.

'But who's going to say "Senge Mukha" to a dog?' Uma laughed. 'So it was Mukha, and she's very fluffy, so it got to be Muffy. It suits her, too. She's a marvellous person.'

*

In early 1995, Uma received a call from the renowned French director Louis Malle about a thought-provoking project. Malle was a prolific and highly respected filmmaker who had worked with some of the screen's biggest sirens in their most pivotal roles, such as Jeanne Moreau in 1959's sexually explicit (for the time) *Les Amants* (*The Lovers*), Brigitte Bardot in 1962's *La Vie Privée* (*A Very Private Affair*), allegedly based upon the actress's life, and Brooke Shields in her breakthrough role of a twelve-year-old New Orleans prostitute in 1978's *Pretty Baby*.

The role Malle had lined up for Uma could have been as much of a breakthrough for her as *Pulp Fiction*'s Mia Wallace. He was planning a biopic of the legendary German actress Marlene Dietrich, whom it had often been said that Uma resembled. *Marlene* would have been the perfect vehicle for Uma, with Malle's completely original perception of the icon, but tragically the director became very ill with cancer over the following summer. He passed away aged sixty-three on 23 November 1995. Overcome, Uma declared she couldn't even think of continuing *Marlene* with anyone else, and the project was shelved for good.

Another ideal part that unfortunately fell through during 1995 was the eponymous lead in Miramax's spoof spy comedy *Modesty Blaise*. This update of the role first played by Monica Vitti in Joseph Losey's 1966 version was reportedly to be directed first by Robert Rodriguez, then by Luc Besson, with Quentin Tarantino producing, and Uma would star opposite Sean Pertwee as Willie Garvin. The film's emergence in Uma's life was uncanny, as there are several references to the comic-strip character Blaise in *Pulp Fiction*.

However, months after the film was first announced in May 1995, Uma dropped out amid rumours that she was unhappy with the excessive amount of nudity required for the part. For a while it was reported that Natasha Henstridge (who happily spent much of her film debut, 1995's *Species*, entirely naked) would replace her, but the movie has yet to materialize.

So Uma was left with a massive void in her career – not one but two dream roles had fallen through, and time was marching on. Would Hollywood forget about her?

14

YOU'RE DAMNED IF YOU DO AND DAMNED IF YOU DON'T

'It's gotten to this point where actresses are painted into a corner to play women who are intelligent and should be respected, as if there should be some agenda in roles you play.'

UMA THURMAN

It was a bitter winter in Boston and *Things To Do In Denver When You're Dead* screenwriter Scott Rosenberg was holed up, waiting on a deal with Disney (which resulted in *Con Air* with Nicolas Cage, John Cusack and John Malkovich), when he realized he was sitting on a story.

'Snow ploughs were coming by, and I was tired of writing movies with people getting shot and killed,' he says. 'I realized there was more action going on in my hometown with my friends dealing with the fact that they can't deal with turning thirty or with commitment – all that became *Beautiful Girls*.'

A story examining men's differing perceptions of women set around a high-school reunion in a snowy New England town, *Beautiful Girls* became a Miramax project with Ted Demme at the helm.* The director was 'like one of the guys in the movie,' said Rosenberg. 'He comes from a working-class background, is thirty years old, and is this big, loveable beer-drinking fellow. Ted was just perfect for the movie.'

Demme had originally envisioned a career as a professional football

---

* Coincidentally, the producer for this movie was Cary Woods, the agent who first looked after Uma when she was sixteen and newly arrived in New York. Uma had since moved on to the entertainment giant Creative Artists Agency (CAA).

player until he suffered a devastating knee injury. Instead, he worked as a production assistant at MTV, and, having risen through the ranks of rock-video direction, he moved into TV and feature films in the early 1990s. *Beautiful Girls* was to be his second high-profile feature after 1992's *The Ref*, starring Denis Leary.

Amusingly, Demme felt the pressure working at the studio that produced *Pulp Fiction*. 'I was scared to work for Miramax because I felt like it was the "house that Tarantino built", and how the fuck do you top that?' he joked. 'But I'm a different filmmaker and a different guy . . . I've actually been treated like a prince.'

Essentially an ensemble 'buddy movie' with some thirteen principal players, *Beautiful Girls* boasted a strong cast including Timothy Hutton, Matt Dillon, Mira Sorvino, Lauren Holly, Rosie O'Donnell, David Arquette, Michael Rapaport and a stunning thirteen-year-old Natalie Portman, who until then had been best known for her role in Luc Besson's *Léon* (in which Gary Oldman also starred as a corrupt, psychotic DEA agent).

When Demme and casting agent Margery Simkin approached Uma to play the character Andera, he was impressed by her intense concentration during the audition. 'When you're talking to her she looks right into your eyes, and if you look away you're finished,' he said. 'Let your guard down around Uma and you're in trouble.'

In *Beautiful Girls*, Willie, a New York pianist (loosely based on Rosenberg himself) returns to Boston and meets up with all his old school friends. He realizes that many of them have hardly matured since their schooldays. As they sit in a bar examining and re-examining their various romantic relationships, they are ruffled by the entrance of Andera, the attractive cousin of the bar owner.

According to Demme, Uma was perfect to play Andera 'because she's traditionally knockout beautiful and accessible and funny and charming. She's a regular chick. She'll sit down at a bar and chat with you.'

Shortly before filming commenced, Demme requested his entire cast live together for a fortnight or so, so that their friendships would come across as genuine on screen. When they were all present and correct, he rented out a small theatre and, stocking up on beer, Irish whisky and popcorn, he screened the 1978 classic *The Deer Hunter*. Although in essence a three-hour violent Vietnam War epic starring Uma's ex, Robert De Niro, its first third is essentially a buddy movie, and everyone thoroughly enjoyed their shared viewing experience, afterwards feeling inspired and closer as friends.

Filming was to take place in Minnesota. Before the shoot

commenced, the crew had consulted with meteorologists about which location would be the most wintry, snow being integral to the plot.

'They all said, "Go to Minnesota. They'll have 6 feet of snow the whole winter, it'll be great,"' recalls Natalie Portman. Snow was not predicted for Massachusetts, which was where the story was supposed to take place, but predictably, when they duly arrived in Minnesota, despite the mean temperature being some 20 degrees below zero, there was a distinct absence of snow. Of course, it was 3 feet deep in Massachusetts.

'We had to make our own,' Portman continues. 'The crew got chunks of ice from a lake in Wisconsin and ground it into little snowflakes to be put on land.'

*

By all accounts, the shoot of *Beautiful Girls* became one long party for the large cast and crew. When filming got behind schedule by a couple of days, Harvey and Bob Weinstein both visited the set to view the dailies and address the budget, but ended up playing an impromptu game of baseball with the rest of the guys.

Although *Beautiful Girls* is set in 1994, Ted Demme decided to give it a dated feel, so that the situation could reflect any town, any time within America. As he said, 'If I was ever going to make a buddy movie, which I never thought I would, I wanted to make sure it had some real depth to it.'

Again taking his inspiration largely from *The Deer Hunter*, Demme achieved his time-warp effect by not using anything that looked at all new, and picking mid-tone colours such as greens, oranges and browns for his costumes, props and sets. Uma found this approach fascinating and engaged in long discussions with her director about translating the script onto the screen effectively.

'Without a doubt she should direct,' Demme said. 'She had incredible ideas on the set. She helped me figure out what the characters and the movie were about.'

Beautiful Girls was released in February 1996 in the US. Although critically acclaimed, it only fared moderately well at the box office, but enjoyed a healthy afterlife when it was released on video and DVD.*

---

* A sad epilogue to this film is that Ted Demme died of a heart attack less than six years later, at the peak of his career having just released the controversial *Blow*, starring Johnny Depp. True to his amiable all-American nature, Demme's death came after being taken ill while playing basketball in a charity tournament on 13 January 2002.

Humorous and perceptive, the film takes a light comedic look at relationships. While its central theme is relatively undemanding and certainly unoriginal, it is nonetheless entertaining as the men of the town examine their attitudes towards women, beauty, responsibility and commitment, and generally do a lot of much-needed growing-up. One criticism is that, considering it addresses certain moral issues such as extra-marital affairs and paedophilia (Timothy Hutton's character Willie develops a crush on Natalie Portman's Marty, seeing in her all the things he'll miss if he commits to his current girlfriend), the film could have delved a lot deeper in its character explorations.

Every critic seized upon the performance of the luminous Portman, forgoing all others. The adolescent girl-next-door effortlessly steals every scene she is in and leaves the older, more experienced actors standing in the shade. Hutton's performance is actually excellent, as he bravely mixes vulnerability and wisdom with lechery and yearning, making for an interesting and somehow dignified relationship between the two characters.

Unfortunately, given the Willie–Marty storyline and such a large cast, the other characters, however competently played, are less developed, and Thurman is a prime example of this. As Andera, her performance is commanding; she holds her own in the bar and is particularly good fun when she first dances with the bumbling Michael Rapaport, then storms out when he gets fresh with her. Thurman seems more relaxed in this film than in other recent efforts, her delivery natural and genial, helping the men of the town realize that far from being an unattainable 'beautiful girl', Andera is just a normal person after all, however charming in countenance and spirit.

But her character was only ever passing through the town, meaning that Uma's screen time is less than twenty minutes. Her impact, although thoroughly engaging, is questionable – the film would certainly have existed in much the same way if she hadn't been part of it.

It has to be said that Uma's motives in taking this role were dubious. For all her claims that she didn't aspire to be a Hollywood beauty, here she was playing just that, adding her name to a collective of A- and B-listers, just as she had for *Pulp Fiction*, but without the depth. *Beautiful Girls* wasn't really a progression in her career, it was a sidestep, much as *A Month By The Lake* had been. It was true that the unfortunate loss of both *Marlene* and *Modesty Blaise* had held her back, but while her fellow *Pulp* co-stars were all achieving greater things by now, Uma was seriously lacking in direction.

Uma's next turn as tabloid totty was a result of her dining once again with Richard Gere, this time in London towards the end of 1994. Speculation about the nature of their friendship pumped up a notch when her old pal and co-star split with his wife, the supermodel Cindy Crawford, a few months later, eventually divorcing her in 1995.

When quizzed on her fondness for leading men (Robert De Niro; the current Richard Gere rumours), Uma defiantly responded, 'Boredom is a great motivator – but you have to remember I've been linked to everyone I've ever had coffee with. Let them write what they want!'

Another of Uma's former co-stars, Keanu Reeves, would heartily agree with her devil-may-care attitude, commenting, 'You show up at a premiere together and the next thing you know, they've got you married . . .

'If you have relationships with the [people] you work with then you become part of the Hollywood gossip-mongers . . . If you don't, then people say you're gay. You're damned if you do and damned if you don't!'

But for Uma, amusingly the attention was just a big fat red herring, as since the filming of *Beautiful Girls*, she had indeed hooked up with one of her co-stars: Timothy Hutton. A dark-haired, blue-eyed, brooding kind of guy, key elements of his past strikingly resembled that of a certain Gary Oldman.

A decade older than Uma, Timothy's childhood was shaped by his relationship with his absentee father, the actor Jim Hutton, who died after a regrettably brief period of reconciliation when Tim was only nineteen. The pain of this loss stayed with Timothy throughout his career, which saw him balancing Oscar-winning screen roles (*Ordinary People*) with stage work on Broadway (*Prelude To A Kiss*). When he met Uma, Timothy was divorced from the actress Debra Winger (Richard Gere's co-star in *An Officer And A Gentleman*), with whom he had a son, Noah.

As well as these close resemblances to Uma's ex, he shared with the actress an itinerant childhood, having been born in Malibu, then living in Cambridge, Massachusetts before relocating to Boston when his parents divorced. The rest of his early years were spent just as regularly upping sticks. 'When friends talk about the room they had as a kid, it's strange and foreign to me because we were always moving and living in so many different places,' he recalls.

Having survived the freezing Minnesota winter together, Timothy and Uma embarked on a whirlwind affair as the weather improved in 1995. Over the summer they were seen holidaying in the Hamptons and enjoying regular dates.

Possibly inspired by her new love, who thrived on the stage actor's routine, Uma spoke of a yen to expand into theatre work. She adored Harold Pinter's recent offering, *Moonlight*, saying the playwright was 'so on point' and praising his usage of 'eight-dollar words'. Towards the end of the year she made it known in interviews that appearing on stage was a dream of hers – Ibsen would be her first choice of material – but she was suffering from a lack of confidence. After all, the last time she had trodden the boards had been in her school production of *The Crucible*. 'Basically,' said Uma, 'I've become intimidated because I haven't exercised the different muscles that performance acting is about, and have kept busy doing films.'

While she waited for the right stage role to come along, Uma's relationship with Hutton fizzled out after just six months, and by December 1995 they were no longer an item. The problem was not balancing the careers of two major stars as one might think ('Hollywood relationships are just like relationships everywhere,' says Hutton, 'it doesn't matter what you do for a living'), rather a certain reluctance to settle down.

Both had been through divorces, and Hutton especially had doubts as to whether he would ever marry again. Unlike Uma, he had a child to consider. Speaking about his commitment-phobic character, Willie, in the film on which the two had met, Hutton commented, 'I've certainly been through what he's been through. Everybody has a problem with commitment until they find the one person who makes that fear disappear.' Sad as it may seem, Uma just wasn't the one.

Chalking it up to experience, she flew to St Barts for a holiday in the New Year.

*

Uma's next role was as Noelle Slusarksy in *The Truth About Cats & Dogs*. Much encouraged by the positive reception whenever she attempted light comedy, this was Uma's attempt to break into that genre properly.

Her chosen director, Michael Lehmann, was the ideal person to start her off on this path. Known for his quirky black comedies, his career was prolific but rather uneven, with the excellent *Heathers* in 1989 and the following year's *Meet The Applegates* achieving new cult heights, before the director's winning streak was halted by the box-office turkey that was *Hudson Hawk* in 1991. In 1993 Lehmann was dismissed from *The Good Son* after refusing to work with child star Macaulay Culkin, instead quietly resurfacing the following year with *Airheads*, which suffered from being overly safe and unadventurous. *The Truth About Cats & Dogs* was his next feature, and Lehmann certainly had something to prove.

The plot is an updated and gender-reversed variation of *Cyrano De Bergerac*. Abby is the smart and funny host of the titular daily radio phone-in giving advice about people's pets. When Brian calls in asking for help with his Great Dane (who has developed a worrying penchant for roller skates), he falls in love with Abby's voice, smart jokes and smooth reassurances. When he asks her what she looks like, Abby, a short 'cuddly' brunette who is painfully insecure about her appearance, finds herself describing her new fashion-model neighbour, the tall, slender, blue-eyed blonde Noelle. Enchanted, Brian asks Abby out and she initially agrees, before getting cold feet.

Panicked, Abby persuades a confused but agreeable Noelle to stand in for her, and Brian is understandably perplexed when his blind date is unarguably attractive but rather more inarticulate than his radio conversation had led him to believe. As the authentic Abby woos Brian on the phone and radio, Noelle, the pseudo-Abby, takes her place in the flesh. Throughout the course of the movie, both Abby and Noelle fall for Brian and try in vain to reveal their true identities to him.

Abby provided the acerbic comedienne Janeane Garofalo with her first lead after several well-received supporting roles, Brian gave the handsome English actor Ben Chaplin his first Hollywood break, and Thurman took the role of Noelle. When the cast of *The Truth About Cats & Dogs* was leaked to the press, Uma braced herself for a backlash of sorts. For there were no two ways about it: she was about to play a bimbo, which was about as far away as you could get from any aspirations she had ever so much as hinted about in previous interviews.

'It's gotten to this point where actresses are painted into a corner to play women who are intelligent and should be respected, as if there should be some agenda in roles you play,' she answered her detractors. 'I thought, "What the hell, I'll play a stupid bimbo." Besides, it's supposed to be subversive feminist comedy and my character is terribly nice.'

Whether or not being 'terribly nice' was any excuse for Uma's choice of role in this tale of inner versus outer beauty, she had signed up for better or worse. Judging by her experiences on the set of the movie, it may have been for worse.

*

Janeane Garofalo had carefully built her career as a stand-up comedienne and comic actress around her famously insecure, self-loathing nature. Working with some of America's hottest satirists, including Ben Stiller, Garry Shandling and Michael Moore, she was a viciously funny, intelligent woman with a cutting, self-deprecating sense of humour.

However, it was reported that Garofalo and Thurman did not get on – at all. This possibly could have been because the comedienne was dealing with some awkward personal issues of her own, to do with body image and the need to constantly assert herself using her wit. In fact, it seemed as if the clever but self-conscious Abby had been written with her specifically in mind.

Garofalo started the shoot slightly overweight, ranting in her 1995 HBO Christmas special, 'I am such an eyesore . . . I won't lose the weight, I promise you, because that would be a sell-out.' However, she felt uncomfortable portraying Abby during a crucial phone-sex scene, later admitting to *Time Out*, 'I don't feel like [my] image on screen is very attractive at all . . . I'm the last person I would want to see doing that, and I assume the rest of the audience feels the same way.'

By the time *Cats & Dogs* was up for its final reshoots, it was noticeable that she had shed a substantial amount of weight, so much so that the continuity of the film was in question. '[My weight-loss is] a betrayal of what I believe I try to stand for,' she confessed in an interview later. 'It's a huge conflict for me, to have done something I don't believe in, which is to try to fit in to what is considered more attractive.'

She did not try to hide her bitterness towards what she called 'the tastemakers' – meaning the Hollywood casting agents – bristling, 'They don't give a shit what you bring to the table talent-wise; they're very concerned with visuals.'

Whether or not Garofalo was jealous of her willowy female co-star is open to debate, but her hasty weight-loss – apparently against her own better judgement – hinted strongly at her own insecurities. Maybe the characters of Abby and Noelle had begun to blur into the real-life personas of Garofalo and Thurman, or maybe the comedienne just became sick of all the questions about Uma, the 'thinking man's crumpet', but something apparently prompted her to answer any such queries with an exaggerated shaking of her head while answering, with a huge smile, 'She was lovely!'

In 2001 *Talk* magazine reported that Garofalo had said of Uma, 'She's very funny, witty. But she's not overtly wearing a lampshade, so to speak, at the party . . .' Further observations about her co-star included: 'She's probably not pop-culturally intelligent . . . For her it's like, *Atlas Shrugged* – one more time!' It was hard not to view what was superficially a backhanded compliment (*Atlas Shrugged* being deemed the 'second most influential book for Americans today' after the Bible, according to the Library of Congress) as derisive.

As for Uma, she used words like 'clumsy', 'awkward' and 'stressful' when she described the filming of *Cats & Dogs*, but never spoke openly about the cause of her anxiety. Apart from anything else, it seemed she sincerely regretted taking on the part of a bimbo opposite such a firecracker.

'If there's not a character there that seems intriguing, I can't go to work,' she later said in retrospect. 'I've done it before because I liked the picture, and it's too difficult.

'It's *you* in front of the camera, and you have to exist there. And if you don't have a character to support you in that place, it's three months of wanting to commit suicide . . .'

*

The Truth About Cats & Dogs was released in April 1996 in America, where it went down a storm, and in July in the UK. The easy-going romantic comedy clearly aimed at the women in its audience was a success both critically and at the box office, completely belying Uma's unhappy experiences during the making of the film.

It was an excellent showcase for Garofalo, who smoothly steals the spotlight from the relatively inexperienced Chaplin, and from Thurman, whose shallow character makes her generally unsympathetic. A slight but distinct lack of chemistry between the two female leads is confusing – supposedly the two are friends, which is why Noelle kindly agrees to pose as Abby in the first place, but at first this fails to translate to the screen. Perhaps this was due to the actresses' vastly differing acting styles; or maybe their feud was filtering through.

Garofalo need not have worried about her attractiveness on screen: the late-night telephone conversation between Abby and Brian shows her to be sensual as well as beautiful, and when Brian photographs the two women, it is Abby who sparkles rather than Noelle. Other highlights of the film include an endearing series of messages left on

Abby's answermachine by Noelle, and Brian's total and utter confusion as events unfold around him – although the roller-skating Great Dane outshines them all.[*]

Although relatively unambitious and admittedly clichéd in plot and subject matter, all the actors, including Uma, pulled off a convincing, upbeat ensemble performance that charmed the audience. Most reviewers, instead of confusing Uma with her onscreen persona as she had feared, commented that she was a 'sport' for playing the goofy Noelle, the unsuspecting third party in Abby's elaborate scam. Bringing to the role a degree of pathos by highlighting Noelle's own insecurities, something that a lesser actress might have overlooked, Uma otherwise gives a sweet, dizzy performance of which Cameron Diaz, now the mistress of the funny, ditzy blonde, would be proud.

And so Uma had successfully moved into comedy with a seamless, multi-dimensional and thoroughly appealing performance.

[*] A point of interest for Uma fans is that when Noelle complains to Abby that she's 'just the body', the bookstore cashier who replies 'And what a body it is' is none other than Dechen Thurman.

15

A QUANTUM LEAP

'I was in my mid-twenties before I figured out what I wanted out of life and the kind of woman I wanted to be.'

UMA THURMAN

'Ten fingers, ten toes. That's all that used to matter.'

VINCENT FREEMAN, *GATTACA*

Uma's holiday in St Barts while recovering from her failed relationship with Timothy Hutton came back to haunt her in September 1996, when paparazzi shots of the actress sunbathing topless on the beach appeared in that month's issue of *Playboy*. That Uma decided not to take matters further than a low-key statement ('That was really, really disgusting and low') set her apart from other more self-obsessed and less astute celebrities, as her shrewdly feigned indifference resulted in an almost total lack of publicity for the photographs.

In fact, over the last couple of years Uma had become an altogether different woman. 'Somewhere around twenty-six I started getting over old wounds and stumbling blocks,' she explains. 'The road started opening up for me.'

By old stumbling blocks, Uma was referring to her inability to cope with stress in her job – she now admitted to having suffered stage fright for the first time: 'I get sick during rehearsals.'

Under the category of 'old wounds', Uma included all the romantic relationships she had ever experienced. 'I've made a quantum leap,' she laughed. 'It all revolves around not wanting to play games with men and regard them as the other, as a strange foe.' Uma went on to explain that she was being continually disappointed in her search for the perfect partner: someone she could fall in love with *and* admire in a professional sense. In seeking a man she could place on a pedestal, it was unlikely anyone would ever measure up, so Uma endured long periods alone.

But now she had come to a realization: it was time to stop playing games with men and with herself – it was time to relax. 'I don't know exactly what triggered the change in my attitude, but I learned to be less rigid and dogmatic and take things as they come without constantly trying to organize, categorize and structure everything to my taste,' she said. 'Then one day – boom! – life no longer seemed like this chaotic abstraction.'

Uma acknowledged she felt younger, healthier and altogether more enthusiastic now than she had in her late teens, rightly joking she was a 'late bloomer'. It was finally time to take herself and everything else a lot less seriously – and have some fun.

Around this time, Uma was linked in the press to a distinguished parade of male celebrities, Robert Downey Jr, Nicolas Cage and Mick Jagger being among the famous names regularly dropped by the press. The last caused the most waves: after Uma was photographed locking lips with the ageing Rolling Stone at the Viper Room in L.A., tabloids gleefully reported that his long-term partner, Jerry Hall, was gunning for the actress and seriously considering splitting from Jagger.

'I have many friends, and people always assume the wrong thing when they see a well-known woman with a well-known man,' was Uma's only explanation as she unapologetically launched herself back on the New York dating scene.

*

In mid-1996 Uma appeared briefly as the character Maya in the short TV film *Duke Of Groove*. Directed and co-written by Griffin Dunne (*An American Werewolf In London, After Hours, Me And Him*), the respected actor who had decided to try his hand behind the camera, *Duke Of Groove* boasted an impressive cast and an unusual spin on a very personal coming-of age storyline.

Based during the heady turn of the 1960s into the 1970s, Rebecka (Kate Capshaw) takes her self-conscious teenage son Rich (Tobey Maguire) to a crazy Hollywood shindig, to ensure he will not be at home when his father leaves for good. During the course of the evening, Rebecka gets stoned and Rich looks on in astonishment as various pop icons arrive at the gathering, including Janis Joplin (Jennifer Lloyd). As the wild night continues, Rich discovers much about himself, as he receives a kiss from the beautiful hippie Maya (Uma Thurman), a gift from the party's host (Kiefer Sutherland) in the form of a bootleg tape of his idol Bob Dylan, and the eventual devastating news from his mother that his father has left.

Bursting at the seams with Dunne's celebrity connections, *Duke Of Groove* also featured Elliott Gould and Udo Kier in cameo roles. Its TV debut was well received, with the only criticism being that the distinct bittersweet tone soured somewhat in later scenes due to the writers' 'reactionary' attitude toward hippie culture and women. *Duke Of Groove* proved successful in its field and garnered an Oscar nomination for Best Live Action Short.

Much encouraged by the positive reception to this thirty-one-minute film, Dunne made his cinematic directorial debut with the hit romantic comedy *Addicted To Love* the following year, and *Duke Of Groove* was released in a compilation of four shorts called *Four Tales Of Two Cities*.

*

However, it was time for Uma to take on another major role on the big screen. This came in the form of Irene Cassini in Andrew Niccol's chilling vision of the future, known at the time under the working title of *The Eighth Day*.

This was the cinematic debut of the New Zealand-born writer-director, who had spent the last decade filming commercials in Britain. *The Eighth Day* was an ambitious science-fiction-meets-murder-mystery script, set in a future where a person's life is determined by expensive genetic engineering rather than education or capability, and racism and sexism are replaced with discrimination against a person's inherited physical and mental traits.

Vincent Freeman is one of the last natural babies, an 'In-Valid' conceived of his parents' love rather than any test-tube tampering. Disturbingly, his future is known at the very moment of his birth: he will be shortsighted, suffer emotional problems and has a high probability of dying from a congenital heart condition by the age of thirty. Distraught, his parents shell out for an engineered baby to complete the family, and Vincent's younger brother Anton is born a 'Valid', destined to be taller, stronger and healthier, and to benefit from a secure future in a well-paid job. Sibling rivalry and a keen interest in space exploration only serve to push Vincent further in his quest to become an astronaut – a career about as far out of his reach as the stars themselves.

While working as a janitor at the Gattaca Corporation, a leading aerospace firm, Vincent comes into contact with an illegal DNA broker, who arranges for him to meet Jerome Morrow, a Valid athlete secretly crippled during an accident. The men make an illicit agreement in which Jerome sells his identity and superior physical materials – samples of his skin, blood, urine and hair – to Vincent, who is then enabled to enter and quickly ascend the ranks of the Gattaca Space Program, with the extra assistance of some coloured contact lenses and fake fingerprints.

There Vincent begins a romance with Irene Cassini, a beautiful Valid from a wealthy family, whose one personal genetic imperfection (her own heart defect, predicted to cause her death at the age of sixty) precludes her from space travel, although her accelerated mental ability enables her to work at the Corporation. Just as Vincent is poised to embark on his life's dream, a manned mission to Titan, Saturn's fourth moon, the Corporation's director is murdered and Gattaca is soon crawling with cops. The problem is that Vincent has unknowingly shed one of his own eyelashes close to the scene of the crime, providing the detectives with enough genetic proof that an impostor is present among the employees.

As the hunt for the murder suspect closes in on Vincent, Irene, assigned to assist on the case, becomes more and more suspicious of her lover's true identity and, only days away from the Titan launch, Vincent helplessly watches his once-in-a-lifetime chance at space travel begin to dissolve alongside any hope of a future.

Despite Niccol's relative inexperience and the comparatively small role of Irene, Uma signed on early in the project – it was just too intriguing to pass up and Irene seemed almost to have been written with her in mind.

'Uma's character is a diamond,' says Niccol, 'perfect to the naked eye, but with the most minute flaw. Apart from her talent, there is the physical aspect to Uma – she has this otherworldly quality.'

'I see her as a nineteenth-century heroine,' says Uma of Irene. 'She lacks a genetic dowry, and that condemns her to spinsterhood – not unlike some women in Jane Austen's books. She's isolated and clearly haunted by her condition.'

Uma was particularly inspired by Irene's diametric opposition to Vincent, in his refusal to believe in his early death and in his determined fight against the system.

Having Uma on board early on was an unexpected bonus for Niccol, as her name alone helped him gain financing for the project from producers including Danny DeVito, who had also funded *Pulp Fiction*. Uma's commitment, including being involved in rewrites of the already excellent script and her unshakeable belief in the unknown director, helped attract other big names to the mixing pot. It has since been acknowledged by those who worked on the movie, finally renamed *Gattaca*, that without the actress's determination, it may never have got off the ground.

*

After Uma agreed to take a gamble on Niccol, Loren Dean signed up as Vincent's brother Anton, and Jude Law won the part of the wheelchair-bound Jerome. The talented British actor was amused but delighted that his classical good looks should win him the role of the perfect specimen of future society. 'I won't be cast as Quasimodo,' he joked, 'but I'm lucky that people think I'm quite attractive!'

With the three main Valids in place, the critical part of In-Valid Vincent provided a major headache for Andrew Niccol. 'I was looking for a very precise, fastidious character – especially to play the Jerome side of it,' says the director.

When Ethan Hawke expressed an interest in the role, Niccol was doubtful. Although unquestionably an actor of considerable talent, Hawke was notorious for his unkempt slovenliness off set. The character of Vincent would require him to shape up and clean up – with conviction. So things did not initially look promising, as the director remembers: 'When I first met him, he was a really scrawny character . . .'

Fortunately, Niccol was persuaded by Hawke's brilliant audition and his keen interest in the project itself, and relaxed a bit when the actor reluctantly took on a gruelling fitness regime to pass as a bogus athlete ('Getting in shape is a pain in the ass,' he grumbled). That was not to say that Hawke didn't keep Niccol on his toes until the last minute, though, as the exasperated director exclaims: 'He wouldn't shave off his goatee until the day before shooting!'

The question of whether or not Hawke could convincingly brush up physically was only one of the issues standing in his way, however. In his career thus far Hawke had specialized in angst-ridden adolescents, sons and students; he was arguably most famous to date for his proclamation of 'Captain, my captain!' as the sensitive schoolboy in *Dead Poets Society*. Both Niccol and Uma were very worried the twenty-six-year-old simply didn't seem old enough to play Vincent.

'I was concerned that he was too young,' Uma recalls of her disapproval. 'I expected a more mature actor for this film.'

'I hadn't played romantic parts in a long, long time,' she continued, harking back to the days of playing opposite the likes of John Malkovich and Robert De Niro. 'I couldn't imagine myself opposite someone under the age of forty-five.' She had perhaps overlooked the fact that, as he prepares for his space mission, Vincent is perilously close to reaching his supposedly fatal thirtieth year.

Although their paths had crossed on two previous occasions, Uma neither remembered nor knew much about Hawke and it wasn't until they began read-throughs together that she recognized his commitment to the film was equal to hers.

'It's very uncommon for a young actor to be presented a part that has any complexity at all,' said Hawke. 'And this part has so much going on, Andrew is such a good writer. It's so rare these days to see a movie that's so rich in metaphor . . .

'What I liked about the character was that his ambition and drive was not based on wanting to get any outward acknowledgement. What he was going to get was the opportunity to prove to himself his own self-worth.'

It was an apt observation. The same could perhaps be said for the actor himself.

*

Uma thoroughly enjoyed the shooting of *Gattaca*, in more ways than one. Early on, she spent some time in Ethan Hawke's company, and surprised herself by liking what she saw.

'We got to know each other before filming started,' she said. 'I realized that this was someone I wanted to spend a lot of time with.'

Standing 3 inches shorter than Uma with blondish-brown hair, and seven months her junior, Hawke wasn't her usual type. But he sparked in her a hitherto unseen mischievous sense of humour as they teased each other flirtatiously.

'Apparently, we had met years earlier at a bank machine in New York, but I had never paid any attention to him,' said Uma with a glint in her eye. 'I don't remember him at all!'

Hawke had always had a soft spot for the graceful actress, but it was not long before his crush rubbed off on Uma. It seems the actor accomplished this by playing hard to get.

'He wasn't overly nice to me right away,' Uma revealed. 'He didn't kill it with kindness. I remember saying to myself, "Why can't you just have fun with this young guy? He's sexy; just enjoy that. Give yourself a break!"

'I initially thought he was too young for me. I did not see him coming. It was only after we were somewhat involved in what I thought was just a pleasurable dalliance that I realized I was in love with him.'

It had taken a little while, but when Uma fell, she fell hard and suddenly.

'It was shocking,' she continued. 'I think he worried a bit about my level of intensity! It was funny in a way because he was in love with me first . . . Love sort of snuck up.'

For his part, Hawke was very attracted by Thurman's admirable focus on set, crediting her with a sense of discipline he had only previously seen during his stage work.

'In many ways, [Uma is] the most impressive peer of mine I've ever worked with,' he said. 'She's really disciplined, works really hard, *loves* acting, is really smart, and because she's 6 feet tall is also intimidating . . .'*

Hawke obviously wasn't that intimidated by Thurman's height, though, admitting, 'I'm crazy about her!' Fortunately, the crew were charmed rather than dismayed by the co-stars' increasing closeness. In fact, the director himself took all the credit.

'I don't like to gossip,' said Niccol, 'but being a director is like being a very expensive matchmaker.'

*

One unexpected result of the on-set romance unfurling in front of everyone during the making of *Gattaca* was that Uma unveiled a new cheeky side to her personality.

A million miles away from her projected image as a glacial blonde ice queen, here was a naughty schoolgirl capable of sneaking up behind her on- and offscreen lover during the filming of an especially intense scene and tying his shoelaces together. It was surely not something she would even have considered with the likes of Oldman or De Niro.

'She's funnier than you might think,' said Niccol. 'She has all of these wonderful vices. I would never attempt to drink her under the table . . .'

In Hawke, Thurman was revelling in the opportunity just to be herself with a man of her own age. 'He has a great sense of humour,' she said, 'which I always find attractive in a man. We spend a good deal of our time laughing, which is wonderful.'

Jokes aside, Thurman and Hawke soon buckled down to the task in hand. In his shift from scriptwriter to director, Niccol was meticulous

---

* Amusingly, during his quest to assume Jerome's identity in the movie, Vincent has his legs surgically lengthened to match the athlete's 6-foot-1-inch frame, but Irene still towers over him. That is until the lovers engage in a dance scene – by the wonders of standing on a box, Vincent has miraculously sprouted an inch or two!

Tall, striking and entirely naked, the effigy of Uma's grandmother welcomes visitors to the Swedish port of Trelleborg.

'I had a big nose and a big mouth and these far-apart eyes which looked like I had two fish swimming in my ears,' Uma says of her youthful features.

Having spent her formative years believing she was hideous, the teenage Uma suddenly found she could make a relative fortune from her looks as a model.

'We can always complain about our parents, but until we actually get involved in running our own families, we don't know how difficult the process can be,' remarked Uma after giving birth to Maya. She remains close to both her father (*above left*) and mother (*above right*).

Uma is especially proud of her famous father, Robert Thurman, and is always happy to lend her support to his quest to free Tibet.

'I was the only girl, but I was basically one of the guys,' says Uma, pictured here with brothers Dechen (*above left*) and Mipam (*above right*). She counts her siblings among her closest friends.

'She has this Jayne Mansfield body and a horrifyingly great brain,' said John Malkovich of Uma during the *Dangerous Liaisons* shoot.

When Uma was filming *Les Misérables* with Liam Neeson, she formed a firm friendship with his wife, Natasha Richardson.

'It was a mistake … a crazy love affair which needed to end,' commented Uma of her marriage to Gary Oldman.

'Tall, dark, damaged and handsome' was Uma's type and Robert De Niro was no different.

Erstwhile boyfriend Timothy Hutton's past was strikingly similar to that of Gary Oldman.

'Marriage definitely requires commitment, discipline, love, self-investigation, and patience,' said Uma in all honesty of her relationship with Ethan Hawke.

Top: The Thurman-Hawke family enjoyed a low-key lifestyle.

Above: Uma and Ethan maintained a close friendship after their split for the sake of the children.

Uma won the Best Actress Golden Globe in January 2003 for *Hysterical Blindness*.

Uma with Ben Affleck and director John Woo promoting *Paycheck*, December 2003.

Relaxing on holiday in St Barts, 2004.

Michael Madsen, David Carradine, Uma, Quentin Tarantino and Daryl Hannah promoting *Kill Bill Volume 2* in Cannes, May 2004.

'We love each other, but we're almost too close now to be a couple,' said Tarantino. 'We had our life together on *Kill Bill*. It was like a marriage in every way.'

In November 2003 Uma began dating hotelier Andre Balazs.

about what was necessary to portray his vision of a clinical, pristine future with strong undertones of isolation and paranoia.

'With Andrew, it was like, "OK, we're going to pick up the vial, and then you got to do the thing . . ." It was a whole different style,' said Hawke. 'But the writing was so specific and so good that it warranted that kind of precision in doing it just the right way . . . no matter how hard I worked, I know Andrew worked five times as hard, and it's hard not to respect that.'

*

The completed *Gattaca* was released in October 1997. The timing couldn't have been more perfect if it had been planned – which, in fact, it wasn't.

Dolly the sheep was born in 1996. She was the first mammal to be cloned from an adult cell and her birth was announced seven months later, during the filming of *Gattaca*. The arrival of Dolly simultaneously heralded potentially the most important scientific breakthrough of the decade and opened up a still-ongoing debate over the ethics of cloning, be it animals or humans.

As this formed the exact premise of the future as depicted by *Gattaca*, Hawke, Thurman and anyone connected to the film found themselves entertaining all sorts of fanciful notions during promotional press interviews.

'I've been shocked, actually, by the number of interviewers who've been titillated by the idea of what you'd change about yourself if we had this *Gattaca* technology,' said Hawke. 'There's too much "If I weren't bald" or "If I were pretty, my life would be good", instead of "I'm going to be the best I can because that's all any of us can really be".

'You're just reminded that we fought this huge war against this so-called beacon of evil and sin, Adolf Hitler, who was trying to engineer his own master race. Yet now we go, "Ooh, but if I could do my own master race . . ." '

As they fielded questions about reaping the benefits of modern medicine and the ethics of science versus nature, sometimes the actors grew frustrated that the more positive aspects of *Gattaca* were being overlooked.

'You know, there's not a gun in this whole movie and I know the advertising people would not like me to announce that,' said Hawke. 'If you really wanted to make sure this movie was a hit, you'd ask Uma to take her top off and have me carry two guns the whole time, and *then* you'd sell a lot of tickets.'

Hawke in particular could get a bit tetchy about surely unreasonable claims that *Gattaca* was cynically cashing in on Dolly's miraculous gambol into the public's consciousness. 'Well, that all happened only after I decided to do the movie,' he snapped. 'All the press about the sheep happened while we were making the movie, not before then.' Still, even he had to admit, the unexpected media interest didn't hurt.*

*

Gattaca's release was unusually low-key and it took a while for the movie's timely and compelling messages to begin to hit home. Over time it began to take off, acquiring an audience passionate about what was ostensibly the most artistic and original science-fiction film to appear for years. European audiences warmed more to the philosophical epic of love, betrayal, science and the plight of the individual in the face of oppression; America didn't seem so keen.

Ridiculously, one of *Gattaca's* key strengths also prompted its downfall. The film is visually incredible to behold: Niccol's future is embodied by a stylish production set in no specific year, but not too far away from a recognizable world.

Purposefully clinical and detached, and richly furnished with metaphor, cars and clothes take on a neo-1950s design, offices and homes are clean, sparse and functional. Countless sparkling glass walls symbolize Vincent's struggle against a predetermined future, and the whole film glows with an odd, otherworldly yellow tinge. Michael Nyman's majestically hypnotic score brilliantly heightens the overwhelming mood of sober austerity and sense of dark foreboding, and the pace of the movie is slow, deliberate and fatalistic. Exhilarating, edge-of-your-seat entertainment this is not, but it is a ruthlessly intelligent, subtle and rewarding exploration of what 'being human' actually means.

The key criticism was that the intentional air of detached coldness somehow leaked into the story itself, and those viewers too in awe of the sterile premise and surroundings found themselves unable to relate to the characters or the plot.

'*Gattaca* is highly recommended for its looks, but it's lost its heart to science,' said *Time Out*, while *Empire* commented, 'For all its style and promise, *Gattaca* is far easier to look at than actually watch.'

---

* Sadly, just as in *Gattaca*, even the custom-built Dolly had a flaw: she was put down at the relatively youthful age of six when alleged accelerated ageing was said to have caused a progressive lung disease and form of arthritis. She is survived by four lambs.

'A miserable, coldly dispassionate setting is no excuse for making a miserable, coldly dispassionate film,' railed *Total Film*. But even the biggest entertainment publications couldn't deny that *Gattaca*'s following was assuming cult-like proportions.

It is true that whether or not one enjoys this film is a question of taste. Hawke's Vincent isn't an easy man to get to know, but you cannot fault him for his rage against the machine. He has the capacity to uncover the most human traits in everyone, be it the primal competitive streak with his brother, the increasingly liberating relationship with his lover, or the unlikely, profound and surprisingly sweet bond that grows between him and Jerome. Both Hawke and Jude Law are magnificently well cast and thoroughly believable in their shared determination to beat the system.

Without a doubt, Uma is once again playing third fiddle to two more compelling characters, but as Irene she competently fulfils and even stretches her brief. Physically she looks perfect, with a dazzling strong screen presence; icy and immaculate, she varies her demeanour from being almost robotically detached while at work to a surprising old-fashioned glamour and vulnerability outside the Corporation's walls.

The role unquestionably limited the actress, however, as Irene is intrinsically stifled by her society and lack of future, so that she seems a rather empty, superficial character. Thurman's onscreen chemistry with Hawke came in for reviewers' criticisms time and time again, but it's important to recognize that only through the course of their brief romance does Vincent convince Irene to search within her numbed soul to find a potential individuality. Their relationship is doomed as both realize (even before the murder) that they don't have a future together: the looming mission to Titan ensures that. But certainly during the dance scene the viewer can imagine they are falling in love.

Uma's performance as a whole is memorable, dignified and multi-faceted, Irene's slow realization that Vincent is not who he says he is effectively portrayed by her palpable inner turmoil. The film does notably suffer from an absence of any form of final farewell scene between Vincent and Irene.

Gattaca deserves praise for standing the test of time. It is not all detached coldness: at times, well-punctuated humorous moments are effective and disarming, and unanticipated plot twists keep the viewer guessing till the end. Niccol's main concepts are sharply defined without ever labouring the point, sensibly leaving many threads open for the audience to decide the answers for themselves.

Yet despite its numerous plus points, an Oscar nomination for Best

Art Direction and a Golden Globe nomination for Best Original Score, *Gattaca* still went down in history as 'one of the season's worst box-office flops', as noted by the *New York Times*. It actually gained more coverage and notoriety for facilitating the romance between Thurman and Hawke.

Andrew Niccol would fare far better with the release of his next film, the similarly themed *The Truman Show* in 1998, featuring comedian Jim Carrey in his first 'straight' starring role, and earning three further Oscar nominations, including Best Original Screenplay for Niccol.

16

THE LATEX EXPERIENCE

'I try to sample different genres. Do I sound defensive?'

Gattaca marked a romantic period, and not only for Uma Thurman and Ethan Hawke: in 1997 Jude Law married Sadie Frost.

Love was in the air, and Uma was 100 per cent ready for it. 'I was in a better frame of mind and ready to be with someone who was so much fun and so easy to be with,' she said. 'I have always had the tendency to question things and look for deeper answers when sometimes the simple truth is just staring you in the face. So I gave myself the freedom to enjoy Ethan's becoming part of my life.'

Predictably, as soon as Hawke stepped off the set of *Gattaca*, his old slovenly ways returned and Uma had her work cut out keeping him in shape.

'He jokes that I got really conned, because when I met him he was clean-shaven every day,' she sighed. 'He likes to slop around looking grungy. I've tried so hard to clean him up! He still looks great when he tries but I have to remind him.'

Uma's scruffy companion was perhaps better suited to her than some might think. Born to teenage parents on 6 November 1970 in Austin, Texas, Ethan was brought up by his mother after his father walked out when he was just a toddler.

This alone was familiar territory to Uma, given the background of her exes Gary Oldman, Robert De Niro and Timothy Hutton. The four leading men in Uma's personal life to date may well have shared an altered and hopefully more sympathetic perception of women due to each one's experiences with his mother.

Then, of course, Ethan was also an actor. Andrew Niccol's initial assumption that he was at his best playing a tortured adolescent was in fact severely out of date. Hawke was an accomplished, intelligent performer on both screen and stage, his active enthusiasm for the theatre demonstrated by his co-founding of the not-for-profit New York theatre company Malaparte, with a group of actors including Robert Sean Leonard, Frank Whaley and Josh Hamilton. Uma's fascination for the stage (an arena conquered to varying degrees by Oldman and De Niro) had recently been reawakened by Hutton; she was deeply impressed by any actor who made his mark in that field and longed for the right vehicle in which to make her own debut.

Finally, Hawke also inspired Uma with his creative courage and ability. In 1994 he had worked behind the camera for the first time, directing the music video for Lisa Loeb's single 'Stay'. In the same year he broke out of his *Dead Poets Society* schoolboy rut with his portrayal of a brooding slacker in Ben Stiller's *Reality Bites*, and following a $400,000 publishing deal he penned *The Hottest State* – a semi-autobiographical coming-of-age novel said to be based on his relationship with Loeb.

Hawke's background mirrored Thurman's to an extent. His upbringing and career had taken him from Austin, Texas, to Princeton Junction, New Jersey, to Carnegie Mellon University in Pittsburgh, Pennsylvania, and finally to Bohemian Manhattan. His mother, a character to rival Robert or Nena Thurman, had notably sold all her possessions and joined the Peace Corps in Romania, working with orphans and the homeless.

Hawke had also been something of a child star, making his screen debut at the age of fourteen opposite River Phoenix in 1985's science-fiction fantasy *Explorers. Dead Poets Society* was his equivalent of *Dangerous Liaisons* – an auspicious early performance in a highly regarded movie that resulted in the frustration of being pigeonholed. First his age and youthful demeanour thwarted his ambition, compounded by a series of appearances as a goateed, overly sensitive, angst-ridden Generation X-er.

He was also no stranger to tabloid scandal with fellow celebrities, having been linked to Kiefer Sutherland's ex, Julia Roberts, in 1994 while she was still married to Lyle Lovett.

*

As with her previous partners, Uma tried to keep her flourishing relationship with Hawke a secret. Their mutual attraction had been obvious to anyone on the set of *Gattaca*, but both actors knew a degree of cynical suspicion would be attached to a new couple who had a movie to plug and so they tried to keep their feelings for one another under wraps. Besides, 'I wouldn't respect somebody who frivolously talked about people in their life in a bar – let alone for an audience,' Hawke remarked emphatically.

For nearly a year, the couple kept their affair quiet, staying out of the public eye and thereby avoiding the gossip columns. 'I'm in love with someone right now who's very special,' Uma told an interviewer persistent enough to crack the veneer. 'Does he really have to have a name? Isn't that enough?' That journalist was savvy enough to mention Uma had attended the interview wearing one of Hawke's old jackets.

When the secret finally leaked out in 1998, both parties graciously answered endless questions without visibly tiring of the subject. Perhaps keeping their love hidden had genuinely helped to preserve the initial thrill of the relationship.

'His talent is really clear; it doesn't take a microscope,' said Uma about Ethan.

'He can do anything. He has a will and a positive energy in him that is fearless.'

Hawke was equally complimentary. 'She's better than Hepburn. She's a better actress,' he raved. 'Uma's best quality is her frightening intelligence.'

Notably, perhaps to gloss over any embarrassment caused by Uma's previous 'blankings' when they met for the first and second times, both actors were guilty of pretending they'd never met before *Gattaca* in interviews, claiming they met on the set.

'Until *Gattaca*, we'd never crossed paths. I only saw him in *Reality Bites*,' said Uma. Elsewhere she was quoted as admitting, 'We had met a number of times but I didn't really know him.' 'I had never met her before starting this job,' added Hawke, who confusingly would be only too happy to later recount tales of the encounters at the cash machine and the *Pulp Fiction* premiere.

Whatever the couple's motives for their secrets and lies, there were no two ways about it: Uma was happier than she had been in years – happy to put on frequent displays of togetherness and rave about her new-found soulmate.

'It feels really truly right,' she said. 'He was the right person, and it was the right time for me . . . I think that I've always had this uncanny ability to seem like I was floundering in the water, but actually be anticipating, ahead of time, my plan in life. [Our relationship was] even shocking to me, because I think I didn't give myself credit for as much predestination as I actually had.'

*

Love aside, Uma needed more than ever to concentrate on her flagging career after *Gattaca*, and so she accepted an unusual role.

Joel Schumacher is a versatile director who made a name for himself with the classic Brat Pack 1980s movies *St. Elmo's Fire* and *The Lost Boys*, which he followed with several solid successes. In 1995 he turned his attentions to the *Batman* films.

When Tim Burton relinquished the reins as director of the first two cinematic versions of the caped crusader's adventures starring Michael Keaton, Schumacher eagerly jumped on board. While Burton had employed a very dark approach to Gotham City in his offerings, true to the original DC Comics, Joel Schumacher made his mark by realigning the tone with the lighter feel of the 1960s television show.

Schumacher's first attempt was *Batman Forever*, which starred a new Batman (Val Kilmer), introduced Robin (Chris O'Donnell) and pitted them against The Riddler (Jim Carrey) and Two Face (Tommy Lee Jones). While it took over $100 million at the box office, making it one of the top-grossing films of 1995, it was slammed by the critics. Burton and Keaton were sorely missed in this third instalment, and at the end of the day it was little more than a vehicle for the rubber-faced theatrics of comic superstar Carrey.

The following year Schumacher intended to try again, but he ran into early problems. Kilmer had clashed with the director on the set of *Batman Forever* to the point where he broke his contract and refused to appear in the fourth film, *Batman And Robin*. Schumacher looked to George Clooney to don the cape, and, as the actor was still struggling to shake off his *ER* image, he readily accepted for a fee of $10 million.

With Chris O'Donnell still on board as Batman's sidekick, Schumacher brought in a new crime-fighting heroine, Batgirl (Alicia Silverstone). He then had only to cast Bruce Wayne's love interest (supermodel-turned-actress Elle MacPherson) and the requisite duo of baddies. While Arnold Schwarzenegger joined as Mr Freeze for a cool $20 million, the role of Poison Ivy caused quite a stir as she was advertised as 'the most beautiful woman in the world, but if you kiss her you die'.

'Those are fighting words in Hollywood,' acknowledges Schumacher. 'The minute that was printed, every woman in

Hollywood, from the Olsen twins to Granny in *The Beverly Hillbillies*, thinks she's the most beautiful woman in the world. We were fighting off movie stars, their agents, managers, lawyers, and publicists.'

Demi Moore and Julia Roberts, both of whom had worked with Schumacher before, were in the running, along with other leading contemporary actresses such as Sharon Stone. In a soundbite reminiscent of his casting a very young Nicole Kidman as the intelligent girlfriend in *Batman Forever* ('I know, I know, she doesn't look anything like a criminal psychiatrist,' conceded Schumacher. 'But it's my Gotham City and I can do what I want! I've had my eye on her since *Dead Calm*'), the director confessed that he knew exactly who he wanted for Poison Ivy.

'It's my Gotham City, and for me, there was only one Poison Ivy. Uma is the most beautiful woman in the world,' said the director, who had been enraptured by her appearance a decade earlier in *The Adventures Of Baron Munchausen*.

Uma was graciously flattered and surprised by the offer, and, although this film would naturally throw her back into the limelight as a sex object, she had her reasons for accepting the role.

'I had never made a movie like that, a bizarre, pop-culture movie with larger-than-life, ridiculous characters. It was an experiment. I try to sample different genres,' she explained. 'Ivy's not so much a fighting character – more of a manipulator who can talk Batman into anything. I found something intriguing in Ivy.'

For the fourth outing, Batman and Robin are joined by butler Alfred's niece, aka Batgirl, to foil the plans of two diverse villains. Mr Freeze has had to keep his body temperature sub-zero since a botched medical experiment and consequently wants to put Gotham City on ice. In another scientific catastrophe, a shy horticulturist is reunited with Mother Nature and is transformed into Poison Ivy, a vamp who wants to eradicate humans so that she and the plants can rule the world. Meanwhile, Alfred is dying – but are the heroes too busy saving Gotham to find a cure for him?

Perhaps Uma saw *Batman And Robin* as an obvious Hollywood blockbuster: unfortunately, the film's success was far from guaranteed and it appeared that she had joined a rapidly sinking ship.

*

In preparation for her role as 'the most beautiful woman in the world', Uma was keen to tone up her body. She started going to the gym and took up Pilates. The new sportier Uma was finally beginning to feel comfortable with her gangly frame. This was just as well, as the role of Poison Ivy required her to wear a green version of Michelle Pfeiffer's Catwoman suit.

'I've had the latex experience with Poison Ivy. You can't put an actor through more unpleasantness than latex,' laughs Uma. After spending four hours in make-up daily, including donning an enormous red wig, Uma acknowledges, 'They made me look wonderful because that was how my character was meant to look, so I have no problem with that.'

In fact, Uma, who usually preferred smaller films to large movie sets, had a whale of a time. 'I really got into it. It's so much fun to play a completely uncomplicated but uber-confident creature who's unconcerned with and unintimidated by everything,' she says. 'There's nothing as much fun as having total licence to kill with regard to going over the top, which is normally career suicide.'

This light-hearted attitude, which had often been missing for Uma on set, seemed to be carried over from *Gattaca*. Her relationship with Hawke was clearly the breath of fresh air she needed.

'Much of the wit and wickedness you see, Uma brought to the part,' says her enamoured director. 'She is clearly a legendary beauty along the lines of Garbo or Dietrich, she has that same timeless quality, but she can also be very funny and goofy. The great thing about Uma is that she can be all dressed up in a ball gown and look like the queen of Romania, and still act like one of the guys.'

Uma researched unusual sources for this role, including the stylized hand movements of Japanese kabuki theatre, a popular traditional drama with songs performed by men. 'I've always felt that Batman is the extreme hyperbolic American kabuki, in the cartoon sense,' she says.

The only thing Uma baulked at was the physical confrontation with Batgirl in the final scene. 'Poison Ivy was an opera character. I found it ludicrous having to throw a punch in that character,' she continues. 'That whole fight at the end was the one thing that I really objected to. It seemed so beneath the character to actually have to scrap.' And she had a fair point, as that is exactly why Poison Ivy created her overgrown henchman, Bane. Also, her swift defeat is a bit of an anti-climax, given that it's only Batgirl's first fight.

When filming wrapped in 1996, it would be a few months before it was discovered whether the fourth volume could save the series.

*

While *Batman And Robin* opened in June 1997 in America and rolled out worldwide over the next two months, Uma was a little overpowered by Schwarzenegger in the promotional press conferences. But would she hold her own as a Batman baddie?

The mammoth $100 million budget is certainly in evidence; there are numerous lavish sets and the action sequences are truly spectacular. Such exuberance, however, begs the question of whether the movie is faithful to Batman, or if Schumacher's variants have taken on a life of their own. The extended action-packed opening credits set the tone for the rest of the film: fast-paced, flashy, and full of corny lines and close shaves, with justice always prevailing.

As for the acting, Clooney is a little too understated as both Bruce Wayne and Batman, and it doesn't help that the script opens the character up emotionally. 'I know I did a pretty bad job of a certain rubber-suit film,' admits Clooney, 'but that's part of my learning process. I learned that I don't have to do those films any more.'

O'Donnell fails to hold his own as Robin and becomes a whiny sidekick, while Silverstone is adequate, if a little wooden, unfortunately also earning herself the tabloid epithet 'Fatgirl'. Schwarzenegger as Mr Freeze is entertaining, but no more than a parody of himself in *The Terminator*, armed with endless terrible puns.

Uma, on the other hand, is convincing as the unkempt nerdy scientist, and simply excels as the wonderfully larger-than-life Poison Ivy. Sometimes it feels as though she is about to burst into song, but that mock-opera-singer stance was exactly what she was aiming for.

'What's great about her is that there is a vulnerable, fragile, sensitive person there, too,' raves Schumacher. 'I know no one at her age with that beauty, that talent, that intelligence, and also that humour. It's a very rare combination. She's so much fun. A lot of great beauties just take themselves too seriously.'

Poison Ivy smoulders as she lures both Batman and Robin into her traps of desire and, given the film's child-friendly appeal, certainly pushes the sexual-reference boundaries. 'In perhaps the sexiest turn ever seen in a PG rating, she melts celluloid every time she touches it, camping it up but never denting her cool cred,' drooled *Empire*'s Neil Jeffries. 'Silverstone and Elle MacPherson (as Bruce Wayne's squeeze) don't even come close.'

Thurman was the new Catwoman.

Ultimately, *Batman And Robin* is far too reminiscent of *Batman Forever*, leaving the viewer wondering what, if anything, is different about the new film. One villain is set up with an accident, the other's story is shown in the media, one chooses green and red, the other dark icy colours, havoc is wreaked at a city ball, there is a new hero in waiting to discover Wayne's secret life – even diehard fans have to question the lack of originality. 'A film which tries hard but seldom manages to be anything more than moderately entertaining,' summarized Derek Malcolm of the *Guardian*.

Despite the lacklustre reviews, fans of Batman, Clooney, Schwarzenegger and Thurman all queued up to see the film, ensuring that it was among the top-grossing movies of 1997. This was the second picture in which Uma had appeared that had pulled in more than $200 million worldwide – *Pulp Fiction* being the other – but bearing in mind the staggering costs, the huge takings were essential for *Batman And Robin* to make a profit.

'I knew that the movie made a fortune, but not a triple fortune which is what they were hoping for,' said Uma. 'It wasn't well reviewed but I felt I came out of it pretty good.'

17

CORSETS AND CATSUITS

'I like skin-tight black leather.'

UMA THURMAN

'It's been a year of becoming unselfconscious.'

UMA THURMAN

A combination of events worked in Uma's favour to finally make her more at ease with her body and looks – growing older and more mature and getting fit for the role of Poison Ivy, to name a couple – but it was clear that her loving relationship with Hawke gave her the stability and grounding that had often been missing in her life.

'These days, if a magazine describes me as a sexy woman, I can take it as a flattering compliment and it does not freak me out. I feel in tune with the world and I'm pretty oblivious of any image the media might choose to play up these days,' she said.

It seemed that she was so relaxed with her image that she went a step beyond shapeless, sexless outfits, adopting Hawke's trademark scruffy attire. She was regularly snapped around New York wearing baggy clothes and no make-up. 'I dress like this because I'm comfortable,' she said. 'I wish men could see past the physical side and into the soul, then maybe we wouldn't waste so much time and have so many problems. When you look a certain way, people forget that you have a personality.' Her blunt responses to journalists demonstrated that she still harboured resentment about her early stereotyping. Perhaps she was regretting her alluring appearance in *Batman And Robin*.

'I am not attached to how I look,' she explains. 'I have nothing to protect. I see my body as a very transient thing. I am very rubber, very changeable, and I have looked very different in almost all of my movies. My body and face can be twisted into something that looks iconoclastically pre-Raphaelite in one movie and very cheap, ugly and downtrodden in another.' And as if to prove a point, Uma's next film saw her looking the complete opposite of the temptress Poison Ivy.

In the spring of 1997, while Uma was waiting for *Batman And Robin* to be released, she signed up for two new projects. Although both were very exciting, the commitments meant she would spend most of the rest of the year abroad, only returning to America in late autumn. While the second movie was a return to the kitsch world of 1960s television with *The Avengers*, the first project she tackled was a whole new genre: the gritty historical drama *Les Misérables*.

Victor Hugo had conceived his story about unjust legislation and social misery in the 1830s and produced a rough first draft of the novel in 1840. Many of the characters were based on Hugo's friends and acquaintances, and Marius, the idealist student in love, is a depiction of the author in his youth. Finally, after numerous interruptions, Hugo produced his magnum opus, *Les Misérables*, in the spring of 1862. Politically it caused an uproar and the French establishment became extremely concerned about the spread of dissent – the Catholic Church even went so far as to say the book had been written by Satan in an attempt to discredit it.

Regardless of these attacks, the novel, which was split into four parts, quickly became assimilated by society and the issues it highlighted were discussed in the National Assembly. *Les Misérables* has since become regarded as one of the most important works of the literary canon, and the story has been adapted for all media. In the film industry, the Bible is the only other literary work that has been remade more times.

There are almost twenty versions of *Les Misérables* in existence, ranging from a silent movie in 1909 through Charles Laughton's talkie in 1935 to a television miniseries with Anthony Perkins in 1978. But perhaps most popular is the musical interpretation, adapted by Alain Boublil and Claude-Michel Schönberg, produced in thirty-eight countries in twenty-one different languages and seen by an estimated 50 million people.

In spite of a surely saturated market, one director, Billie August, felt he could offer something new with a fresh adaptation. August, a Dane, started his film career as a cinematographer before becoming a director in the 1980s. With an eye for period detail, he became renowned for creating deeply personal stories with three-dimensional characters. In

1987 he helmed *Pelle The Conqueror*, which marked not only his most internationally successful film, but also his growing interest in revising seemingly impenetrable novels. By the time he embarked on *Les Misérables*, however, his highbrow literary adaptations were popularly considered tiresome.

August commissioned *Fearless* screenwriter Rafael Yglesias to adapt Hugo's novel for the big screen, but as the original stands at over 1,500 pages, clearly there would have to be some hefty culling. The script concentrates on the relentless cat-and-mouse game between Valjean and Javert, and many of the subplots are abridged or axed altogether.

Valjean, a reformed criminal who vows to change when given a second chance, works his way up to the rank of mayor and factory owner in a new town. But he is hounded by his former prison guard, Inspector Javert.

One of Valjean's workers, Fantine, is discovered to have an illegitimate child and is sacked by her supervisor. Fantine's daughter, Cosette, is looked after by greedy innkeepers, the Thénardiers, who constantly demand more money. Taking to prostitution to pay for Cosette's keep, Fantine gets into a fight with a customer and is nearly arrested by Javert. Instead, Valjean intervenes, sets her free and cares for her as she is seriously ill. Promising to look after Cosette when Fantine dies, Valjean and his adopted daughter hide in a convent for ten years.

Then the story jumps forward to a student uprising, when an adult Cosette falls in love with a militant young man named Marius. For the sake of keeping the film simple, Yglesias's rewrite ends here, deleting many of Hugo's plot twists. But the greatest omission, which upset Hugo purists, is Eponine, daughter of the Thénardiers and rival for Marius's affections. While Eponine is a lynchpin of the novel, the musical and the 1935 film adaptation, August simply said, 'She doesn't serve the purpose of this story.'

*

As the focus of Billie August's version of *Les Misérables*, the two male leads, Valjean and Javert, had to be cast carefully, and the director chose Liam Neeson (*Schindler's List*, *Rob Roy*) and Geoffrey Rush (*Elizabeth*, *Shakespeare In Love*) respectively. With such a heavyweight duo already in place, he looked to a competent actress to bear the trauma of Fantine's lot.

Uma was thrilled to be offered the part, not least as it was the perfect antidote to the big-studio commercialism of *Batman And Robin*. 'I've always wanted to work with Billie August,' she said. 'I've been after him for a long time as one of the directors that I thought was really artistic and special.'

But it was not just the director that appealed; Uma was in love with Hugo's epic. 'That's one of the things I wish we had more of in modern cinema, the telling of great stories,' she continued. 'It's a profound tale about the complexity of human life, about justice, and about redemption and forgiveness.'

Uma phoned her agent the same night she read Yglesias's script and accepted the part instantly. 'I felt that [Fantine] was a beautiful character, a beautiful person who had a legitimate, poignant, traumatic historical experience,' she says. 'This novel, when Victor Hugo wrote it, was one of the first big indictments of the societal treatment of women. What makes it interesting is she's not just a victim [who] accepts her fate and gets whacked around and feels miserable about it. There's something strong and stubborn in [her] character that probably brought trouble down on her.' Uma had clearly done her research into the background of Fantine, as laid out in the first quarter of the novel, where she had fallen for a dishonest man and borne his child out of wedlock.

Hans Matheson (*Bodywork*) took on the role of young Marius, and his lover Cosette was played by Claire Danes (*William Shakespeare's Romeo + Juliet*), who would be heading for Yale in 1998.

With a first-rate cast and a condensed script, filming started in Prague in May 1997. The Czech capital was a place Uma had always been interested to visit, and the surroundings were about as far removed from everyday life as she could imagine.

'I remember looking around and not being able to figure out what was so different,' she said. 'It looked kind of like Europe but then not like Europe, and I couldn't put my finger on it. And finally I realized what it was: there were no billboards. And it was so beautiful, just to see the buildings and the sky and the vegetation.'

As Uma had hoped, August turned out to be exactly the type of director she enjoyed working with – like Tarantino, he brought out the best in her. 'I really felt as it went on that we had some sort of understanding,' elaborates the actress. 'I think he looks for the truth in performing. He's not easily satisfied. He's not the most communicative person, which is usually the sign of a good director, one that doesn't ever overspeak or overstep. They leave things alone, but provoke what they're looking for.'

Unfortunately, as Uma's character dies after the first hour, she spent only a limited time with August, but she made the most of his experience. She was particularly concerned about how he would handle the various scenes in which Fantine was beaten up. She told August in no uncertain terms that she did not want to make Fantine seem cheap or coy.

'I hate movies where you see someone who's supposed to be dying [or] has just been sexually assaulted and they're in a brand-new pair of white panties and a really prissy little lacy bra,' said Uma. 'It becomes obnoxious. It becomes obviously about the actress, not about the piece.'

Uma was determined that Fantine should not seem weak and outlined her thoughts to August, who actually wanted the character to be more desperate and totally crushed. The director was impressed with Uma's understanding of the story, and he eventually allowed himself to be persuaded into representing a more forceful Fantine.

'She is very brave,' praises August. 'Uma's very courageous. She's taken a lot of risks.' He might have been talking about her penchant for tackling demanding and diverse roles, but it also applied to the physicality of this particular part. 'I got really bruised, because there's no way you can pretend you're flying through the air and landing on the ground,' says the actress, 'you actually have to do it. There's also a scene where Fantine is physically assaulted by three men, and I found that very intense to shoot.'

*

Les Misérables was released on 1 May 1998 in America with little fuss; it was neither loved nor hated by critics and so was widely overlooked. This was a great shame; it seemed as though the studio was unsure about its product. The visuals are impressive, August's attention to detail is immaculate, and the acting is solid with evocative performances from all five leads.

The first half of the film is exceptionally well crafted, with Javert searching for the truth while Valjean tries to look after Fantine, building to a beautiful climax. As the story jumps forward ten years, a new plot is introduced with Cosette and Marius, but Javert's relentless chase of Valjean gives continuity. Danes and Matheson hold their own, but the driving force comes from Neeson and Rush, both excellent actors who demonstrate believable emotions of mutual hatred and pity. Although many storylines are missed out, Hugo's main themes of love, redemption, mercy and compassion resonate throughout.

Some critics felt the ending was unfulfilling, and it has to be said that Rush's final speech could have been improved. 'The film ends on what's supposed to be an inspirational note, but it's more likely to produce a shrug than a swell of the heart,' commented Andrew Johnston from *Time Out*. Perhaps it was down to the liberal losses and the change of focus from the original story, but many felt something was not right.

It is hard not to contrast August's version with the tremendously successful musical. While it is unfair to compare different mediums, there is a valid point to be made: namely, in the musical it is undoubtedly the emotive lyrics and stirring score which help one section segue into another, while August's retelling sometimes feels stilted and awkward.

For Uma, however, while *Les Misérables* was not an obvious blockbuster like *Batman And Robin*, it was a respectable film and she gave a marvellous performance which certainly did not harm her career. 'Uma Thurman shares many of Fantine's qualities,' summarizes August. 'Throughout her professional career Uma has dared to take big risks and, in most cases, won great victories. In Uma's interpretation, Fantine has become an extremely subtle and moving character.' Uma is especially poignant in her portrayal of the character's bond with her daughter – all the more remarkable considering she had no experience of motherhood – and as a result she gained some of the best critical reactions of her career.

On a personal note, Uma not only enjoyed filming *Les Misérables*, but she also made two lasting friends with Liam Neeson and his wife Natasha Richardson. Neeson's lasting impression of Uma is 'a mixture of wonderful intelligence and incredible shyness'.

Natasha Richardson, the classically trained stage and screen actress, had starred opposite Neeson in 1993's acclaimed Broadway revival of *Anna Christie*, marrying him the following year. The daughter of actress Vanessa Redgrave and director Tony Richardson, perhaps it was Richardson's strong sense of independence, gained through her parents' pursuit of their respective careers, that Thurman found so familiar.

'In Uma there's a little lost girl who's put on very grown-up clothes to appear completely together, and as someone wonderfully sophisticated,' comments Richardson, likening Uma to her favourite children's character, Pippi Longstocking.

*

It had been a terrific shame that Uma's studied performance in *Les Misérables* had gone largely unnoticed. For better or for worse, there would be no likelihood of a muted release and reception for her next role.

The Avengers was a 1960s television series like no other. Uniquely set among the stiff British upper classes, debonair secret agent John Steed (Patrick Macnee) of the secret intelligence unit Ministry was paired with a succession of modern, capable female partners, variously played by Linda Thorson, Honor Blackman and, most memorably, Diana Rigg.

A curious bastardization of Bond-style national-security protection, *The Avengers* plotlines were always fantastical, embracing cyborg armies, invisible men and baddies armed with cold viruses, set against eerily deserted backdrops. 'No woman should be killed, no extras should populate the streets,' outlined writer and producer Brian Clemens. 'As a fantasy, we would not show a uniformed policeman or a black man. And you would not see anything as common as blood in *The Avengers*.'

Other than its outlandish themes, the most noted detail of the programme was the attire – Steed was always impeccably dressed, but, far more importantly, his partner Mrs Emma Peel (her name a play on M. Appeal, standing for 'Man Appeal') was clad in a skin-tight black-leather catsuit. The show was a smash hit during the 1960s and subsequently revived in the 1970s.

Independent film producer Jerry Weintraub had been trying to adapt the cult series for the big screen since the mid-1980s. His dream project had been an uphill struggle from the start as key personnel joined and left the venture. When Nicolas Meyer bowed out of the director's role, Weintraub hired Jeremiah S. Chechik, whose inconsistent CV comprised the impressive and ambitious *Benny & Joon* and *Tall Tale*, but also the flop remake of *Diabolique*, starring Sharon Stone.

The next task was to find a screenwriter who could create a script that remained faithful to the series' spirit for ardent fans, yet updated for a modern audience. 'I was concerned with keeping the true, quintessentially English background and characters of the show,' says Weintraub. 'That's tough when you're making a big action-adventure movie. Your natural tendency is to Americanize it, [but] I didn't want to.'

He brought in Don Macpherson, a relative newcomer who was keen to preserve the inner essence of *The Avengers* – 'the wit, the style, the lunacy, the strange *Alice In Wonderland* terror,' Macpherson elaborates. The screenwriter was also adamant that *The Avengers* would essentially be a romance, a 'will they, won't they?' scenario exacerbated by Steed's formality and Peel's rebelliousness.

'Patrick Macnee was very pleased that I got the relationship between

Steed and Mrs Peel absolutely as it should be,' continues Macpherson. 'She is the character who causes trouble. She is very antagonistic to Steed, but they come to realize they need each other to progress.' Macpherson was also specific about the language used ('very Noel Coward,' says Chechik), although his style may have alienated younger sections of the audience.

Focusing on the flirtatious rapport between the pair, Macpherson was less concerned with the plans for an evil takeover bid which Steed and Peel were supposed to foil. Rather than trying to transport *The Avengers* to the 1990s, he looked to the TV series for plot inspiration. 'There were a number of episodes that dealt with the weather,' he explains, 'and I came across some research about the 1950s and 1960s when the Soviets and Americans were involved in cloud seeding.

'It seemed that the weather was both something that they would talk about in a very British manner and be very dangerous and very global.' Consequently, in the big-screen adaptation the duo have to track down Sir August de Wynter, a former secret agent turned villain who is attempting to control London's weather in order to hold the capital to ransom.

With a script of sorts in place, Weintraub needed a big-name cast to rival the other cult television-to-film remakes *The Avengers* would be following: *Mission: Impossible* with Tom Cruise (1996), *The Saint* with Val Kilmer (1997) and the *Batman* series with Keaton, Kilmer and Clooney. Initially, Mel Gibson had rather incongruously accepted the lead role of Steed, but, like Meyer, he withdrew before production began. Without the box-office pull of a celebrity such as Gibson, Weintraub considered an equally unlikely selection of British stars to no avail, including Sean Bean, Alan Rickman and Robbie Coltrane.

After much toing and froing, the producer slowly began to piece his cast together. 'It took ages to find the right Steed,' he bemoans. 'It was the most difficult role of all to cast. I went through a lot of people.' Intriguingly, Weintraub chose the serious classical actor Ralph Fiennes for the part. While Fiennes certainly had the right accent and required Englishness, his fine performances in highbrow fare such as *Wuthering Heights* and *Schindler's List* did not obviously lend him to a madcap comedy. Moreover, he was filming *The English Patient*, another gritty, heart-rending saga, when Weintraub signed him up.

The actor's reasons for accepting the part were a combination of a lifelong love of the TV series and a need for light relief from all those sombre dramas. 'I think the British get a lot of stick in a lot of films, and it's time for the return of the British hero,' he said as he donned

Steed's bowler hat. In contrast to conventional action heroes built like Arnold Schwarzenegger, Sylvester Stallone and Bruce Willis, the Bond-style agent who relies on wit and gadgetry was the perfect guise for slender Fiennes.

The illustrious Emma Peel was originally to be played by Nicole Kidman, but instead she took on her own action role in *The Peacemaker* with George Clooney. Next up for the role was Gwyneth Paltrow, but after her success in *Emma* she was busy filming *Sliding Doors*, *Great Expectations* and *Shakespeare In Love*. Then the director considered Uma Thurman and realized she had all the right qualities. 'I wanted somebody smart and sexy who would be able to deliver a certain modern sensibility,' says Chechik. 'That's Uma – she is both quirky and odd, funny and interesting.'

Although Uma had recently played a camp caricature in *Batman And Robin*, she signed up without hesitation. 'I'm a drawing-room actress used to sitting around drinking tea and talking,' she said. 'I thought it would be fun, a new genre to experience. *The Avengers* is popcorn. It's squeaky-clean. Kids can go.'

With the two leads cast, Chechik searched for *The Avengers*' villains, and the Ministry bosses Mother and Father. The part of the evil meteorological wizard Sir August de Wynter was snapped up for a cool $17 million by Sean Connery. 'Well, it's an amusing irony, isn't it, that the one Scotsman who did once play the epitome of the British hero thirty years ago, turns up in *The Avengers* playing the baddie,' observed Fiennes. After relinquishing the mantle of 007, Connery had forged a successful career unhindered by his trademark thick Celtic accent, and finally he was now legitimately cast as a Scot.

Connery's unlikely henchmen consisted of the unpredictable transvestite comedian Eddie Izzard (who had originally been slated to play Mother) and former Happy Mondays frontman Shaun Ryder. With the role of wheelchair-bound Mother going to Jim Broadbent, Dawn French lost out on the part of blind Father to Fiona Shaw.

With a tip of the bowler for approval, the cast were honoured with a vocal cameo by Patrick Macnee as Invisible Jones.

*

Top production, set and costume designers were brought in to help give *The Avengers* the dual sense of taking place in the late 1990s, while still stuck firmly in the 1960s.

'Stuart Craig, the production designer, brilliantly mixed far-out and modern, pop designs with rather old fuddy-duddy English things,' explained Fiennes. 'To me that is visually true to the original.'

Furthermore, the designers adhered to the uncluttered sets of the low-budget series, thus meaning there were no extras, no London traffic – just clean, empty streets. While many of the interiors were shot at Shepperton Studios, outdoor locations included Blenheim Palace and Greenwich Naval College, among other British landmarks.

Weintraub was obsessive about Steed's pinstriped suits and bowler hat, taking Fiennes to Savile Row for lengthy fittings. For Uma, as well as the variety of skimpy outfits, there was of course *the* catsuit. 'It feels pretty funny,' she laughed as she was shoehorned in with the aid of talcum powder and then sewn up each day. 'Luckily I had my *Batman And Robin* experience to break me in, my Poison Ivy latex sheath. It's been a year of becoming unselfconscious.'

Unlike Fiennes and the rest of the British population, American Uma had not been particularly aware of the original series and so watched hours of old tapes for research. 'I didn't know I'd seen it before,' she admitted. 'When I watched some of the episodes to prepare for this film, I realized I had seen some of them as a child.'

Further homework included a detailed study of Rigg's portrayal of Peel. 'When I saw Diana Rigg's work I was so impressed. Her Emma Peel is the real Emma Peel and unforgettable,' said Uma. 'I loved her, and certain questions were answered by her interpretation which I used to colour the Emma Peel in the script.

'But I didn't try to model my character on her in any way, because I am too different and it would have been weird to try to impersonate her.'

For Uma, the hardest part was the distinctive upper-class English accent. 'It's very difficult to do it properly and not lose character,' she says. 'I'm sure to the English ear it's not going to be perfect, but perhaps elsewhere it won't sound too bad.' Indeed, to a Brit she does sound very stilted in the finished film, but in the context of the movie and alongside Fiennes's clipped accent it is just about passable.

From the second she signed on the dotted line, Uma was bombarded with comments about how sexy Emma Peel was, and so the actress set about analysing the character's appeal. 'There was this really delicate, fine line between this fresh, cheerful, always-got-a-good-idea person and this unselfconsciously self-confident dynamic of female sexuality,' she noted. In fact, in the feature-length version of *The Avengers*, Emma Peel is cloned – a theme familiar from *Gattaca* – and so Uma was required to depict two different sides of the character.

Ironically, in one of the scenes deleted from *Pulp Fiction*, Uma as Mia Wallace interrogates John Travolta as Vincent Vega to find out more about him. After quizzing him about some popular-culture preferences, she finishes by asking if he has ever fantasized about being beaten up by a girl.

'Sure,' Vincent replies. 'Emma Peel on *The Avengers* . . .'

*

Apart from the sparse sets and fetish-driven outfits lovingly re-created from the original *Avengers*, the crux of the film was the hinted romance between Steed and Peel. 'It's very ambiguous,' elucidated Fiennes. 'They're both able and unable to show their concern for each other and they constantly won't be caught out as the one being soft on the other. And that's kind of the sweet thing.'

Uma confirmed that they don't actually have an affair as that would be 'an *Avengers* sin . . . but there is the suggestion that it is always about to happen. Maybe a kiss.'

The actors looked forward to the filming, which began in London during June 1997 with a generous budget of $60 million from distributors Warner Brothers. However, it became clear from day one that all was not well.

Fiennes's first day had got off to a bad start. Uma, who had been watching, joined him afterwards and said reassuringly, 'It doesn't matter.' Her shoot then began with Peel encountering a naked Steed in a gentlemen's club steam room, his modesty preserved by a copy of the *Financial Times*.

'I was extremely nervous,' recalled Uma. 'I thought I sounded awful, so I was very uptight. I came stumbling down the steps and I didn't know Ralph intended to do it without his pants on.

'Sadly, they didn't have a close-up camera on my face to get my genuine reaction, as I was trying to hold back my laughter! Ralph was very shy, but I assured him that as I am deeply near-sighted I couldn't assess his equipment.'

Suddenly it dawned on her what she had signed up for. 'We had a good time, but we realized from the first day on set that we wouldn't be achieving much on an artistic level with our performances,' admitted Uma. 'The film is too campy and we don't test any serious emotional chords or depths. We were both disappointed at first that there wouldn't be more of a challenge.'

It seems surprising that Uma was so unprepared for the tone of *The Avengers*; it never set out to be an intellectual drama and wasn't promoted as such. Perhaps she expected it to resemble the overblown camp of *Batman And Robin* – again something the film's creators never intended. Either way, she did little to disguise her dissatisfaction.

While Thurman had previously mastered the art of comic timing,

Fiennes found the genre both demanding and stimulating. 'I have to say that kind of light comedy, like Cary Grant, David Niven and Jimmy Stewart were known for, required a relaxation of delivery I found quite hard,' he said. 'It can't just be throwaway charm, although it might appear to be. It has to be bloody precise. That was a very tough thing, but I loved doing it.'

Thurman may not have been enamoured with the direction in which *The Avengers* was going, but she did at least enjoy the company. 'Ralph is such an angel,' she elaborated. 'He's such a particular person that I find him deeply amusing. He's so extraordinarily specific. And beautiful and intelligent and sensitive, and totally removed.'

Despite Uma's misgivings, she managed to please the director. 'Actors train in different ways,' explained Chechik. 'She examines and questions everything. Even if she is not convinced, she will be very enthusiastic and say, "OK, let's give it a try." That is part of her process.'

One of the things that Uma insisted on trying was her own stunt work. Weintraub was aware he needed some fast-paced action to maximize the film's appeal, as he said, 'I thought sexual tension, innuendo and the repartee between Steed and Emma was important, but you can't do a Noel Coward piece as a big blockbuster movie.'

While Fiennes had previous experience of stage fighting, Uma was not versed in combat scenes, and the pair spent a long time preparing their swordplay. 'We had Bill Hobbs doing the fights,' said Fiennes. 'He was the number-one fighter, especially with swords – he's brilliant.' Hobbs had a solid background in stunt work and choreography and taught the pair every minute move, which both would execute admirably on set.

The grand finale fight scenes were ambitious and required considerable training. 'There is a final fight with Sean, but that was the learning of the fight as opposed to the learning of the technique, which took some time,' recalled Fiennes.

Uma's confrontation with Eddie Izzard was one of her most taxing sequences, as she was balancing on a set of high wires, trying to perform complex hits and kicks without falling off. 'Being in spiked heels 40 feet above cement with no protective barriers makes me feel very uncomfortable,' she said, acknowledging her intense fear of heights.

In another nerve-wracking scene she was suspended 20 feet in the air, clinging on to the side of a hot-air balloon. 'I remember the look of mortal fear on her face,' said Chechik. 'She was not pleased about being up that high.' Once up there, Uma then had to dislodge pipes to reduce the balloon's power.

'We were dealing with fire and some kind of gases that make pipes very hot,' she explained, shuddering at the memory. 'I coped – irritably – but I did it step by step. I just tried to do it and stay in a good mood.' When a fire broke out on set during the early days of filming, an impish Uma joked, 'Actually, it was me, running around with a torch, trying to get a few days off.'

18

YEAR OF THE MOTHER

'I was really ready for a life change. I was getting a little bit lost in my professional life. You know, change is usually preceded by some kind of drift.'

UMA THURMAN

When Uma finally left the set of *The Avengers* and returned to America in 1997, she stayed with her brother in New York for a while until she and Ethan Hawke found an apartment. A brownstone ideally situated in Greenwich Village costing just shy of £1 million, it was a solid sign of the couple's commitment to each other. The actress was delighted to be properly reunited with her lover and keen to see where the romance would take her.

With the benefit of hindsight, it seems very strange that Uma didn't discover she was pregnant until she was more than three months gone, but the stress of a heavy schedule can do funny things to the regularity of a woman's monthly cycle. Perhaps Uma hadn't noticed the passing of her first trimester because her pregnancy had been so smooth; there was no sign of morning sickness or cravings, and any tiredness was put down to her workload.

Like many expectant mothers, one of the first things Uma did when she found out there was a baby on the way was to shelve her unhealthy pack-a-day cigarette habit. 'I stopped smoking the day I knew I was pregnant,' she recalls. 'Ethan and I both stopped on that day. It was the Super Bowl.'

Although they sat through the rest of the Super Bowl happily stunned by the news, it wasn't really that much of a shock. The couple had first started thinking about having a baby when Uma began filming her role as the mother Fantine in *Les Misérables*. After mulling it over for a while, Uma, who had always wanted to have children, decided it was time.

'It's the year of the mother,' joked Uma of the Fantine connection. 'It took me a while, but I managed to convince Ethan. It's wonderful when the circuitous nature of things comes together.' So the contraception went out of the window and they were now on top of the world. 'I think it's the most optimistic choice I've ever made,' she said. 'It means you believe love is worth living for, despite everything else.

'When I was younger I used to think, "Who could bring a child into this world?" Now I've come to accept that love has made my life worthwhile.'

Of course, it takes two to make a baby, and many people wanted to know how Hawke was adjusting to impending fatherhood. 'He's been a champ, an absolute champ,' Uma gushed. 'It's been a really happy time for both of us.' Hawke too was eager to discuss his new favourite subject.

'I'm thrilled, I'm scared, I'm nervous,' he said, echoing the thoughts of a million prospective dads. 'Right now, I just really want to make sure that Uma's healthy and stays healthy.'

And so, just a few months after moving into their first apartment together, Uma and Ethan found themselves house-hunting for a home that was more suitable for a baby, as their current spare room was so tiny it would barely accommodate a crib.* It was faintly ridiculous – they hadn't even unpacked the boxes from their first move – but it was fun.

'People say moving is so stressful,' she said, never having believed this herself. '[But] I find being in a space [where] you can't ever feel like you should really unpack your boxes is even more stressful. The reason I move is the hope of new space.'

With the pregnancy now guiding her hand, Uma admitted, 'A little bit of the folly goes out of it. I always used to say, even when I was in my teens and going from apartment to apartment, that I had a sneaking suspicion that I would never be able to make a home for my own sake.' Uma had quite rightly suspected that her endless need for travel and domestic reinvention would not come to an end until she had somebody else's best interests at heart.

---

* Amusingly, at this time certain journalists obviously not 'in the know' reported the couple were moving out so soon because their apartment was haunted.

It was admittedly a half-hour drive north of their beloved New York City, but Uma and Ethan eventually fell in love with a $1.25 million four-bedroom house in a small country town called Sneden's Landing on the Hudson River. 'One day Ethan and I were out driving, and we saw it and started screaming, "We have to buy this!" ' she recounted.

On the one hand, the house was stately, magnificent and elegantly placed overlooking the river; on the other, it was an ageing, crumbling shambles requiring total renovation. While this might not initially have seemed like an obvious abode for two A-list film stars, the neighbours did at least include Al Pacino and Bill Murray.

But Uma had always been one for rolling up her sleeves, and even as she grew heavier by the day, she confidently tackled contractors, gardeners, electricians and builders with aplomb. Ethan too made a concerted effort, but as the main breadwinner while pregnancy temporarily took Uma out of the running, he needed to find a way to pay for this most expensive acquisition and so signed up for *Snow Falling On Cedars*. That shoot would soon take him away to film on location in Vancouver, leaving Uma in charge of proceedings.

Considering the extent of the restoration, there was never much chance that the house would be ready by the time the baby was due to arrive in July, but that was part of the challenge. 'It's a never-ending story,' gasped Uma, wholly consumed by the progression of the building work and decoration. 'The house is a wreck. [But] I didn't know I could have so much fun and not be at work!'

*

Despite the five months of filming in the summer and autumn of 1997, several of *The Avengers* cast were recalled in February 1998 for further filming. Apparently, the test screening in Phoenix, Arizona, had revealed that nine out of ten people hated the movie.

Uma, now several months pregnant, was not only required on set again, but also had to re-create some of the daredevil stunts that had scared her previously. The special-effects co-ordinator, Joss Williams, was aware of her condition and noted, 'We had to be very careful with her.'

The press soon found out that the film had required retakes so late in the day and quickly paired this information with Uma's overt unhappiness during the initial shoot to spell disaster. Escalated reports of fires on set, script difficulties, poor test screenings and undercover reshoots dogged the film during post-production.

Compounding matters, Warner Brothers were being unnaturally protective of their forthcoming release. All they leaked were a trailer and a few sexy images of Uma as the leather-clad Emma Peel. The press and public alike were forced to wait until the summer to form their own opinions.

*

After the *Avengers* reshoots, it was time for Uma to take a step back and enjoy the rest of her pregnancy.

Alongside keeping a constant eye on progress at the building site she hoped one day to call home, Uma was spotted attending the annual Tibet House benefit concert at Carnegie Hall in March 1998. She and Ethan quietly fulfilled their family brief to act as chairpersons at the upbeat occasion, which featured musical support from Sheryl Crow, Natalie Merchant, Patti Smith and Live.

'This is the fun side of the Tibetan movement,' said her father of the yearly event. 'It has to have a fun side; you have to be able to dance in front of the flames.'

Although always happy to lend her support to Robert and his quest to free Tibet, Uma grouchily admitted her pregnancy left her tired, 'so my threshold for public life is extremely low – and it was never very high to begin with'.

So, after a sole appearance on *The Clive James Show*, and a trip to Canada to visit Ethan on the set of *Snow Falling On Cedars* (where the couple were endearingly spotted practising parenting skills on a doll in Vancouver's Absolutely Diapers store), Uma largely melted away from the public's gaze to see out her last trimester. However, she still granted interviews, eagerly extolling the excitement of late pregnancy.

'It's really hard to concentrate on anything else right now,' she would say. 'All the things that used to be so important to me have been swept away. I felt the baby kick the other day and it was like no other experience in my life. I feel blessed and very peaceful.'

Uma would happily chat away about the joys of eating Oreos and getting fat (she refused to exercise), the benefits of painkilling drugs during labour, and the desire to know the sex of her baby ahead of time, although this last wish remained unfulfilled. Jane Austen was replaced on her bedside table by a tall pile of books on pregnancy, birth and childcare, she drank stinging-nettle soup for the iron content, and would regularly erupt into peals of helpless giggles due to her surging hormones.

Feeling fulfilled, Uma made plans for after the birth that notably didn't include any film work. She stopped reading scripts and enthused, 'I'm more excited about motherhood than any role I've played and feel I deserve a sabbatical.' In her own words, Uma felt she had discovered the meaning of life and was truly 'in heaven'. 'When you become pregnant, there's a force inside you that you can't escape,' she said. 'This is your reality, you are becoming a mother – and it cuts through the bullshit.'

One question that was open to debate was baby names. For years Uma had detested her parents' unconventional choice, until she realized it helped her stand out from the rest – in a positive way. Uma and Ethan agreed that the name should be unusual, so the baby would feel like part of a tribe.

'Somebody named Jack would have an identity crisis in my family!' quipped the mum-to-be. Of course, the unmarried couple also had to consider which of their surnames their first-born would take, but they didn't take this too seriously; Uma jokingly brushed off the question, saying the child would use the last name of 'whichever parent he or she hates the least'.

*

That Uma and Ethan's baby would be born out of wedlock didn't really seem to be an issue for the couple. Notions of the sanctity of marriage were rather outdated in modern New York, and besides, with a new house and a planned baby on the way, they were clearly committed to each other.

Still, as she had fallen pregnant, rumours began to circulate that they were planning a secret wedding. Uma denied all speculation. 'No, no, no!' she responded to a persistent journalist. 'I love the guy, I'm having his baby and I don't want to worry about a wedding. It'll happen – all in good time.'

The truth was rather different. Ethan first went down on one knee towards the end of March, but his romantic suggestion initially met with resistance, as Uma neither wanted a 'shotgun wedding' nor to repeat the mistakes she had made with Gary Oldman. But after three weeks of more in-depth consideration, the actress realized she really wanted her partner to be listed as her 'next of kin' on the hospital forms.

So Uma turned the tables and quietly proposed; Ethan accepted and soon enough his fiancée was spied with a diamond ring on the third finger of her left hand. Still the couple denied anything was going on, but reports persisted in the media, especially after they were spotted attending a New York City marriage licence bureau, then leaving the potential venue of the Cathedral of St John the Divine, in Manhattan.

It was actually Uma's brother Dechen who let the cat out of the bag once and for all. Accompanying his sister to the premiere of *Les*

Misérables, he blabbed to the *New York Daily News*, 'I've been sworn to secrecy about the place and the day but it's going to be soon, very soon, a small ceremony . . .'

Dodging reporters and photographers, the engaged couple were unable to escape prying eyes on Uma's twenty-eighth birthday. Dining at Brooklyn's River Café, Ethan pulled out a sheet of paper and began reading aloud to their unborn child as Uma, smiling, blissfully rubbed her belly. 'They looked like two teenagers in love,' said Stephane D. Hainaut, the maître d'.

The big event took place two days later, in the early evening of May Day.

Concerns about Uma's safety, especially being seven months pregnant, meant that many guests weren't even told the location until the morning of the wedding. Five police cars escorted the bride and groom to the ceremony and five others were parked outside to deter uninvited guests and prevent anyone entering with cameras or other recording equipment.

Despite the imposing security measures, the ceremony was lovely. Uma and Ethan had decided on the Cathedral of St John the Divine after all – the Episcopalian setting to please the Hawkes, with a Buddhist blessing to please the Thurmans. Reportedly, a prenuptial ceremony was sanctified by the old family friend the Dalai Lama himself.

The cathedral was filled with flowers and lit by candles. 'It was such a beautiful wedding,' said Uma. 'It was just close family and friends. We didn't want a huge Hollywood wedding with agents and tax advisers cheering us on. It was simple, peaceful and a night I will always cherish.'

Guests watched Uma walk up the aisle in a traditional lacy gown designed by Vera Wang, a veil and subtle jewellery. 'Big as a house!' the bride later exclaimed, '*and* I wore white!'

The reception followed in an adjacent chapel, where Uma ecstatically showed off her wedding ring, a band featuring a lucky seven diamonds on the outside and a secret eighth jewel hidden inside.

*

Uma and Ethan's wedded bliss was soon interrupted with the arrival of their daughter.

Born on 8 July 1998 at St Luke's-Roosevelt Hospital in New York, she weighed in at a healthy 7 pounds 11 ounces.

Uma went through a long eighteen-hour labour to bring her little girl into the world, the slowness of the delivery eventually sped up by an injection of Pitocin. 'It was a pretty scary thing,' said Uma several months later. 'When you think of something that big inside you, it's either going to be the knife or you that's going to get it out . . .

'Ethan was there for all of it, and he got high accolades from the doctor!' The glowing new mum pronounced her daughter 'heaven on earth'. Ethan had generously allowed Uma to choose the name in the end, and she settled on the pretty and not overly wacky Maya Ray Thurman-Hawke.

Right from the very beginning, Uma took to motherhood like a duck to water. Her close friends and family proudly praised her commitment.

'Uma's adult life was spent preparing to be a mother,' said Dechen. 'You'll never find a more loving parent than her.' Meanwhile, her former director Joel Schumacher suggested that to truly appreciate the actress, you have to view her as a mother. 'I always felt that if I had a crisis of the head or heart I could rest my head on her shoulder. She has great compassion for how difficult it is to be a human being.'

The effects of motherhood on Uma were more profound than anything she'd ever experienced before. She'd certainly anticipated and dreamed of the unshakeable bond that exists between mother and child for most of her twenties, and stated on more than one occasion that in her desire to be a relatively youthful mum, she would have had a baby on her own if necessary.

But Uma wasn't alone. In Ethan Hawke she had found someone she felt she could trust with bringing a new life into the world – and she has often said he was the first and only man she could envisage as a father to her children. Despite her enthusiasm, Uma wasn't strictly ready for the immense stretch having a dependant places on both parents' emotions, and the almost alien change of perspective it gives on life.

'Before I had my child, I thought I knew the boundaries of myself, that I understood the limits of my heart,' she said. 'It's extraordinary to have all those limits thrown out, to realize your love is inexhaustible.

'Starting a family was my way of taking responsibility for my life . . . It made me realize how empty it was just to live for myself [and] gave me a chance to redefine my whole life.

'I am simply in awe of the miracle of it all. I think it's the bravest act of hope a person can exhibit in the whole world.'

Like many women, Uma found she became closer to her own mother now she had a daughter, and she began to view all those faraway childhood struggles in a fresh light.

'We can always complain about our parents, but until we actually get involved in running our own families, we don't know how difficult the process can be,' she acknowledged, while specifying her own methods would be unlike those of her parents. 'We're an odd family,' she said, referring to the Thurman clan. 'Bohemian and definitely eccentric. I'm not saying it was a bad thing, but I know my daughter's upbringing will be totally different.'

As for Maya herself, Uma said she was 'adorable', 'confident and smart – just like her dad', and tried her hardest to savour every single day with her. 'Already I can't remember what I did before she was my daughter and I was a mum . . .'

Settling into a comfortable routine of what she laughingly referred to as the 'constant rotation of messes' a small baby brings, Uma felt utterly fulfilled and content. It seemed nothing or no one could spoil her mood.

19

SWEET AND LOW-KEY

'Like a soufflé, sometimes films don't rise.'

UMA THURMAN

The marked absence of preview screenings for *The Avengers* fuelled rumours that the feature-length version was no match for the original series. Having declined advance press viewings, an approach usually reserved for B-movies, Warner Brothers finally allowed a couple of public airings just days before general release. As before, when the reshoots were ordered, the feedback was of overwhelming apathy, but by then it was too late and Warner Brothers had to roll out distribution as planned.

Although the release of *Les Misérables* on 1 May 1998 had barely caused a ripple at the box office, Uma was too busy marrying Ethan to be concerned. Just a couple of months later, however, there was a lot riding on the opening of *The Avengers*.

'I used to carry a lot of different kinds of doubt and insecurities,' admitted Uma as her latest offering was about to be shown for the first time. 'Now I have relaxed in some profound way.' No doubt this new repose was due to marriage and motherhood, but did she really not care about the fate of the intended blockbuster?

She was certainly quick to defend it before release. 'I think fans of the shows will be happy with our interpretation,' she said. 'The film's a bit of a surprise – it's an antidote to the action-man films like *Armageddon* and *Godzilla*.'

Those two of the summer's biggest blockbusters aside, as Jeremiah

S. Chechik's fifth film was unleashed on 14 August 1998, it followed in the footsteps of a string of television shows that had been given the big-screen treatment, some more effectively than others, and was subsequently compared to its predecessors.

The Flintstones in 1994 was not one of the success stories, despite a strong comedy cast and some thirty-two screenwriters. *The Addams Family* and *Addams Family Values* held their own as films, but never quite matched the quirkiness of the original black-and-white television shows.

The *Batman* series had been doing well until Joel Schumacher took over as director and undermined the dark comic-book beginnings with his over-the-top caricatures. *The Saint* notably flopped in 1997, as Val Kilmer ignored its roots in the cult series and applied his distinctive Method acting to the role of Simon Templar.

Mission: Impossible, however, the most popular attempt in terms of box-office takings, was undoubtedly a hit *because* it modernized the show – to the point where it was almost unrecognizable.

Most unfortunately for *The Avengers*, two similar films were already in the pipeline that would overshadow it. *Austin Powers: The Spy Who Shagged Me* was due out ten months later and promised a hilarious mix of 1960s surrealism and high camp, while the much-hyped *Charlie's Angels* the following year would amply redress the gender imbalance by introducing three female action stars.

The Avengers as a series was low-budget with farcical plots, and, perhaps misguidedly, Chechik tried to make a blockbuster movie within these parameters. In his determination not to update anything about the show, the director alienated a large section of the audience used to flashy special effects and polished action sequences.

Ultimately the film is so caught up in its own homage that it lacks any substance. Although great attention was paid to the sets, costumes, dialogue and British stiff upper lip, the characters show little or no emotional development, while the plot is lame and riddled with holes. The accents are off-putting, the dialogue is stilted, there is no chemistry between any of the actors (to the extent that they might as well have all filmed their scenes separately), there is no suspense and the action sequences are presented in a tame 1960s fashion.

Remarkably short at just under an hour-and-a-half, *The Avengers* feels as though whole chunks have been removed in a desperate bid to restore interest during an overly brutal edit. The sporadic appearances of Peel's clone are never really explained, yet instead the viewer is confounded by a car chase with giant mechanical shooting wasps, a gun-toting granny and a boardroom meeting where members are dressed up in giant brightly coloured teddy-bear suits.

'Incoherent, flat and lacking any spark whatsoever,' complained John Millar at length in the *Daily Record*. 'How can moviemakers get something so wrong when all that money and talent is concentrated on one project?'

None of the cast was excused from blame. Fiennes was ridiculed for being the only Brit ever to look daft in a bowler hat; Uma was tirelessly compared to Diana Rigg, who was placed on a pedestal as the 'one and only' Emma Peel; Connery was lambasted as the worst screen baddie, regardless of the kilt; and Izzard was deemed frankly absurd as a henchman.

Far removed from the vision of Chechik and Weintraub, *The Avengers* picked up a selection of Razzie nominations, notably for Worst Actress and Worst Couple, implicating Uma twice. Michael Medved, critic for the *National Enquirer*, jumped on the bandwagon, adding the Golden Turkey Award for Worst Picture. The paper later commented: 'The film is a combination of horrible acting, wretched special effects and a completely incoherent script. Normally, if they mixed up the reels, and showed them in the wrong order, the audience wouldn't understand what a film was about. With *The Avengers*, it might actually help.'

Finally, critics at the British magazine *Total Film* voted Uma and Fiennes the worst double act of all time. 'There's a lot of competition for the worst film duo, but you have to go a long way to beat Uma Thurman and Ralph Fiennes,' blasted the magazine's Ceri Thomas. 'They look as if they've never even met before, just plonked on the set together on the day of the shoot and told to flirt. Completely unconvincing.'

For the first time, Uma had been brought down along with the ship.

*

Having already pulled off camp comic action in *Batman And Robin* with some success, *The Avengers* seemed an odd task for Uma to undertake. Yet it was her style to try something 'bold and unique'.

The greatest slur she suffered as a result was that she had a fickle attitude to image and looks. The woman who started her career by baring all quickly became self-conscious and refused to strip at all. Once satisfied that she was no longer being stereotyped as a sex symbol, she then felt unattractive and took on a series of roles that exploited her looks and figure. With *Batman And Robin*, she could use the excuse of trying something completely different, but a second figure-hugging outfit in another television-to-cinema movie was a step too far for her detractors.

'That's part of my contrary nature. Often I look for things in life that don't suit me,' Uma tried to explain. 'I did this on purpose. Because when I started out, I was so afraid of being pushed into some false image of womanhood. Now it's more about not being afraid of *any* image.'

Similarly, Uma tried to put a positive spin on her recollections of filming *The Avengers*, perhaps trying to salvage what she could from the unmitigated flop. 'It's very close to the spirit of the series,' she said in the picture's defence. 'My only regret was I didn't have that much chance to work intensely with Ralph Fiennes. He's a brilliant actor and it would have been interesting to develop our characters. But *The Avengers* isn't about dense dialogue and complex motivations; it's more about romping around with an attitude. It's great fluff.'

Time heals all wounds, and after a while she began to talk more openly about it. 'I think you should take your backlash on the chin . . . up front, square, even on the face, just take it like a man,' she says bravely. With a little distance, she was even able to admit that it had been a disaster from the outset. 'Even though it was kind of a pleasantly silly experience on the set,' she says, 'it's kind of depressing to realize that your film is a dead duck from the start.'

Faced with an embarrassing blip in her career, Uma suddenly started opening up about how hard it was to be away from Hawke all the time, how monotonous it was living out of different hotels, and how tiring it was working so hard on projects back to back. She saw the debacle as 'an incentive to get back to my roots as an actress, to get back to drama, working with a certain type of director. A more actor-centred director and more emotionally story-based material.'

She also offered an alternative career path: 'I'd love to try directing. I think it'll be much more interesting than being in front of the camera.' Of course, there was now the small matter of Maya and her new family to provide distraction.

*

Reeling from the adverse reaction to *The Avengers*, Uma decided it was high time for a break. Having appeared in twenty films since 1987, she defiantly stated, 'I essentially put off having a life to have a career, but that's going to change now.'

So Uma continued to ignore the scripts that appeared on her agent's desk, refusing to plan anything for her future other than bringing up Maya. Besides, as she wryly noted, 'Once you have a child, you're always busy and never sleep.'

After the initial flush of motherhood faded and normality resumed to a certain degree, Uma realized that her relationship with her husband was changing. Like many new parents, she found that they no longer spent much time together. It was not exactly that they drifted apart, more that things which had become less important to Thurman still interested Hawke.

'Ethan is very hard-working,' she said. 'His idea of relaxing is to be doing some work or writing.' Uma was surprisingly candid a couple of years later when she admitted that their instant family had essentially been a 'deal' between them. 'I wanted to have a baby and he wanted to get married. So we both got what we wanted,' she confessed in 2000, also alluding to how much harder it is to maintain a happy marriage when children come along. 'You are either drowning or treading water or swimming,' she continued. 'If you don't work at it, it's simple. You get divorced.'

It was a sobering thought and not one that she would dwell on at the time. Instead, Uma 'worked' on her marriage. Frequently the happy threesome were spotted out picnicking in Central Park with their nanny and their respective dogs frolicking around them in ecstatic canine circles.

*

Uma was clearly reluctant to take on any more work in 1998, although there were still a few directors for whom she would make an exception. 'I had been dying to be in a Woody Allen film for years and he finally popped the question,' she laughed.

Woody Allen redefined comedy during the 1970s as an actor, director, screenwriter and playwright. He brought a unique combination of sophistication and psychological complexity to his movies, successfully tapping into the anxieties of contemporary audiences. His films did not conform to conventional genres and were often more like vignettes on recurring subjects such as art, religion and romance. Allen's directorial debut, *What's New Pussycat?* in 1965, was just the first of a string of award-winning hits including *Annie Hall*, *Manhattan*, *Hannah And Her Sisters* and *Crimes And Misdemeanors*.

Two of Allen's recent films, *Deconstructing Harry* in 1997 and *Celebrity* in 1998, had received mixed reviews, and some harsher critics suggested that he was going through a mean-spirited phase. The director typically addressed these concerns in the next project he embarked on: *Sweet And Lowdown*, a mock-biopic of fictional jazz musician Emmet Ray.

It was simply the 'role of Blanche' he offered to Uma,

complimenting her on being 'a wonderful actress – gorgeous, sophisticated, with the quality of an exceptionally imposing aristocrat'. Beyond Blanche being Emmet Ray's wife, Uma knew little about the part or the plot, which was typical of Allen. 'Sony Classics bought it without having seen it. That's how it works with Woody,' she explains. 'He's very secretive. The actors get to see only the part of the script that they are in. He tells you as much as he thinks you ought to know . . . It's the only thing in showbusiness in which there is actually no way to hedge your bets.'

Even though Maya was only twelve weeks old, Uma could not resist accepting the job, especially as it was small and would not require much of her time.

Sweet And Lowdown turned out to be a 1930s period piece following the life of the eccentric jazz guitarist Emmet Ray. An irresponsible, hard-drinking, arrogant ex-pimp and kleptomaniac, Ray careens from one crazy high to another equally mad low. His hobbies include womanizing, shooting rats at the city dump and performing beautiful music, but he lives in the shadow of a more popular guitarist, Django Reinhardt.

Despite his roving eye, Ray is genuinely touched by a mute laundry girl, Hattie, and falls for her. But his conceited and unfaithful nature ensures that the relationship is doomed, and he ends up marrying a vampish authoress named Blanche. Before long, Ray realizes that Blanche is not the woman for him and he regrets his mistreatment of Hattie. Taking Blanche's advice, Ray lets his feelings out through his music, thus elevating his performance to the level of his rival.

Woody Allen chose Hollywood bad boy Sean Penn for the demanding role of Emmet Ray. Rising to stardom in the 1980s as one of the Brat Pack, Penn's marriage to Madonna and his violent outbursts at the prying paparazzi sadly eclipsed his acting abilities for a time, but during the 1990s he had picked himself up with an Oscar-nominated performance in *Dead Man Walking*.

Uma's filming for *Sweet And Lowdown* took place in October 1998, and apparently it turned out to be the perfect job. 'It was about ten mornings' work and my scenes were all shot in New York. No stress,' she claimed. 'I acted and nursed and went home after lunch.'

On top of the dilemma of combining motherhood with a career, Uma was conscious that her career lacked direction. 'I felt like my life was beginning anew and I realized I wanted to go back to pure dramatic acting,' she says. 'I didn't want to do comedies, or big Hollywood movies.'

Blanche was a short but sweet role for Uma; her only other

involvement was a small amount of publicity around the film's release in December 1999 in America and June 2000 in England. Reviews were mixed, most critics agreeing that while *Sweet And Lowdown* was pleasant enough, it was also more or less instantly forgettable.

Sean Penn is commanding as Ray, but the story is slow-paced with little purpose. 'Woody Allen's latest gives Penn the chance to deliver his most developed comic performance,' commented Andrew Johnston from *Time Out*. 'It's a shame, then, that the movie isn't half as interesting as Penn is in it.'

Penn and newcomer Samantha Morton as Hattie create a strange yet endearing relationship, and in contrast Thurman's entrance as the brash socialite is abrupt and unclear. For the stereotypical sexually aggressive role Thurman leans on her work in *Henry & June*, and while her performance is suitably sultry and dominant, she is hardly breaking new ground. Her departure from the film is as sudden as her appearance, as she leaves with her latest flame, a gangster played by Anthony LaPaglia.

Woody Allen's twist, other than to create a life story of a fictional character, is that *Sweet And Lowdown* is narrated by a selection of jazz aficionados including radio personality Ben Duncan, filmmaker Douglas McGrath, writer Nat Hentoff and Allen himself. This allows for an inspired sequence where each tells a different version of the same story, proving the unreliability of legend.

As much of Allen's work is semi-autobiographical and self-referential, it would be absurd to review this film without mentioning the obvious comparisons between Emmet Ray and Woody Allen: both artists are exceptionally gifted, have troubled relationships with women and harbour peculiar habits.

Despite the varied response, the curiously low-key *Sweet And Lowdown* picked up a selection of awards, namely Oscar and Golden Globe nominations for Penn and Morton. Allen also came out of the project well, garnering some of his best reviews in years and entering into a multi-picture deal with DreamWorks.

20

SAYING HELLO TO THE STAGE

'I'm very happy at home. I love to just hang out with my daughter, I love to work in my garden. I'm not a gaping hole of need.'

UMA THURMAN

During the late summer of 1998, famed Merchant Ivory director James Ivory was relaxing on a plane and turned on his personal TV screen to assess his choices of in-flight entertainment. Somewhat bizarrely, the king of period and costume drama settled on *Batman And Robin*.

Far from switching off in disgust at the lacklustre adventure, Ivory instead leaned forward in his seat for a closer look. Uma Thurman as Poison Ivy had caught his eye.

'She was sensational-looking,' said Ivory, 'but more than that, there was this tremendous presence of the conquering woman.' All of a sudden he was struck that this actress was perfect for a role he was currently struggling to cast.

The director wasted little time in approaching Uma. He was assembling a strong cast for his upcoming film, *The Golden Bowl*, and he wanted her to play Charlotte Stant, 'setting out to conquer New York society'.

But Uma was still recovering from Maya's birth and, although deeply flattered, refused to consider either the exceptionally tricky, unsympathetic part or the ten-week shoot on location in England and Italy – even for cinematic royalty such as Merchant Ivory.

'I said, "I'm so sorry, but I think I can't do it." I was a new mother, and I felt I wasn't emotionally ready,' she explains.

When Ivory pressed her further, understandably puzzled as to why she would turn him down but not Woody Allen, Uma admitted some home truths. She confided that, far from *Sweet And Lowdown* being a simple, easy task as she had claimed, having a baby on set had actually been hellish.

Five years later, Uma was far enough removed from the whole experience to remark, 'When I went back to work after having my first child, it was difficult. I was too worried about that to be able to feel alive in my skin.' But as James Ivory left disappointed, and 1998 merged into 1999, Uma stuck to her guns. Maya was her sole priority, and even the regular flow of temptingly rich roles could not shake her conviction.[*]

*

The question of how to balance Maya with her career, and in fact whether to continue her career at all, occupied Uma at around this time.

'I'm going to try and be particular about the films I do and always take her with me,' she said with all the best intentions, amusingly describing Maya's resilient personality as 'very butch and self-possessed'. But she also admitted to not wanting to raise a child 'who can sing every TV commercial because she's been brought up on a film set'.

During her many years in the trade, Uma had noticed that actors' children tended to be given deferential treatment simply because of their parents' celebrity, and she knew enough to discern she didn't want that for Maya, although some form of compromise would probably be necessary seeing as either she or Hawke was likely to spend a large portion of time each year on a film set. Together they decided that, whatever direction Uma's career might take, they would try never to work at the same time, so that at least one of them would always be around to look after Maya.

Uma was very proud of her husband, often praising him as an 'amazing father' in public. Wanting to be just as involved with Maya's daily needs as Uma, the actor rolled up his sleeves and got into nappy-changing with the best of them. Hawke joked that he approached fatherhood by imagining there was a 'Dad of the Month' award and behaving like he was competing for it constantly.

'It's my view that being a father means being there every day for

---

[*] Uma would not always lay claim to the upper hand, as she had when turning down *The Golden Bowl* – roles she was considered for but did not get in recent years include the leads in *Bedazzled*, *Charlie's Angels*, *America's Sweethearts* and *The Others*.

your child,' he said. 'It's a very important thing for me.' The actor was also very honest about how the pressures from lack of sleep and the responsibility of caring for a new life can lead parents to squabble about the most trivial, mundane things, and he and Uma were no exception.

The couple were aware that Maya's birth had initially provoked extra scrutiny of their lives. Both were known for shrugging off their fame and leading a relatively anonymous existence in Manhattan and upstate New York. 'We definitely don't feel or behave like a celebrity couple,' said Uma. 'We don't pay attention to what's written about us and I don't think many people are interested.'

The city itself had a lot to do with it. 'New Yorkers are calm,' she continued. 'That's one reason I love living here. Nobody faints when they see me on the street.' Also, as Maya grew, the public's curiosity waned, actively encouraged by Uma herself.

'You're boring when you're married with kids,' she explained. 'They want to photograph the guy staggering out, adjusting his tie at 2 a.m. – they want drugs, sex, the money shot. Me walking down the street with a stroller and no make-up is only newsworthy to the point that they say, "God, look at her!" '

Additionally, Uma was also beginning to practise what she willingly admitted to be a turn-off in interviews, appearing boring and insipid. 'You meet someone and you can't quite tell what's going on, or they seem to have an agenda and I immediately deflate,' she said. 'I don't become guarded; I just get very, very . . . small. I use very few colours.'

Judging by interviewers' comments from around this time, Uma also took great delight in meeting at the most expensive restaurants, eating and drinking the best food and wine at the expense of the magazine or newspaper, and even taking home doggie bags of leftover food! It wasn't great for her career, but it worked a treat for protecting her private life.

Uma claimed never to read either her own press coverage or that of her husband, unwilling to expose herself to negative feedback as it would discourage trust in future interviewers, and not wanting her self-image to become 'distorted' by the positive.

'It's hard to be the subject of a stranger . . . I've always found the interview process a little bit embarrassing. I don't want to become more paranoid.'

Of course, Uma's attitude towards this necessary part of the job was coloured by the shyness she claimed still permeated her life as an adult.

'Maybe people think I'm mysterious because I retreat,' she said. 'I envy that [extrovert] personality – the bravado. That's what being on screen lets you do.' Endearingly, she would admit to suffering from anxiety in public situations, where putting on an act didn't stop when the director shouted 'Cut!' and the cameras ceased to roll.

'I can be introducing two of my brothers to two of my best friends, and I'll be searching my mind for a name,' she said of the tongue-tied creature she became at the drop of a hat.

*

Barry Edelstein had been a freelance director around the United States for some time, helming *Merchant Of Venice* at the New York Shakespeare Festival, and a revival of Arthur Miller's *All My Sons* which became a Broadway hit. For two years he had been hawking Martin Crimp's adaptation of *The Misanthrope* around New York's theatres to no avail, as it fell in the no man's land category between old and new. He sent the play to an actor friend, Roger Rees (Tony award-winner for the RSC's celebrated *Nicholas Nickleby*), and together they were determined to find a home for the production.

The Misanthrope, a comedy by Molière, was first produced in Paris in 1666. The story follows Alceste, an intellectual snob disgusted by the sycophancy and hypocrisy of the court of Louis XIV, who vows only to speak the truth. His philosophical friend Philinte tries to dissuade him, explaining that honesty does not mean purposefully being hurtful – a few favourable words might help him advance in court. Alceste remains steadfast, burning several bridges along the way, but meets his match when he falls in love with a much younger woman, Célimène, a self-confessed flirt.

'The play's genius is to make these two very opposite people fall in love with one another,' explains Edelstein. 'Ultimately, Célimène's worldview wins and Alceste must leave. The play's a satire – Molière shows that the rather silly, cynical mores of court will seem to push out the sober, artistically 'pure' values of an Alceste. It's all very complex, multi-layered, ambiguous and thought-provoking.' The play ends as Éliante, Célimène's cousin, and her beau Philinte determine to change Alceste's outlook.

The idea of a man too busy criticizing others to see his own faults remains relevant today, but many of the attitudes surrounding the main story were archaic and needed updating. When Crimp set about modernizing the work, he did not use Richard Wilbur's translation from 1954, as favoured by most writers, but had the play retranslated from scratch. Adhering to the central themes, he revamped the location and characters.

'Crimp's adaptation is set in contemporary [1998] London,' explains Edelstein. 'He makes the snippy world of the Brit glitterati and media elite the equivalent of the royal court of Versailles. He turns Alceste into a semi-successful playwright, sort of an 'Angry Middle-Aged Man', and Célimène is Jennifer, an American movie star who's come to London to promote a film. The 'courtiers' fall all over themselves to get close to her; she flits around having exactly the good old time that a young, rich, sexy, famous twenty-something would have in the circumstances.'

By filling the new version of the play with fashionable references, Crimp is poking fun and mocking real people, just like Molière some three centuries earlier. He derides fellow playwrights Tom Stoppard and David Hare, mocks New York magazine editor Tina Brown, makes digs at film director Steven Spielberg, insults Andrew Lloyd Webber's musicals and dismisses Alan Ayckbourn's plays. Even British theatre critics Michael Coveney and Michael Billington did not escape Crimp's biting satire as they converge in the character of a 'middle-aged, menopausal white male specimen named Michael Covington'.

Crimp's version of *The Misanthrope* opened in London starring Elizabeth McGovern and Ken Stott to great acclaim; even Coveney and Billington approved.

'I'd known Martin Crimp for many years,' recalled Edelstein, 'and when his adaptation of *The Misanthrope* opened in London I loved it immediately. Funny, very smart, and so much more energetic than the standard English translations of the play. It captures the essence of the Molière and renews it, forging a direct connection between the court of Louis XIV and our world.'

*

The Classic Stage Company is an off-Broadway theatre in New York renowned for productions that present classics with a fresh interpretation for the contemporary audience. Founded in the late 1960s, it has a reputation as an exciting venue; its intimate 180-seat auditorium near Union Square is cherished by actors and public alike.

Barry Edelstein was appointed the artistic director of Classic Stage Company in May 1998 for the upcoming season, beginning in October. Crimp's modern take on *The Misanthrope* complemented the Classic Stage Company's mandate to produce the classics from a contemporary point of view, rather than just reviving them, much to Edelstein's delight. 'When I got the job at Classic Stage, everything came together – the right play, the right place, the right artistic match, the right star,' he recalls. 'I decided to make it the centrepiece of my inaugural season. All that remained was to cast the rest of the actors.'

Edelstein had earmarked Roger Rees for the part of Alceste, because 'he has exactly the right combination of technical facility, to get through the huge long speeches, and emotional depth, to get in touch with the guy's rage and comedy skills.' But who to cast as the alluring madam he falls for?

At the time it seemed that the trend was to entice stars of the screen on to the stage. Alec Baldwin and Angela Bassett both did *Macbeth* at the Joseph Papp Public Theater, Nicole Kidman had just opened in David Hare's *The Blue Room*, and veteran Kevin Spacey was due to tread the boards again in *The Iceman Cometh*. Furthermore, John Turturro had recently finished the Classic Stage Company's version of *Waiting for Godot*, Edelstein's first production for the theatre.

Despite the critics calling copycat, it had been commonplace for actors to cross over between the two mediums since the early days of cinema, with such greats as the famed Barrymore trio. 'The American theatre has always been enhanced by visits from movie stars,' Edelstein maintains. 'And it's hard to find a period in New York theatre when there were no film actors in major productions – Lee J. Cobb, George C. Scott, Marlon Brando, Dustin Hoffman, Al Pacino, Meryl Streep, Kevin Kline, Sarah Jessica Parker, etcetera.'

For the demanding role of Célimène, now renamed Jennifer, Edelstein drew up a list of names, but one stood out as his ideal – Uma Thurman. 'She's the right age, the right type, and – bonus – a real movie star to play a movie star. She's elegant and has a great sense of humour. In short, perfect casting,' he says. 'Though she'd not done theatre before, her work in film suggested she could easily handle the complex text of *The Misanthrope* (which, though it is in modern English, is also written in rhyming couplets as in the original French). I had no doubt that she'd be wonderful.'

Although the director had known Ethan Hawke for many years as they had both worked in the close-knit New York theatre community, he followed traditional procedure and contacted CAA. The script was dutifully passed on to Uma, and in early December Edelstein heard that she was interested and wanted to discuss the matter further.

'I went to her house on 13th Street – Ethan was there to make introductions – and we talked about the play, my ideas about it, her thoughts on the role,' he continues. 'She read a bit of it with me. Then Uma suggested that she get together with me and Roger Rees and read some more.

'I've always thought this was a very savvy move on her part. While the conventional wisdom is that an actress of her stature would never audition or read for a project as small as a play in an off-Broadway theatre – and I would never have dared suggest it – Uma knew that this kind of Hollywood status-consciousness was beside the point. She understood that really having a go at the material, in the theatre, with the actor she'd be playing opposite, and with the director she'd need to trust, was the best way – the only way – to determine if it would be a good idea or not. Not to mention the fact that this would be *Uma's* chance to audition *me*, and see how I worked on the material, and if she responded to my methods.'

So, in mid-December 1998 Uma met with Roger Rees and Barry Edelstein at Classic Stage for a trial. 'We spent over an hour working together,' says Edelstein. 'We all felt generally positive, and agreed to take a few days to think about the logistics, scheduling, etcetera, and to give everyone a chance to consider it all before committing.'

Edelstein and Rees were convinced and officially informed CAA that they wanted to cast Uma as Jennifer.

Uma then left a long message on Edelstein's voicemail the next day explaining that after careful consideration, with a young baby in tow, she felt it was the wrong time to do such a project.

'I was devastated, of course,' says the director. 'I reached Uma on the phone and she told me more about her reservations, apologetically. I thanked her for the time she'd already put in, and said goodbye. Rehearsals were set to begin in a few weeks, so I hustled to find another actress.'

The following morning the phone rang at Edelstein's home.

'Don't do anything,' said Hawke mysteriously. 'I can't say any more than that, but hang on before you cast someone else.'

'I will hold on, but I can't wait more than a day,' replied Edelstein.

After another twenty-four hours, Uma telephoned the theatre and confirmed that she was on board after all.

'To this day I don't know what went into her *volte-face*, but I'm grateful it happened,' smiles Edelstein.

For Uma, there was a lot to consider. 'I thought he just wanted me for hype,' she said, but she was persuaded otherwise by the director's passion for the piece. When she realized the offer was genuine, she had to weigh up her long-harboured desire to appear on stage against motherhood.

'I'm going through an interesting time in my life, I'm willing to begin again,' she explained. 'I felt compelled to do something in which I would be forced with pain or pleasure to grow.'

The rest of the cast seemed to fall into place naturally as Barry Edelstein was friends with many of them: Mary Lou Rosato, Nick Wyman, Adina Porter, Brian Keane and Seth Gilliam – some of whom he'd worked with previously.

'I should point out that of all the artists, only a few came on board after Uma,' states Edelstein. 'All these people committed to this low-paying project out of their belief in the material and the theatre company, and not merely to bask in the reflected glory of a huge movie star. Which is not to say that they weren't overjoyed when I called them to say who'd been cast!'

*

In late January 1999, Edelstein and the Classic Stage Company started rehearsals on *The Misanthrope*. Uma soon discovered the distinct contrasts between stage and film work. They rehearsed for six days a week with only Mondays off. The actors were contracted to work a maximum of six hours a day, so Edelstein devised a staggered rota to achieve a seven-hour day without anyone breaking their limit. They spent three-and-a-half weeks in the studio, before lengthy twelve-hour sessions in 'tech' on stage.

But it was not just the working hours to which Uma had to adjust; she had to alter her whole approach. 'In my experience, film actors who are used to working with a camera 12 inches from their nose (literally) can often find acting for the stage unnaturally big,' Edelstein observes. 'After all, you have to act with your whole body, you have to project your voice, you have to make sure the back row gets what you're doing. Even in a theatre as small as Classic Stage, that requires a much bigger energy than on film.

'Plus, there are so many *words* in a play, especially a Molière play. In a play, a character talks about what she's feeling. The same moment in a movie, the character would just *feel* what she's feeling, and the camera would look in her eyes, read her thoughts, and get it all.

'So at first, Uma kept it small. We worked on letting the language be more expressive, letting emotion be communicated through the words. She watched Roger Rees, Mary Lou Rosato, Nick Wyman – theatre vets – and saw how much energy they were able to put through the words without being fake or too big. And she got it. To this day I've never seen anybody take to it so quickly.'

Once she understood the new method of working, Uma was on more familiar ground as she grappled with the intricacies of her role and the story. 'It's exciting and intimidating to play such a fantastic and complex character, especially coming from the film industry, where the roles for women are so two-dimensional or of one level of consciousness or agenda,' she said. 'Jennifer is a series of paradoxes and contradictions: youthful coquette and femme fatale; strikingly intelligent and painfully frivolous; remote and passionate.'

Some of Jennifer's traits – the love/hate relationship with her celebrity status; being labelled an object of desire – were issues with which Uma could identify all too well. 'It's an interesting cross to bear for her,' she said. 'As a sex symbol, the image that precedes her is so powerful, it overwhelms anything that she may be. Being famous has a way of contorting the air around you.' Undoubtedly this was spoken from bitter experience.

Although Uma was a film star brought in to play a film star, she affected no airs or graces and fitted in easily with the rest of the ensemble. 'We all became a kind of family, as always happens when you're in close quarters with people for a short and intense burst of time,' remarks Edelstein. 'If she was nervous about it being her first time on stage, it didn't show. When Uma came across stuff that was unfamiliar, traditions and folklore that are part of theatre life and not necessarily film life, she just figured it out, picked it up. If it was unfamiliar to her, she'd ask what it meant. No fuss, no bother. She was a champ.'

'She's a great stage actress, a real find,' confirms Roger Rees. 'It doesn't matter if you've been in 450,000 plays or one play. If you're a great actor, you're a member of the club. She's loving, frank, and honest in the way great actors are, and she has a wonderful work ethic.'

Uma had again found a director to whom she responded. 'She was open to my ideas, full of her own ideas, had great impulses, made things real, made things fun,' says Edelstein. 'Ours was a real collaboration. I wasn't some dictator; she wasn't some puppet. We figured it out together, which is as it should be.'

Of equal importance to a good relationship with her colleagues was a harmonious balance between working and home life. Uma was able to look after Maya relatively easily around rehearsals for *The Misanthrope*, since her character Jennifer was not in every scene and Edelstein's rota meant that she probably worked three or four hours a day. During the time she was not required, Uma would cycle back to the apartment to relieve the nanny and nurse Maya, who was still breastfeeding. As the preparation involved a number of twelve-hour days, Hawke or their nanny would bring Maya to the theatre for some quality time with her mother during breaks.

'It was sweet to have a baby around, and sweet to see Ethan and

Uma juggling their schedules to make this work,' recalls Edelstein. 'I trusted that Uma would know how much she could handle and would not hesitate to ask for help if she needed it.'

*

After two weeks of previews consisting of afternoon rehearsals and evening performances, Classic Stage Company's rendition of *The Misanthrope* opened on Martin Crimp's birthday, Valentine's Day 1999. 'There was an opening-night party at a now-defunct restaurant called Belgo on Lafayette Street,' remembers Edelstein. 'The place was about to open in early 1999 and saw our party as a way to get some advance publicity. And it got it – celebrities, TV news crews, paparazzi. The party was crowded, noisy and fun. The audience of 200 plus some friends came to celebrate the production, and Uma.'

The run was seven shows a week, Tuesday to Saturday evenings and Saturday and Sunday afternoons, for a month. Nearly twenty seats were added to the small theatre to accommodate the demand to see Uma Thurman in her professional stage debut. Extra security guards were also hired to monitor the lobby area immediately before and after each show.

'That season I had two sold-out productions starring big movie stars,' recalls Edelstein of his first year as artistic director. 'It was great for the theatre, though one critic did waggishly re-christen my Classic Stage Company as 'Celebrities Seeking Credibility'!

'Of course the attention that came to all of us was a fun benefit as well. Classic Stage Company never had both Michael Stipe of REM and Deepak Chopra in the house before, let alone on the same night. Our productions were not routinely covered in the national, as opposed to the New York City, press, as this one was. Our opening-night parties were not usually covered by TV crews. All this attention emanated from Uma, and it was wonderful to be on that train, however briefly.'

But once all the excitement and fuss died down, the burning question was whether Thurman could cut the mustard on stage with heavyweight theatrical actors, night after night.

'She has a rich stage voice that easily accommodates the high-tension revulsion she expresses at Rees's self-debasing sexual advances,' observed *USA Today*. 'She also has the physical magnetism, poise and charm to keep everyone adoring her even after she has publicly insulted them.'

Most reviewers were similarly overawed by Thurman's beauty and undeniable stage presence, but the *New York Post* seemed more realistic: 'Her actual performance gets better as the play goes on; her nervousness seems more controlled and she stops hitting all the rhyme words and relaxes, although we never quite believe she's this devastating intellectual.'

While the *New York Times* was critical, they still felt Uma had potential: 'Ms Thurman exaggerates her gestures and delivery with pained self-consciousness. Her valuable stock-in-trade on screen, a sly, feline confidence, evaporates here. She has her moments, including a brutal confrontation with Rees that suggests the strange, misguided interdependence between their two characters.'

'But Thurman and the rest of the company are faced with the law of diminishing returns as they deal with Crimp's stilted, sour script,' commented the Associated Press reviewer. Indeed, the few negative criticisms to be made were about Crimp's adaptation, rather than the actors or direction. While Uma did not exactly take the theatre world by storm like Nicole 'theatrical Viagra' Kidman in *The Blue Room*, she certainly showed a credible future on stage.

*

The support Uma received from colleagues, friends and family during *The Misanthrope* was far more important than any review, and she soon developed her own little rituals. 'Every night, when Uma came in before the show, she'd go out on stage in the empty theatre to warm up her voice and do some stretches,' says Edelstein. 'She called it "saying hello to the stage".'

'[*The Misanthrope*] was an education,' acknowledges Uma. 'Every night there was that sensation of the audience being with you, or not. It's quite brutal. The entire experience was equal measures pleasure and pain. I had a great time.' When Natasha Richardson came to see the play, the experienced stage star had only one piece of advice. 'She told me to change my shoes,' says Uma. 'She said I didn't look comfortable in my shoes. Which was very astute of her – I was worried about slipping out of them.'

Charmingly, the new mother was still able to cycle home during the extended interval to feed Maya and see her husband. 'I used to spy Ethan, who sometimes came to the theatre to pick up Uma at 10 p.m. when the show ended, hiding out at the auditorium's entrance, sometimes with Maya sleeping in his arms, dancing,' smiles Edelstein.

The greatest moment of all was *The Misanthrope*'s nightly climax, as the director recalls: 'The play ends when Jennifer throws a costume party in her hotel suite. The theme is Louis XIV so, wonderfully, although the bulk of the play is in modern dress, we end up in Molière's period. Uma wore an amazing white gown designed by

Martin Pakledinaz, that had photos of her own face appliquéd to it – her eyes, her mouth, etcetera – it was extraordinary-looking.[*]

'The set had a huge mirrored wall cantilevered on an angle over the stage, a reflective steel floor and candles everywhere. So the effect was that we ended up in the hall of mirrors at Versailles. The party ends when Jennifer asks her friend Simon, earlier the bell captain at the hotel, to turn on some music so everyone can dance. We used the Pet Shop Boys, loud.

'Simon held a couple of small mirror balls in his hands, which reflected dots of light everywhere, and Uma came to centre stage, her pale face and white costume glowing in a bright pool of light, an image of her visible on the mirror upstage, and, her ice-blue eyes aglow, she raised her arms in the air in triumph. It was a real *coup de théâtre!*'

The run sold out prior to the first preview, which financially enabled the Classic Stage Company to expand, and the notoriety of such a project attracted renewed support from donors and patrons. 'I loved the play before we did it, and even more after,' Edelstein enthuses. 'It was a gorgeous physical production, and Uma's name helped the costume designer convince major fashion houses to donate clothing that made the actors look far sharper and more stylish than is typical at a theatre Classic Stage's size.

'And Uma was great in it; assured, charming, electrifying, fun.'

There were talks about a Broadway transfer, but the astronomical costs would have required such enormous commitment from Uma and the rest of the cast that it was decided to keep the experience as the precious gem it was. The closing-night drinks, held at the Telephone Bar on Second Avenue, were informal and relaxed, with a birthday cake for Edelstein.

'I've tried to get her in a couple of projects since,' says the director, 'but her busy film schedule has made it tricky. I hope we'll have the opportunity to work together again – it would be my great good fortune.'

---

[*] Martin Pakledinaz was awarded a *Village Voice* OBIE for Costume Design for his work on *The Misanthrope*.

21

THE HIP VICIOUSNESS OF
LA-LA LAND

'She gets up out of a chair and you want to applaud.'

KATE BECKINSALE ON UMA THURMAN

In March 1999, with the immense confidence gained from *The Misanthrope* behind her, Uma moved seamlessly into her next role: the character Anne de Montausier in *Vatel*, to be directed by Roland Joffé. Coincidentally, the play and the film shared two common elements: a French author and the court of King Louis XIV.

After a promising start in the Old Vic theatre troupe and TV work, Joffé's 1984 feature-film debut, *The Killing Fields*, a brutal tale of the Khmer Rouge's Cambodian holocaust, met with an ecstatic response from audiences, critics and the Academy Awards. Staying in a political vein, Joffé's next film, 1986's *The Mission*, was almost as ground-breakingly successful, with its story of an eighteenth-century Catholic mission in South America.

Then, throughout the 1990s, Joffé's output became chaotically mixed in nature and quality. His poor choice of material is perhaps best exemplified by 1995's gratuitously erotic *The Scarlet Letter*, in which Gary Oldman's memory-obliterating drunken stupor and various unlikely sex scenes nearly sunk Demi Moore's career for good and sent the director into a period of self-imposed exile from the film world.

In 1999 Joffé was to direct *Vatel*. It was a case of make or break. Around this time, journalist Stephen Lemons described the director as 'gaunt, bearded and slightly dishevelled' and shrewdly noted:

'There's something a little too sensitive about Joffé, as if he can't really get with La-La Land's hip viciousness. That's a genuine handicap for him.'

Tom Stoppard's English adaptation of Jeanne Labrune's French-language screenplay, *Vatel* is based on a true story: set in 1671, it follows the plight of the titular steward of the French Prince du Condé. Hoping to win the favour of Louis XIV, the prince invites the king and his entourage to spend three days of extravagant festivities at a chateau in Chantilly. François Vatel is in sole charge of every last detail from the hosting of feasts and pageantry to more personal and often demeaning or cruel tasks as requested by the visiting king.

A man of honour, principle and no little talent when it comes to crafting confectionery out of sugar, Vatel manages to keep his dignity even as he finds himself attracted to Anne de Montausier, the king's latest mistress. The gentle courtesan is charmed in turn, seeing in Vatel a man very different from the merciless noblemen and politicians with whom she normally associates. In the light of each one's position and social status with their respective employers, their courtship is surely doomed from the start.

Joffé was especially taken with the character of Vatel. 'When I read the first draft of the screenplay, I thought, "My God, this is about being a director,"' he said. 'In some ways you're God. In other ways you're just a servant. That role reversal is fascinating.'

Like Edelstein before him, the director had his principal player in mind from the beginning: 'I didn't want Vatel to be too much of an aesthete. I wanted a working-class element to him – with big hands, face and neck.' Gérard Depardieu, he decided, was physically suitable for the role, the accomplished French actor himself noting on many occasions that he was an unlikely candidate to play a typical heartthrob.

Joffé thought Thurman 'would understand Anne's dilemma of being stuck between being a public and a private figure', and he was right. The actress was at last back on the market for film work and thrilled, if a little nervous, about working with her prospective leading man.

'I love Gérard Depardieu!' she gushed. 'It's just that it's very intimidating to have to say his name in front of him. He has this big, huge . . . personality.' Julian Glover, Julian Sands and Tim Roth joined her in the task of perfecting their best French pronunciation in the respective roles of the prince, the king and his evil aide, the Marquis de Lauzun.

*

When Maya reached the grand old age of ten months, an altogether more predictable and manageable part of babyhood, Ethan took on the lion's share of her care and balanced time away from acting with work on his second novel. The trio relocated to Paris so Uma could shoot *Vatel*, and things actually went far more smoothly than the actress-mother could have anticipated.

While Uma was on set, Maya – famous for rising early, according to her bleary-eyed father – spent much of the time asleep in her trailer, under the watchful eye of a nanny. Any time Uma was needed for a feed or a cuddle, she could slip back to the trailer, relaxed in the knowledge that she and Maya were never really apart.

Hoisting her postnatal figure into a corset ('It's the only way to go after having a baby!'), Uma's love of her work was reactivated on location at the beautiful chateau of Vaux-Le-Vicomte. The surrounding scenery and sets were fabulous in their opulence, but Joffé was aware he had compromised himself in order to get the $37 million budget.

'[The French are] none too happy with Gérard Depardieu,' he admitted, referring to the star's decamping to a production backed with American money, and a native story played out in a foreign language. 'I knew that would happen. But the only way we'd get the money was to shoot in English. I didn't feel there was any betrayal at all.'

The director went to rather touching lengths to get his actors into character. 'I wrote each of them letters or memoirs, which I said I'd found in the museum,' he revealed. 'I had them printed up rather neatly, bound in little books. I wrote them all in the first person from my research, and they were written with a slight bias toward the scenes they had to play.'

Another fun touch added to make proceedings sparkle as much as Vatel's own court creations was that Joffé instructed the costume designer not to cut corners at all, instead taking her to a Parisian shop that made clothes for pop stars and asking her to use the shiny material as inspiration. Then, as the actors were fitted into their costumes, pop music would be playing in the background as Joffé raved about his beloved Rolling Stones, giving them the sense that they should act like superstars.

In describing the character of Anne de Montausier to Uma, the director likened the courtesan's dilemma to that of a 'neophyte celebrity', whose emotional entrapment between Vatel and Lauzun mirrors any Hollywood actress's thirty seconds of fame: 'It's very like a card game.' De Montausier clearly touched Joffé deeply, as he admitted, 'In all fairness to Vatel, I'm probably more like Uma's character, Anne ... I don't have Vatel's strength of character, that simplicity and greatness. I'm more like Anne because I'm between those two elements – the virtuous and the venal.'

Still, the real-life actress clearly had some principles of her own. One day, during the filming of a hunting scene, Uma stormed up to Joffé, red in the face with fury.

'Roland,' she cried, 'I'm ashamed of you!'

'Why?' asked the director, taken aback by the unexpected attack.

Uma pointed an angry finger at a Nubian boy perched in a nearby cart. A gold collar was around his neck. The dismay of the new mother was clearly apparent.

'What do you think is going on in his head?'

*

Joffé put as much love and effort into *Vatel* as the hero does into his own work: the research and passion that went into the film were unsurpassed. Indeed, it paid off, as the banquets and entertainment are truly sights to behold, encompassing highly original pop-up theatre, extravagant firework displays and ornately carved ice sculptures. Apparently one of the director's greatest problems was preventing certain greedy cast members from devouring all the lavishly prepared food before the scenes were complete.

Produced in both English- and French-language versions, *Vatel* was the obvious contender for the coveted opening spot at the Cannes Film Festival, held during the week beginning 10 May 2000. Uma was present at the premiere, together with Joffé and Depardieu, basking in the sunny atmosphere of the glamorous annual event.

Despite this most promising showcase, *Vatel* only received a limited release, starting on Christmas Day 2000 in America and the UK following a May run in France. No reviewer could deny the spectacular visual appeal of *Vatel*, and it won as many plaudits for its luxurious appearance as it deserved, eventually culminating in Oscar nominations for Best Art Direction and an award in the same category from the French Academy of Cinema; the latter board also nominated the film for Best Costume Design.

But the critics were equally united in judging *Vatel* to be unexpectedly dull, soulless and an altogether unrewarding experience. '*Vatel*'s sumptuous weekend banquet . . . is a feast for the eyes,' said *Time Out*. 'The viewer's mind and soul, however, will emerge somewhat less nourished.' *Variety* wholeheartedly agreed: 'This ultimately downbeat tale, though most lavishly designed and choreographed, is otherwise a disappointment in almost every respect.'

Maybe Joffé had spent too much time researching and investing in the exquisite details of his production, leaving the human aspect untouched – or maybe the film had been severely miscast. Depardieu, often praised for his intense, emotive performances, comes across as unreservedly wooden as Vatel, far outshone by Thurman and various others in the acting stakes. It has to be said that, as he has the only thick French accent in the whole cast (the rest, including Uma, speak in convincing, precisely modulated English), he was always going to stand out like a sore thumb, and his own admission at Cannes didn't help his case. 'I love the French language, but I get caught in the trap of my own language because I haven't had any profound education,' he confessed, continuing that he was happy to deliver the English lines assigned to him as an actor, but did not always understand all of them.

A decidedly depressing ending and Joffé's refusal to utilize standard Hollywood cliché resulted in a melancholy, hollow and largely humourless picture. Much like *Gattaca*, it was noted that the restrained, undemonstrative nature of the characters made for a restrained, undemonstrative movie.

As had been the case with so many of Uma's less successful films, the actress was probably the least affected by the poor reception, due to a strong individual performance. Predictably she looks spectacular in costume: elegant, regal and haughty with a swan-like neck and an intricate hairstyle. With little dialogue (a problem reminiscent of *Even Cowgirls Get The Blues*), it is left to the actress to depict her character's gradual shift in perception with subtle reaction shots, carefully directed glances and delicately erotic edginess.

Uma has not spoken about the failure of *Vatel* to win over its audience, but Joffé was uncharacteristically vociferous. 'I'd always thought that you made a movie and you showed it to a neutral world who absorbs [its] truth. What I realized is that you show your movie to a roiling, furious, angry world, all with their own opinions. And if by any chance you don't happen to match their clichés, they get furious at you,' he fumed. At the time of writing, the director had yet to complete a follow-up film, although he was toying with the idea of turning his attention to the thriller genre.

*

Although Uma had turned down James Ivory's invitation to appear as Charlotte Stant in his upcoming production of *The Golden Bowl* in favour of looking after Maya in 1998, it had been a difficult decision, as she was quite taken by the prospect of working with Merchant Ivory. As she and the director shared the same agency, the actress instructed her representative at CAA to keep an eye on the project's progress, and through the grapevine she heard that production had been delayed by several months.

Merchant Ivory are period-drama moguls with a hugely successful string of lavish English novel adaptations to their credit. Director James Ivory and producer Ismail Merchant formed the company in 1961, around the same time they became acquainted with screenwriter Ruth Prawer Jhabvala, who has collaborated with them on all but a handful of their films.

Their reputation was sealed with the Oscar-winning adaptation of E. M. Forster's *A Room With A View*, starring Maggie Smith, Helena Bonham Carter and Denholm Elliott. This was soon capitalized upon with another Academy-favoured Forster venture in 1992, *Howards End*, featuring a wealth of talent including Anthony Hopkins, Vanessa Redgrave and Emma Thompson. Hopkins and Thompson were then reunited the following year for *The Remains Of The Day*, another smash hit. In a surprising move, the company turned away from literary adaptations for the next few productions, but they all met with disappointing reviews and takings. By the end of the 1990s, Merchant Ivory's fortunes were in need of revival.

Focusing all his attentions on *The Golden Bowl* in 1999, James Ivory's search for the perfect Charlotte Stant continued. 'Whoever played the part would have to bring a particular kind of glamour to it, because Henry James very much wrote her that way,' he said. Apparently, Ruth Prawer Jhabvala had taped Uma Thurman's picture to the back page of the first draft of the script – they clearly knew the image they wanted for the role.

'There was only one person who came to mind,' confirmed Ivory, 'who was our first choice from the very beginning, who was full of that kind of vitality and life, with a beauty that is very individual and completely beguiling – and that was Uma.'

Finally, Uma received a personal letter from Ismail Merchant, reputedly the most relentless member of the Merchant Ivory production team. 'I wrote her that she reminded me of Vivien Leigh's character in *Gone With The Wind* . . . I felt strongly that there was something unique about Uma, that she alone could bring that character to life and capture her strength and at the same time convey a certain mad desperation.'

One day Uma was having coffee with Natasha Richardson, now a working mother of two, and they were discussing their careers and the film parts currently on offer.

'Excuse me, but did you pass on *The Golden Bowl*?' enquired Richardson.

'Yeah, I did,' Thurman replied nonchalantly.

'Well, I think you're just crazy,' said her friend.

Feeling chastised, Uma spoke to Ethan when she returned home that night. While he fully supported her choice to maintain a career, he always wanted her to be sure it was the right choice. 'My husband puts a lot of pressure on me, so that if I feel I have to work, I have to be very passionate about the film, whereas before I used to love to try this and that,' she said.

As they discussed the role and the production, it became apparent that Uma was indeed very keen. 'I knew that I wanted to do dramatic work, and do things that I wanted to do,' she said. 'Just do things that would satisfy me personally and play hard roles that I could fail in or succeed in. Challenge myself.'

Having looked deeper into the part, Uma realized that it would be one of the greatest challenges of her career to date. 'Charlotte is outwardly polished and refined, but inwardly, she's out of control, passionate and belligerent. She's a very sensual character, and that will be an interesting exploration for me,' said the actress.

As usual, she was also drawn by the director, or in this case the trio of Merchant, Ivory and Jhabvala. 'I'd always wanted to work with the Merchant Ivory team,' she later admitted, 'because they're among the few filmmakers who have consistently investigated the human condition. Performances in their movies are complex and brave – not homogenized. They love people, they love acting and they have something deeply glamorous about them.'

The following morning she telephoned CAA to find out if the role was still available.

*

The Golden Bowl was Henry James's last completed novel, the treacherous tale of a close father–daughter relationship and the pair's flawed marriages. Without a dowry, Charlotte Stant is forced to give up her Italian prince lover, Amergio, so that he can marry for money. Ironically, the lady of his choice is Maggie Verver, best friend of Charlotte and daughter of a widowed American billionaire, Adam Verver. In order to remain close to her lover, Charlotte ingratiates herself with the ageing Adam and the two are soon wed.

While Maggie dotes on her father and insists on keeping him company rather than going out, Charlotte selfishly attends social gatherings without her husband, taking Amergio along as her escort. Out of sight, if not mind, the former lovers rekindle their relationship. The question is whether they will be found out and what effect their careless cavorting will have on their respective partners.

Relieved to have Uma securely cast as Charlotte Stant at long last, Merchant Ivory looked to other respected actors to fill the remaining roles. Adam Verver was to be played by Nick Nolte (*The Thin Red Line*), his naïve daughter Maggie by Kate Beckinsale (*Much Ado About Nothing*), and Prince Amergio by Jeremy Northam (*Emma*). Anjelica Huston and James Fox were given wonderful cameos as busybody socialites offering commentary throughout.

'She was brought up to be a completely dependent creature,' explained Uma of her character, 'but because she had no money of her own, she was unable to compete in the great race to make a good marriage.

'She's so polished on the surface – just like the golden bowl – but also deeply damaged and deluded.'

The titular golden bowl (an intended wedding present) is outwardly beautiful, but closer inspection reveals a hairline crack threatening to destroy the whole piece. This 'lovely, but flawed' motif is a metaphor for Charlotte, who is undeniably attractive but on the brink of an emotional breakdown.

Charlotte certainly was a stimulating role, and although Uma was happily married and content with her little family, she drew on previous heartaches to portray the desperation her character felt in her all-consuming love for Amergio. 'I've been with one person now for such a long time that I've finally reached a pleasant amnesia about my previous awful encounters,' she recalled, '[but] I recognized the hurt pride, the disappointment, the shock.'

Yet Charlotte is much more than a woman scorned. 'She's so out of control emotionally. She betrays everyone for love,' explained Uma. 'She hung her whole life on it, staked everything including her honour, and as long as she believes in it she feels clean in whatever she does.'

For the first time in a long while Uma became deeply involved in her character – considerably more so than for *Sweet And Lowdown* or *Vatel*; this was on a par with the dedication required for *The Misanthrope*. 'It was really emotionally stirring to play her for three months,' said Uma. 'She's a character who is somewhere between a diva and someone having a nervous breakdown . . . It took a while to get back into life at home after I finished.' Uma did admit there was an amusing side to Charlotte: 'It's quite delightful to play someone who is kind of wicked with no conscience, no guilt, no twentieth-century psychology wrapping her up. She is quite free.'

Director James Ivory was pleased that Uma seemed to understand the multi-faceted Charlotte, but he was even more enthralled with how perfectly she looked the part. 'Her beauty is a bit off, that's why she's so fascinating,' he marvelled. 'She changes all the time. She has this extraordinary glamour, and then she can be this incredibly healthy, sensual girl in the next breath. But she's also very sophisticated, a natural aristocrat.'

Merchant Ivory set about filming *The Golden Bowl* in the last three months of 1999 with a comparatively small budget of just $15 million. On location in London and Rome, the cast and crew also visited eleven stately homes in Britain to fully capture Henry James's world.

Alongside adapting to the change of scenery and grasping a wholly unlikeable character, Uma faced an added test. Since *Vatel*, when Uma ably juggled motherhood and work with the aid of her nanny and husband, she was keen to have her daughter on set no matter where she was in the world. 'I had Maya with me in my trailer for ten weeks and I had to concentrate on the part,' recalls the young mum.

'Having a small child and doing a movie was very, very challenging. You're trying to do everything, trying to be a superb human being. I think all working mothers can relate.'

Overall, Uma found the few months of filming very pleasant, and part of the reason was the support she received from her co-stars. 'When you think you have a handle on what it is that Uma is, she's something else,' marvelled Beckinsale, who became good friends with the older actress. 'She has this goddess body, but she's not just a goddess. She's smart, but not just smart. She's kind of goofy and naughty . . . and you can see it all kind of moving underneath the skin on her face.' James Ivory was also impressed by Uma's ability as well as her presence, and took to calling her 'The Beautiful Giraffe'.

*

The Golden Bowl was first shown at the May 2000 Cannes Film Festival, which Uma was already attending with Joffé and Depardieu to promote another period drama, *Vatel. The Golden Bowl* was received well at the festival, for which she was joined by co-star Nick Nolte – sadly, Ethan was too busy with his own burgeoning career to accompany her.

Merchant Ivory's latest offering was then released in October 2000 in the UK, although the American circulation was held up until April 2001 by the distributors Miramax, replaced by Lions Gate Films. Although the film created a positive buzz at Cannes, reviews upon general release were much more scathing. Most of the criticism was aimed at Merchant Ivory for producing yet another costume drama, one which was deemed staid and lacking in inspiration. To be fair, the Henry James novel is a tough piece to adapt successfully: incredibly complex and overloaded with metaphor. The Merchant Ivory production is a respectable attempt to translate the tale of love and infidelity to the big screen, preserving much of the character-driven saga and its finer nuances.

One significant downside, however, is the visual realization of James's unsubtle symbolism. The heavy-handed overuse of the comparison between the golden bowl and Charlotte, on top of the opening and closing play depicting the incestuous story in brief, is patronizing. It feels as though Merchant Ivory don't believe the viewer can understand James's implications unless spelt out in words of one syllable.

Furthermore, while all the actors are experienced in period drama, none is allowed to fully develop his or her character. Thurman's performance often comes across as stilted and posed, Beckinsale and Nolte's unnaturally close relationship is not properly explored, while Northam's phoney Italian prince is more irritating than irresistible. 'Lavish, but suffocating' was the accurate summation by Rebecca Flint for *All Movie Guide*.

Even Uma, in a candid moment, admitted that she was not completely satisfied. 'I'd have to be honest and say that as I finished I really wished I could do it again. I could easily probably have improved it,' she said.

At the end of the day, it is hard to see *The Golden Bowl* as any form of career progression, as Uma had ably proved herself to be proficient in period pieces already, with her appearances in *Dangerous Liaisons*, *Henry & June* and *Vatel*. While the role of Charlotte may have felt like a challenge in preparation, that Uma's performance and the film as a whole were unsatisfactory rather negated her effort. Uma was in need of a fresh persona and a plot with a difference to revive her career once again.

22

BEAUTY IS IN THE EYE OF
THE BEHOLDER

'Hollywood is filled with beautiful, unhappy women who have shut down.'

MICHELLE PFEIFFER, ACTRESS, *DANGEROUS LIAISONS*

'The idea of seeing my child abuse herself by buying into a lot of the negative perceptions of our culture, of seeing her limited or derailed from her full development, is terrifying to me.'

UMA THURMAN

In March 2000 Uma and Ethan presented an Oscar for Best Documentary Feature at the 72nd Academy Awards. A month later, they celebrated the actress's thirtieth birthday at 27 Standard, a fashionable and cripplingly expensive 'New American' restaurant presided over by head chef Matthew Lake.

It was noted by many that Uma was smoking again that May at Cannes; her near-three-year break ended in 'an appalling fall from grace', as she admitted, caused by spending too much time in nicotine-friendly Europe. Her husband was also part of the problem, as he too had fallen back into the habit, making it impossible for Uma to resist the evil weed.

Possibly Hawke had lit up again because as his career went from strength to strength, so did his stress levels. Currently his perform-ance in Michael Almereyda's thoughtful, modern take on *Hamlet* was receiving rave reviews, as was the film as a whole. For Uma, *Hamlet* was a family affair, for as well as her husband in the lead role, her father appeared – ironically, considering his life's work – as the priest, Dechen played Guildenstern, and Uma herself received 'special thanks' in the credits. Incidentally, Dechen was doing quite well for himself – he next popped up in Ben Stiller's *Zoolander* as a 'funky loft guest'.

Hawke's next project was behind the camera: he was to direct his first feature film, *Chelsea Walls* (working title *The Last Word On Paradise*), adapted by Nicole Burdette from her play of the same name. Having first made a short film called *Straight To One* about a couple living at New York's Hotel Chelsea in 1993, Hawke would now return to the same setting.

Burdette's ambitious play tells five stories simultaneously set in a single day, the link between the characters being that they all reside at the famous Bohemian enclave, haunted by the lingering aura of previous guests including Dylan Thomas, Mark Twain, Tennessee Williams, Arthur Miller, Bob Dylan and Jimi Hendrix. The new residents are all creative, angst-ridden souls with complicated personal lives: there's a novelist, two poets, two musicians, a dancer, a painter, an aged jazz singer and all their various spouses and lovers.

Hawke's involvement had attracted a whole host of respected stars and family friends to the ensemble drama, including Kevin Corrigan, Rosario Dawson, Vincent D'Onofrio, Kris Kristofferson, Robert Sean Leonard, Natasha Richardson and Tuesday Weld. There was even a tiny role for his wife as Grace, who commented wryly, 'I had a small part, so that proves that sleeping with the director does not open all the doors as wide as you may like . . .'

Chelsea Walls was highly experimental, shot on digital video with a minimal budget. 'It's a whole new way of making movies, like painting,' described the director. When transferred to regular 35mm film, digital gives a slightly 'homemade' effect with a washed-out tint, resulting in the cinematic equivalent of a colour photocopy.

Said Hawke, 'This film would've been impossible to shoot in 35mm. It's set in New York's Chelsea Hotel, and the electricity wouldn't be good enough and I couldn't have shut down the hotel for a few weeks to shoot it.' The resulting film would be artistic and aimed at a specialized audience. Hawke was a true convert to digital: 'This technology gives [control] back to the artist,' he claimed.

*

By and large, Uma enjoyed being directed by her husband, although she admitted afterwards, 'He was a little bossy on the set, more than he is allowed to be at home! It was great fun and we are still together, the ring is still on the finger . . .'

In all seriousness, she continued, 'He's really an inspiration to me. He is so creative and so fearless and so his own person, and really belongs to himself and takes chances. I think he's going to "find himself" as a director.

'Ethan is my biggest supporter when it comes to my work. He applies friendly pressure on me to push myself and not be so self-doubting. If I could work like that all the time, I'd be happy.'

Chelsea Walls enjoyed a limited release quite a while later, on 19 April 2002, but most of its viewers would encounter it on video and DVD. Ethan had been right to assume that the potential audience would be 'artistic' film fans: more of an impressionistic mood montage with fleeting character studies than a conventional film with a linear plot, it was vastly inaccessible to the general movie-going public. The characters, although poetic types and initially interesting, tended to blend into one another after a while, and there were too many plot trails to focus on.

As the insecure poet and waitress, Grace, Uma was virtually unrecognizable in an unlikely short dark wig. Her few scenes painted her as fragile, gentle and flirtatious, everybody's sounding board but really no more than tormented eye candy. Like the majority of the highly talented cast, her appearance was far too brief to remotely develop Grace as a full-blown character.

Those who didn't appreciate the digital film's finer points – namely New York's foremost critics – lambasted it as 'pretentious', 'plotless', 'brutally dull', 'shallow' and 'immature'.

Hawke responded to his detractors boldly. 'You can't do anything in this world that's interesting without risking being pretentious,' he said, reasonably. 'The fear of being pretentious keeps so many people from trying. I mean, thank God Francis Ford Coppola was pretentious enough to make *Apocalypse Now!*'

Uma's husband was never one to let his reviewers get him down, although he admitted 'not handling' criticism from his 'very opinionated' partner very well: 'I like unabashed support.' Uma herself confessed that she tried to maintain a respectful distance, only giving advice when he asked her for it, 'because I like to weigh in with my ideas whenever I have the chance. I can't resist those impulses.'

Going from strength to strength in his acting career (including *Hamlet*, the upcoming movies *Waking Life* and *Training Day*, and on stage in the New York production of Sam Shepard's *The Late Henry Moss*), Hawke had also just had his first novel released in paperback. *The Hottest State* had received mixed reviews, the better ones notably hailing from the UK.

Hawke still suffered from the stereotype one writer eloquently summed up as 'tortured, latte-chugging intellectual', thanks to a batch of mid-career Generation X slacker roles, and he was well aware of the dangers of this particular pigeonhole. 'I love being able to throw myself into different areas of culture, but I dread the idea that people think I'm this intellectual poseur,' he admitted.

Although Uma supported him wholeheartedly in everything he attempted, perhaps Hawke realized at this point that he was pushing himself too far. Acting, directing, writing and running a theatre company would stretch anyone, but adding it to fatherhood and marriage to an independently successful film star was surely a recipe for disaster.

Maybe the best way to juggle work and home life was to continue working together? Both actors had enjoyed their brief shared stint on *Chelsea Walls*, so they began to look around for the perfect project. Around this time reports emerged that the husband-and-wife team were up for the roles of Éowyn and Faramir in the second *Lord Of The Rings* instalment, *The Two Towers*, but this information proved to be inaccurate; the parts went to Miranda Otto and David Wenham instead.

*

Although the Thurman-Hawkes maintained their Manhattan base, their country home was now largely restored and finished, filled to the brim with books, folk-art paintings, unusual textiles and a large collection of videos of 1960s and 1970s films of which Quentin Tarantino himself would have been proud.

'I'm really a secret fan of movies, I watch zillions,' said Uma. 'I like bad movies, good movies, trash movies, art movies. That's why I've been in them all!'

Although Hawke didn't necessarily share all Uma's hobbies – her passion for needlepoint is well documented – he did appreciate that she kept him grounded while the rest of his life spun frequently out of control.

It seemed their union was well matched as each balanced out the other's faults, showing qualities the other lacked and vice versa. 'I think we balance each other exceptionally well,' explained Uma. 'Ethan is very restless and ruthlessly optimistic about everything. He needs to be preoccupied with five or six different projects at once or he becomes very anxious.' Since the birth of Maya, Uma was admittedly 'less intense' about her own career and would drag Hawke down to earth when he spun into orbit; simultaneously, she enjoyed the energetic spirit her manic husband brought to her life.

The confident woman so competently in charge of her family was a far cry from the cripplingly shy teenager of old, although she claimed that doubts about her looks and figure still occasionally reared their ugly heads. She admitted to trying various faddish diets to stay in shape, but over the summer of 2000 any residual fears she might have had about her looks really should have dissipated once and for all.

On 11 June it was announced that Uma was the new 'spokesmodel' for the famous French cosmetics firm Lancôme. It was a bizarre move for a woman who had loudly deemed modelling to be 'a really uninteresting way to spend time' during her days at the Click agency, commenting, 'I judge the whole industry as being insignificant,' and who detested the ethos of convincing people to buy products they didn't really need.

Uma's initial explanations of her apparent change of heart were more than a little weedy. 'I was so surprised!' she gushed. 'I accepted it in the end because it was something new to explore. It would also add some glamour to my life.

'I've been working with photographers for years, and that's something I've always enjoyed. It's kind of fun. It's a very nice way to make a living!'

Surely this was a complete contradiction of her beliefs?

'I like their products and I was turning thirty when they asked. Most people don't get make-up contracts when they're thirty . . .'

It didn't sound like Uma at all.

Lancôme's own take on the signing was every bit as flowery, as press statements referred to Uma's 'passion for life': 'That light that shines from within, her ability to marvel, the zest for life that emanates from her smile all make Uma Thurman the ideal choice for the Lancôme Woman.' Or more sensibly, as senior vice-president and general manager of Lancôme USA, Luc Nadeau, put it, 'She is international, uniquely beautiful and women can relate to her as a wife, a mother and an actor.'

One couldn't deny that with this 'new' career, Uma would be raking it in – the lucrative two-year deal was estimated to pay between $8 million and $12 million, affording her more precious time with Maya.

Uma replaced Gary Oldman's ex-fiancée, Isabella Rossellini, and the actress Juliette Binoche as the face of the company who, after a two-year search, were delighted to have found someone they believed to appeal equally to Americans and Europeans. Having lost out on the female lead in Bedazzled to the English actress Elizabeth Hurley, Thurman would now be competing with her again, this time in terms of beauty and advertising, as Hurley fronted Lancôme's greatest rival, Estée Lauder, in a similar role.

Work began immediately on the launch of Miracle, a new perfume featuring 'fruity top notes, a floral heart and a deliciously musky base' that would be launched in Europe that October. As Uma reportedly refused to travel more than an hour-and-a-half outside New York City, a planned shoot in the desert was cancelled in favour of a session in New Jersey; the resulting adverts showed Uma's face drifting wholesomely across a background of pink clouds. Later in her contract, the actress would have shades of Lancôme lipsticks named after her, but these would only be available in Asia.

After all the 'official' business died down, a more recognizable Uma started talking about the huge benefits she received from her new job. Clearly, the working-mum factor featured very high on her list of plus points.

'The Lancôme deal works out well because it enables me to stay home more,' she said. 'Signing the contract also gave me a lot of financial freedom and essentially made it very easy for me to say no to a lot of films which I might have done for more financial rather than purely artistic reasons.'

*

Uma's professional work over the summer of 2000 included her stints with Lancôme, which would see her face plastered on billboards and in magazines all over the world, and a low-key role as the narrator of a TV documentary, *Without Lying Down: Frances Marion And The Power Of Women In Hollywood*. The fifty-two-minute programme, which premiered on the Turner Classic Movies cable channel in August, traced the life of the Oscar-winning screenwriter Frances Marion, the most respected and highest paid of her kind in mid-1920s Hollywood.

Thanks to the influence of this former actress, hundreds of other women would go on to flourish in the production end of the film business as writers, editors, producers and directors. Uma was well aware her own position at the top of the A-list might not have been possible without Marion's fine example.

In September Maya started going to nursery, a huge step for both daughter and mother. Having been so used to her little shadow hanging out in the Thurman-Hawkes' garden, Uma fought back the tears and cheerily waved Maya on to the next stage in her development.

The extra free time gave Uma the opportunity to do a little charity work. She joined the board of directors for Room To Grow, a non-profit organization dedicated to enriching the first three years of babies born into poverty. She also became active within Project ALS, an advocacy and fund-raising group for research into Amyotrophic Lateral Sclerosis (also known as Lou Gehrig's disease, after the famous baseball player who died aged thirty-seven from the rare and incurable condition).

With several similarities to Guillain-Barré Syndrome, including neurological disorders, muscle weakness, impaired respiratory function up to the point of needing artificial ventilation, and impairment of swallowing and speech, Uma may well have been reminded of the painful disease that had previously affected her mother. Indeed, she might even have first learned of the progressive form of motor neurone disease while visiting her mother in the neurological department. However, unlike GBS, the prognosis for ALS is terminal, so she wanted to do all she could to help.

That year's fundraiser, the Tomorrow Is Tonight event, was supported by many other celebrities: the hosts were Katie Couric, Matthew Broderick and Sarah Jessica Parker, and guests included Marisa Tomei, Donna Hanover, Julianna Margulies and Ben Stiller, as well as Thurman and Hawke, the latter giving a moving reading of Lou Gehrig's famous farewell speech. 'We need more fundraisers like this one,' was Uma's proactive stance. 'When you increase recognition and funds, you empower scientists to do as much as they can for sufferers.' Over $1.5 million was raised that night, with Uma and Ethan personally donating more than $5,000.

Over the coming months, Uma also spoke out about her liberal views on politics after Republican George W. Bush was sworn into office on 20 January 2001. Naturally leaning more towards the Democrats, Uma would be deeply disappointed with the achievements of the forty-third president of the United States.

'He should have his own show,' she sniggered, thinking him more a potential TV star. 'He's a very charismatic guy. He's funny.

'I really wish he wasn't running the country. I didn't want him to be elected, but I hoped he wouldn't do a bad job. I have to say it's been less than impressive . . .'

*

As Ethan Hawke simultaneously ditched the slacker label and scored the biggest commercial hit of his career, *Training Day* with Denzel Washington, it became more and more apparent that Uma's own screen output had dwindled to a halt. Joining her husband on location in Los Angeles and then holidaying in Barbados with her parents, Uma's primary focus remained the upbringing of Maya.

Unfortunately, her name was about to become linked with

something other than motherhood or her lately favoured costume dramas.

Just a few months earlier, Uma had spoken of her modelling job for Lancôme in terms that helped make her more accessible to the public. 'I accept it as a way of being an untypical kind of model in terms of the image of what is seen as attractive or what is seen as appealing,' she had said. 'I think at least in a small way I broaden the type of look which is being marketed because I am very different from how most women look.' It seemed a healthy way for Uma to refer to her traffic-stopping physical attributes, grounded in the knowledge that her large, sculpted features were quite far removed from the 'ideal' American aesthetic of button nose, even-set eyes and cupid's-bow mouth.

Then, in March 2001 Uma jeopardized all her sensible self-projections – not to mention her Lancôme contract – with a chance remark to *Talk* magazine.

'Ever since I had my baby I've had that Body Dysmorphic Disorder,' she said. 'I see myself as fat.' The interview also mentioned her inability to eat a bread roll because of its potentially harmful effects on her postnatal figure and a comment from Natasha Richardson: 'Uma genuinely believes she's fat. And she's so thin! . . . I think it hurts her.'

Elsewhere, several choice quotes about the actress's crippling childhood self-doubt ('Even today, when people tell me I am beautiful, I do not believe a word of it') surfaced at around the same time. It was then reported that Uma had finally gathered up the courage to reveal her illness while attending a fundraiser for the Eating Disorders Education Network in Atlanta, Georgia.

Of course, Uma wasn't remotely fat. She never had been. She had shed all her extra pregnancy pounds just twelve weeks after giving birth, but now it seemed she was left with a named psychological disorder. It was a very serious claim to make.

Body Dysmorphic Disorder (from the Greek word 'dysmorph', meaning 'misshapen') is a mental disorder defined as a preoccupation with a perceived defect in one's appearance. Sufferers spend countless hours obsessing in front of the mirror, genuinely believing themselves to be hideous and ugly. Most common complaints concern the face, skin, eyes, chin or lips, whereby a natural lack of symmetry, or a perception that a feature is misshapen, too big or small, or out of proportion can cause an ongoing crippling attack on a person's confidence.

'Most people do have a dissatisfaction about appearance, but whether it's BDD or not depends on the degree of it,' says Susan Minall, a spokesperson for OCD Action. 'Everybody can relate to being dissatisfied with appearance to some degree, but it doesn't make them ill. For a diagnosis of BDD to be made, the preoccupation must cause significant distress or interfere in one's social or working life.'

All sufferers are tormented by their condition, but the level of handicap varies enormously from a general distorted preoccupation with one's appearance, to such a firm conviction of one's unattractiveness that day-to-day life is affected as social and public situations are increasingly avoided to prevent feelings of inadequacy.

Often sufferers develop a form of obsessive-compulsive disorder (OCD) linked to their BDD and feel compelled to repeat certain time-consuming rituals, such as excessive grooming by removing, cutting or combing hair, picking skin, endless comparison to others or excessive dieting and exercise. Many repeatedly seek treatment with dermatologists or cosmetic surgeons. 'This type of compulsive behaviour makes the problem worse because the sufferer rarely feels reassured,' says Minall. 'There's no cure but recovery is possible. Treatment would be cognitive behavioural therapy or medication can be used and you can learn to cope.'

So did Uma really have this most distressing and socially debilitating disease?

'BDD is something that usually starts in adolescence – a time when people are generally more sensitive about appearance,' says Minall. 'If it has become a clinically significant problem, you may manage it very well but you are always vulnerable and then something might happen to set it off again. These anxieties can also start after some sort of trauma or stress in life – having a baby might be one of those life events.'

Clearly Uma had suffered from severe distaste for her looks in her youth, and Maya's birth was the reason she herself cited for her own BDD.

With a rash of popular publications seizing on Uma's comments in *Talk*, BDD swiftly became, quite sickeningly, the latest 'hot' celebrity accessory. There were many glamorous names to add to Uma's in the list of the afflicted. Shirley Manson, the lead singer from Garbage, sees 'a bloodhound' or 'a fish, with big, baggy eyes' every time she looks in the mirror. Mercilessly teased as a child for her red hair and unusual looks, her story wasn't that different from Uma's: 'I was told I was ugly from the time I started secondary school, and I still see everything people used to freak out about.' When Manson was chosen to model for Calvin Klein's 1999 poster campaign, she spent two hours crying in the toilet, refusing to come out. 'They photographed me with no make-up,' she says of that shoot. 'Until that point, I'd never been seen like that in public. I thought that if I went out bare-faced, everyone would think I was repulsively ugly.'

Similarly, Judy Garland never shook off the outdated image she had of herself as an overweight young girl; Michelle Pfeiffer famously described herself as looking 'like a duck'; Elizabeth Hurley lost 15 pounds after seeing unflattering tabloid photos of herself; and Geri Halliwell spoke at length about her eating disorders and deep-rooted insecurities symptomatic of BDD in her two autobiographies. 'I have never liked myself and I have always had self-doubt so I thought that if I am as fit as I can be – and thin – then maybe I'll be good enough,' Halliwell explained of her personal quest to weigh less than was medically advised.

On a more extreme level, glamour model Jordan's insecurity about her breast size led to at least three operations to increase her chest to an enormous and out-of-proportion 36G. 'I did it so I'd feel happier,' she said. 'I love those pictures: they don't look like me.' Lolo Ferrari, the French TV presenter who underwent multiple surgery on her lips, cheeks, nose, forehead, eyebrows, stomach and bust, was surely the worst case of unnecessary and grotesque physical transformation due to insecurity. Before her death from an overdose of sleeping pills, she admitted, 'I wanted to change my face, my body, to transform myself. All these operations have been because I can't stand life. But they haven't changed anything.'

In all cases, being ever present in the media subjected the celebrities to constant physical scrutiny, from journalists to make-up artists to the general public.

Explains Susan Minall, 'Generally BDD sufferers would shy away from the spotlight, but I do know a BDD sufferer who is a model. The thing is, with this illness, it can be quite extreme. You can have one day where the image you see is acceptable and the only thing I can relate it to is a junkie having a fix: you feel better about yourself, but it's very short-lived.

'If you are going into modelling you are actually exposing yourself to your worst fears of being on show and that could actually be quite helpful from a therapy point of view ... Someone who took up something like modelling would almost be [undergoing] what we call "exposure therapy", so they would be putting themselves in their most feared situation, but nothing bad was actually happening, which would be quite helpful for recovery.'

Whether or not the Lancôme contract provided Uma with the 'therapy' she required to finally accept her face for what it was, the actress either recovered from her symptoms in record time or backtracked completely, utterly horrified at the excitable and exaggerated responses her few remarks seemed to have provoked.

'I gave an interview in which I said that I saw myself as fat when I really meant that I saw myself as being heavier than I wanted to be, that I thought I could be in better shape,' she said. 'I knew my perception was very biased, though, and I eventually got over that nagging feeling that I should lose more weight.'

23

KITCHEN-SINK DRAMAS

'I always believe that actors' fragility is their power. It's not about different cultures or different training, so much as individual human beings.'

MIRA NAIR, DIRECTOR, *HYSTERICAL BLINDNESS*

As the BDD backlash raged around her, Uma finally snapped. It was time to get back to doing what she did best.

Uma's return to work featured neither corsets nor smiling for the camera. *Tape* was Richard Linklater's second venture combining Ethan Hawke and digital videotape. The self-taught writer and director had spearheaded something of a renaissance in American independent films in the 1990s, specializing in ensemble pieces, twenty-four-hour plot time frames and youthful rites of passage. In 1991 his highly acclaimed feature-film debut, *Slacker*, had simultaneously coined the media buzzword which would so ensnare Uma's husband and tapped into a twentysomething drop-out culture encompassing artists, musicians, disaffected students and other misfits. There followed *Dazed And Confused* in 1993, which cemented Linklater's brilliant reputation.

Hawke (himself clearly inspired by Linklater's work, if *Chelsea Walls* was anything to go by) was one of the director's favourite actors, sharing with him a love of experimental filming techniques. They had worked together on a more conventional modern western, *The Newton Boys*, in 1998, and most recently on *Waking Life*, in which all the characters and conversations were enhanced in post-production using a ground-breaking 'rotoscoped' computer animation technique, so that the real-life action resembles a cartoon or moving painting.

Tape had originated at the same time as *Waking Life* and was shot with a microscopic budget during the lengthy animation process of the latter. Hawke had fallen under the spell of the one-act stage play *Tape*, written by Stephen Belber, and sent Linklater a copy of the script in February 2000. Meanwhile, he smartly enlisted old friend Robert Sean Leonard and provided Thurman with another opportunity to work alongside him in the three-hander.

The beauty of the whole project was that events seemed to transpire in a wonderful spur-of-the-moment fashion. Belber adapted his play for the screen and the shoot began just two months after Linklater received the script of what he began to call 'a cheap DV movie'.

The director had always wanted to have a film simmering on the back burner, ready to go at the last minute. 'You should be able to work spontaneously like that,' he said. 'Normally the stakes are so high, and it takes so long to cast the movie and get all the elements and all the money.'

Set entirely in Room 19 of a seedy motel in Lansing, Michigan, *Tape* is about the reunion of two high-school friends. Jon (Leonard), a documentary filmmaker, has done particularly well for himself and is revisiting his home town to show his work at a film festival. Vince (Hawke), a firefighter-cum-drug dealer, invites Jon to his hotel room, where they reminisce about old times.

However, as the night progresses, the reunion becomes a deadly sparring match. Vince is still smarting from Jon's great betrayal – stealing his high-school sweetheart, Amy (Thurman), who lives nearby and works as an assistant district attorney. Eventually leading his 'friend' into a confession that he may have date-raped Amy ten years ago, after an initial vehement denial, Vince subverts proceedings by revealing that he has recorded the whole night's conversation on cassette tape. Just as the situation starts to spiral out of control, Amy herself arrives to put a brand-new spin on the old events and soon takes the upper hand.

The filming of *Tape* took just ten days and Linklater stretched the digital-video medium to its limits, experimenting with hundreds of different angles and viewpoints that would not have been possible using a more expensive format. The 'homemade' aspect of the prints lent an edgy, intimate and urgent feel to the film, which all three actors played on brilliantly as they saw out their *pas de trois* of revenge.

'*Tape* didn't feel like a normal film,' Uma said afterwards. 'It was relaxed and freeing and we were able to experiment with the performances.

'I know that Ethan and Robert did actually share a girlfriend at one point in their friendship. So their personal history fed itself into this situation and somehow made it more exciting.'

*

None of the three stars of *Tape* expected that the pointed drama about the boundaries between sex and rape would be a blockbuster, mainly due to its unique filming technique, but also because a one-act film set within just one room could test the patience of a mainstream audience. It was always going to be one of those movies you either loved or hated.

Bearing this in mind, each took a miniscule fee, instead agreeing to a profit-share arrangement that would benefit them all if *Tape* took off. As Uma herself said, 'There can be too much stress and expectation with big-budget projects. The thrill sometimes gets lost.'

Tape and its more assuming big brother, *Waking Life*, both premiered in late January at the 2001 Sundance Festival, held that year in Park City, Utah. The reception for the two films was glowing, and they continued a similar run of critical success at the film festivals held in Toronto before their proper theatrical releases in late autumn.

Tape finally opened on 2 November 2001 in America after Linklater fans had waited nearly a year for the special dose of art-house cinema. British fans would have to wait another six months or so before they could see it, making the film one of Uma's slowest-burning projects for a long while.

It was a stunning piece of work – a true *tour de force* for each of the three actors and the director. From the get-go, Belber's snappy dialogue and Linklater's changes of shot pull the audience to the very front of their seats. The atmosphere is extremely voyeuristic and the real-time action is dark and fast-paced, with well-placed moments of droll black humour helping to break up the friction.

Launching straight into the story, the first part spies on Vince and Jon, who clearly know each other better than anyone and ask each other all the things the viewer wants to know. Each gives the other a grilling, each grates on the other's nerves, and at no point does the tension ease up as the plot twists and turns from one cathartic revelation to the next. Although admittedly *Tape* shows its theatrical roots throughout, cleverly all parts of the set are used, so it doesn't get stale. In fact, the confines of the tiny hotel room only add to the growing pressure-cooker effect.

Hawke is exceptional as Vince: juvenile, abrasive, petulant and dangerous, his 'violent tendencies' genuinely frightening as he fools around in his underwear. Leonard's Jon is respectable in comparison to his old drug-addict buddy, and rather touchingly desperate in his urge to do better and prove himself – that is, until his past is revealed to the audience.

As Vince lures the confession out of Jon as skilfully as any police officer, the strain intensifies as the viewer wonders how on earth either will extricate himself from an impossible situation. A nice touch comes when Vince snorts coke, then throughout the rest of the film gets progressively higher, gradually altering his personality accordingly.

Uma does not enter the film until nearly fifty minutes into proceedings, but her arrival is – initially, at least – a breath of fresh air, and there is a welcome change of pace for a while. The early play of manners between the three (especially in view of the details of Jon's very recent declaration of guilt) is painfully awkward, perhaps the most successful part of the compelling intimacy created by recording on digital tape.

Strikingly pretty, Uma is presented as clearly reminiscent of a schoolgirl, with her blonde hair swept back in a ponytail and Alice band, clutching a satchel-like handbag and innocently dressed in a powder-blue twin set. It's admittedly a little odd watching her and Ethan in such a grainy, home-movie-style piece, as it's hard to forget their real-life relationship, but in a way that knowledge makes it impossible for viewers to tear their eyes away from the screen – a major bonus for the movie.

Although Amy commands far less actual screen time than Vince or Jon, it doesn't take long before she magnificently takes charge of the situation, switching suddenly from helpless, demure and defensive to powerful and unpredictable. The real strength of Thurman's thirty-minute performance is that she builds up the complexity of her character remarkably quickly. Arriving totally unaware and slap-bang in the middle of a potentially dangerous situation, her forced laughter simultaneously confuses the men but reveals to the audience that she is putting on as much of an act to buy time as Vince and Jon have done beforehand. Thurman proves herself in every way the equal of Hawke and Leonard, as the viewer initially feels loyalty to her by default, then is confounded by her own mocking denial and distorted version of events before the ingenious dénouement turns everything on its head.

Although some reviewers unfortunately couldn't get over the demanding camera angles, in general *Tape* met with as warm a reception as it had at Sundance and Toronto, with some critics even preferring it over *Waking Life*; its unapologetically uncommercial style and storyline were in many ways just as exciting as the more expensive film's revolutionary animation.

Uma went on to receive a nomination at the Independent Spirit Awards for Best Supporting Female, and Linklater was such hot property that he could no longer continue to ignore the lure of Tinseltown. 'If there was ever a time to just sell out and become Hollywood, it would be right now,' he joked of the ground-breaking success of *Waking Life* and *Tape*. 'Just kidding ... But you never know.'*

*

In May 2001, Uma and her husband basked in the Cannes sunshine as *Chelsea Walls* received its premiere during the Directors Fortnight of the film festival. Uma was relaxed and happy, cavorting in the extensive grounds of the Carlton Hotel with Maya.

Neither she nor Ethan seemed particularly bothered about going to the parties and the premieres, although Ethan publicly credited his wife for making him feel more confident in those situations. Uma commented at this time that she didn't consider herself a 'slave to the fame game' and suggested her ambitions had been raised because she had less to lose.

But Uma's thoughts may not have focused solely on her career progression during this break. Feeling peaceful and at one with her life, she had conceived around the time of her thirty-first birthday and probably realized she had some important news to break to her husband during their vacation in Cannes. She wasn't ready to announce anything to the media just yet, but it was the second time she had noticeably stopped smoking at public events ...

*

Back in 2000, Uma had actively sought more control over her work. She had enjoyed working closely with Ethan that year on *Chelsea Walls* and *Tape*, and hoped to repeat the experience to some degree. The answer came in the form of a play she and Ethan had seen in a 'tiny off, off, off, off-Broadway theatre' in 1997.

Adapted from the bestselling novel by Laura Cahill, the tale follows the doomed love lives of two desperate women, single and pushing thirty in the late 1980s. The title, *Hysterical Blindness*, refers to a medical condition caused by emotional stress which renders the victim, in this case Debby, temporarily blind, and it is used throughout the narrative as a metaphor for her confused state of mind.

* In 2003 Linklater arguably did 'sell out' with *School Of Rock*, a formulaic high-school romp, gaining the best box-office returns of his career to date.

Debby has had serious issues with men ever since her father walked out on the family some fifteen years earlier, and she craves being the centre of attention at all times. Her best friend and drinking buddy Beth is also on the prowl; although she has a healthier attitude to the opposite sex, she also has a daughter in tow.

Searching for a good time at their favourite bar, Ollie's, the women are spotted by Rick, a construction contractor. Although it is Beth that he eyes up first, he is instead commandeered by the more dominant Debby. It turns out that she is not a pleasant character at all – needy, demanding and selfish – and although Rick is clearly uninterested after their first date, Debby talks herself into falling in love with him and starts telling anyone who will listen about their future together.

Debby is so wrapped up in her own world that she dismisses Beth's flirtations with the barman and ignores her mother's own happiness with a new man. When she is confronted by this touching partnership, Debby becomes jealous, rude and spiteful. But when tragedy strikes, the three women are taught a valuable lesson in love and life, and even if they don't ultimately find new partners, they build on the relationships they already have with each other. It was the poignant emotional journey that particularly attracted Uma to the story.

Keen to start work, she optioned the script and became executive producer for the TV movie, securing a deal with the HBO cable channel. Laura Cahill adapted her play for the small screen and came on board as an associate producer. Thurman also brought in Lydia Dean Pilcher as a co-producer, who suggested Mira Nair as director, with whom she had collaborated several times.

Based in New York, Nair had worked on independent short films for years and won an award for a documentary on Bombay's stripper subculture in 1988. After several critically acclaimed romantic and period dramas, Nair made the art-house hit *Monsoon Wedding*, which established her as a respected international director.

When Nair was approached in February 2001 for *Hysterical Blindness*, she was immersed in editing *Monsoon Wedding*. Furthermore, the timing of the project would have been particularly bad as the threat of a Screen Actors' Guild strike meant that filming had to wrap by June, just months away.[*] Despite this pressure, and although it meant a huge departure from her recent work and an unusual return to cable television, Nair agreed to direct *Hysterical Blindness*.

---

[*] In the event, this strike was called off.

Thurman naturally took on the lead role of Debby, and enrolled Gena Rowlands (*Hope Floats*) as her mother, Virginia, and Juliette Lewis (*From Dusk Till Dawn*) as her best friend Beth. The male contingent were Justin Chambers (*The Wedding Planner*) as Debby's fling Rick, Ben Gazzara (*The Thomas Crown Affair*) as Virginia's boyfriend Nick, and Anthony de Sando (*Double Parked*) as the barman who fancies Beth.

Hysterical Blindness was filmed in June 2001 in the towns of Bayonne and Bellville, New Jersey, half an hour's drive from Manhattan. The ease of the locale meant that Uma could get home in time to see her daughter every evening before bedtime, and it was a short shoot, which was also appealing to the working mother, who unbeknown to many was suffering from a touch of morning sickness.

Nair has an idiosyncratic style, which she carried forward to this film where appropriate. The title sequence is incredibly important as it sets the mood for the whole piece, and Nair thought carefully about the way in which she directed the opening scene.

'For this film, I wanted to address the character, literally having her vision go in and out of focus, which, of course, mirrors her life,' she explained. During the course of the film, Nair provides visual clues each time Debby's condition threatens to arise, to convey the overwhelming fear of hysterical blindness: 'Shooting through glass or using surfaces and textures helps unbalance the frame and field of vision.'

Although well known for her use of bright colours, Nair did not feel that would be appropriate here, given the nature of the film, and so only used occasional splashes when she had fun with the terrible 1980s attire. 'It's about white-trash life,' she said, 'and Uma and Juliette look very tawdry: big hair, acid-washed jeans and shoulder pads.'

The camerawork is perhaps the most distinctive of the director's techniques in evidence, similar to that of *Monsoon Wedding*. 'The type of handheld work for *Hysterical Blindness* was not the usual manic, always-moving approach,' she said. 'It was very still and composed, yet because it is handheld, you can feel the frame is breathing. This pulsating look makes the audience feel right there, in the moment, without getting queasy.'

The intrusion into everyday humdrum life prompted Uma to call *Hysterical Blindness* a wonderful kitchen-sink drama. 'There's not enough movies made like that anymore, about people's lives in a kind of unglamourized, unmanipulated way,' she said.

Debby is about as unglamorous as they come. She is a self-centred, manipulative woman who will throw a tantrum if she doesn't get her own way. Yet all her unattractive traits stem from her constant desire for love and affection. 'That search for love was a search I related to,' admitted Uma. 'The humiliating self-hatred, I think I have been that girl in many ways. So insecure and so full of longing, so going about it the wrong way.'

She went on to explain that Beth's natural ease with her sexuality attracts men far more than Debby's looks ever will, and when the two compete for a stranger's affections, Beth will always win because she is comfortable within herself. Although Uma is often perceived as one of the most beautiful women in Hollywood, it was this connection to feeling awkward and out of place that made her perfect for the role.

*

Hysterical Blindness would be aired as the centrepiece of the Sundance Festival in January 2002, and premiered on HBO in August that year.

The bleak picture of a character close to an emotional breakdown achieved a fair amount of critical acclaim. Uma was singled out for one of her greatest characterizations yet, securing her a Best Actress Golden Globe award in January 2003. Golden Globe nominations were also received by Gena Rowlands for Best Supporting Actress and Laura Cahill for Best First Screenplay, while Uma was nominated for a Screen Actors Guild Best Actress award.

Uma's achievements were no mean feat, given that her character is so intrinsically unlikeable; as the film is based almost solely on Debby and her insecurities, it can therefore be hard to enjoy. Any negative criticisms levelled at the movie highlighted its predictability, the lack of real depth, and its convenient and cheesy, yet unsatisfactory ending.

David Rooney from *Variety* succinctly explained the problems: '*Hysterical Blindness* is a numbingly obvious confection of laughter and tears that's utterly condescending to its one-note characters. There's something that screams "vanity project" about gorgeous blue-blood Uma Thurman playing big-haired blue-collar trash.'

Poorer reviews aside, the fact remains that *Hysterical Blindness* was a short television project, which was part of its appeal to the working mum. Gritty and well acted, it was very low-key for Uma's first try at production; it felt as though she had more to offer.

24

A NEW YORKER, AN ACTRESS AND A MOTHER

'The only pain in motherhood comes from conflict, and conflict is everything other than parenting.'

NENA THURMAN

'Guilt is an inherent part of being a working mother, and that's such a stupid waste of time.'

UMA THURMAN

In September 2001, after a scan revealed her second pregnancy was progressing as normal, Uma felt it was safe to announce her news to the world. Her marriage was secure, her three-year-old daughter was flourishing, her film output was steady and on the whole well received, and she was enjoying a doubly high profile with her modelling for Lancôme. Life was good.

'Things seem to be evolving along a pleasant path,' she said. 'I feel my life's undergone a magnificent transformation and I feel happier today than at any other time in my life.'

Ethan, however, joked that he was rediscovering the value of precious sleep. 'In a few more months I'll be back on a baby's schedule,' he moaned. 'Until you have a baby you never realize how wonderful it is to be able to sleep seven hours straight!'

The couple's happiness was only slightly marred the following month when they sued the actor James Gandolfini, best known for his TV portrayal of the mafia boss Tony Soprano in *The Sopranos*. Now they were firmly ensconced in their house in Sneden's Landing, they no longer needed their base in Greenwich Village. Reportedly Gandolfini had put down a £200,000 deposit on the apartment but got cold feet when he failed to get planning permission for renovations.

Claiming Thurman and Hawke hadn't provided him with the necessary paperwork, Gandolfini had apparently reneged on the deal despite having signed a contract, which prompted the owners to hit him with a lawsuit for the down payment at Manhattan Supreme Court.

This unpleasantness coincided with Uma finally receiving more recognition for her work. Following in the footsteps of such leading lights as Kevin Kline, Christopher Walken, Sigourney Weaver, Harvey Keitel and Susan Sarandon, she was presented with the prestigious Actor Award at the IFP Gotham Awards on 2 October. Introduced by Quentin Tarantino, Uma was the picture of expectant bliss, sweetly concluding her acceptance speech by saying there were three things she aspired to be: 'A New Yorker, an actress and a mother.'

The occasion witnessed Uma crossing paths with Robert De Niro, who was there to accept a Lifetime Achievement Award. The pictures from the ceremony held at Chelsea Piers, New York, amusingly show Uma's 'date', Ethan Hawke, looking typically scruffy with a goatee and long, unkempt hair, while De Niro is the epitome of elegance in his suave suit and tie.

*

Experiencing regular contractions on 14 January 2002, Uma checked into hospital to await the birth of her second child. Unfortunately the labour slowed up, so her doctor advised her to get on her feet and stroll around the maternity ward to help get things going.

Never one to do as she was told, Uma dismissed this suggestion and instead checked out of the hospital and accompanied Ethan and Maya on a long tour of New York's Museum of Natural History. Happily, the threesome explored the Butterfly Conservatory and attended a space show narrated by Tom Hanks. The exercise provided by the ambitious excursion prompted labour to restart, and the next day Uma gave birth to a blue-eyed baby boy weighing 7 pounds 15 ounces. The newest family member was shown his new home the following day, and his big sister took to him immediately, frequently hushing the adults so as not to disturb his sleep.

Unsurprisingly for a descendant of the Thurman clan, the naming of the newborn caused quite a commotion. Journalists were more than a little perplexed when no announcements were made for quite some time after the birth, although it later emerged that the baby was called Levon. However, after Maya persisted in addressing her brother as Roan, it seems that the name stuck, and it was eventually changed to reflect the unusual taste of the three-year-old girl.

Uma thought the whole situation was hilarious. 'If you ask Maya about the name, she'll say, "I got it from another baby,"' she laughed, illustrating the story with her daughter's characteristic nonchalant shrug. To bring more confusion to the tale, the name Roan would continue to be interspersed with Levon way after he reached his first birthday. But it didn't bother his mother, so why should it bother anyone else?

*

With a little help from a nanny and a cleaner, Uma and Ethan threw themselves into family life, enjoying it far more than they ever imagined.

'I feel we have taken things to another state of being where we can explore life together more freely,' she said of her marriage. 'Things are more relaxed between us now than they were when we started living together, even with two children to look after.'

With the experience of Maya's babyhood under her belt, Uma now knew just how 'portable' tiny babies can be and so wasted no time hiding out at home. Instead, the cheery foursome were often spotted out and about, enjoying a snack at a favourite café after nursery school finished for the day, playing in Central Park, or hiking up the hilly 3-mile trek of Runyon Canyon in the Hollywood Hills with the aid of a baby sling. During this time the tribe was joined by Sophie, a long-haired chihuahua chosen and named by Maya.

Still, Uma had certain celebrity duties to attend to, and she was present at the Oscars on 24 March, where Ethan was up for the award of Best Supporting Actor for *Training Day*. Unfortunately he lost out to Jim Broadbent's moving performance in *Iris*, but Uma was no less supportive.

'I was very proud of him because *Training Day* was such a powerful film and he and Denzel Washington were both brilliant,' she said. 'A lot of people thought that Ethan would be overwhelmed because the character Denzel was playing was so ruthlessly charismatic and manipulative, that there's almost no way you can make the quieter role stand out. But I think Ethan did that.' When complimented on her choice of evening wear for the auspicious event, she joked, 'I guess I should thank breastfeeding for adding something extra to my décolleté!'

For a while, Uma's thoughts strayed far from her own career, as family life necessarily took over. 'There may come a time when I'm really passionate about showbusiness again,' she said, 'but at the moment I'm happy at home . . . Work was always the most important thing to me before I had a baby. Now it's not.'

But one thing Uma had struggled with throughout her life was a sense that time was always slipping away, that she was lazy and should be doing something more productive. Any mother of one child – let alone two – will say that this is the least of their worries, but Uma was used to stretching herself to the limit, and then some.

'I'm still trying to make my time more valuable,' she had said when Maya was small. 'I've got a huge problem with getting time to read since my daughter was born – a great luxury, I know, but my mind is rotting.' Now one child had become two, Uma's feet got itchy slightly sooner than they had the first time round. 'I don't want to be one of those women who puts everything into their kids, and then the poor kids have to carry the weight of their mother's frustration,' she mused.

Back when *The Avengers* had flopped, Uma had had the golden excuse to hide away with the arrival of Maya. 'It took me a long time to bounce back, because I was so immersed in the challenges of being a mom,' she recalled. 'I wasn't really the self I knew, the self that was the actor.

'I did do some work, but I was always conflicted.'

Perhaps another reason why Uma hadn't really felt like herself was that, after Maya was born, scripts about earth-mother figures with six or more offspring suddenly began to arrive. 'I kid you not,' she said, shaking her head in disbelief. 'I aged fifteen years in nine months!'

Looking back, even though Uma had decided she would work far less than usual in Maya's formative years, she had actually churned out six films and one stage play in the three years since her daughter's birth – an impressive amount in anyone's book. 'Most of my worries and self-doubts about the parenting–career conflict have given way to a mild state of satisfaction,' she had said when heavily pregnant with Roan. 'I think I've managed to pull things off pretty well and I feel very good about the way Maya Ray is growing up in her own little world with me and Ethan.'

Now Roan was actually on the scene, Uma's ongoing need to test herself seemed more important than ever. As she dragged herself back into the mindset of work, she approached the task in hand pragmatically.

'I think I'm going to take a different approach with Roan,' she said. 'I've seen that children don't necessarily mean you have to put your career on hold . . . Children are fairly mobile, especially when they're so young.' Uma knew that this wouldn't always be the case as her children grew to school age and beyond, but like many working couples with the luxury of wealth, she and Ethan promised to juggle their film projects so that one of them would always be available for the children.

Still, the inherent guilt of the working mother was always going to be there buried in the background, and it was something that only Uma could come to terms with.

'Any working mother will tell you that there is a little tearing,' she said, 'and the thing that tears is usually yourself . . . I try to balance the intense drive to creatively grow and the incredible resentment of anything that interferes with my child's care.'

When questioned on whether her new family status would change her opinions about exactly what work she would take on, Uma didn't hesitate. This time it wasn't about costume dramas.

'I think motherhood will make me try more risqué or braver projects,' she said. 'A lot of people want to do everything family-style after having children, but I'll probably want to do something I feel strong enough to take on.

'The hardest thing is finding a director who's exciting to work with and an environment that's going to work out.'

25

THE TARANTINO TOUCH

'I'm not the kind of actress who's easy to classify and I've wasted a lot of time not finding the right projects. So when you have a chance like [this], you work harder than ever because you know it might not come again.'

UMA THURMAN

Back in June 2000, while Uma was promoting *The Golden Bowl*, rumours suggested that she had another, very exciting project up her sleeve. After the aborted attempt to remake *Modesty Blaise* in 1995, she was apparently about to work once again with Quentin Tarantino.

Having made the leap from quirky cult director to major celebrity in one swift move with *Pulp Fiction*, Tarantino suddenly found that every door was open to him. He adopted a multi-dimensional approach to his career: while he continued directing with a couple of small assignments (one quarter of *Four Rooms* and a suitably edgy episode of *ER*), the aspiring actor in him accepted several film parts, including a cameo in the low-budget *Sleep With Me*, *Desperado*, Robert Rodriguez's sequel to *El Mariachi*, and the comedy *Destiny Turns On The Radio*.

In 1996 he returned to the big screen as an actor, screenwriter and executive producer with *From Dusk Till Dawn*. Directed by Rodriguez and co-starring George Clooney in his first bid to break free from *ER*, the film was vulgar and violent with little coherent plot. The start resembled a *Pulp Fiction*-style gangster flick, but halfway through it disintegrated into a bizarre vampire gorefest. Unsurprisingly, this did little to maintain Tarantino's credibility.

The director redeemed himself the following year, back at the helm of *Jackie Brown*. Working from Elmore Leonard's novel *Rum Punch*, this was the first time Tarantino had attempted a literary adaptation, but his trademark smooth dialogue and soulful soundtrack were still discernible. The film was a quieter, more character-driven piece than his previous offerings, and once again featured Samuel L. Jackson. Proving he still had the knack for reviving actors in semi-retirement, Tarantino cast Pam Grier, queen of the blaxploitation genre, in the female title role, 1970s TV icon Robert Forster as the rueful bail bondsman and Bridget Fonda in an atypical role as the ill-fated beach bunny.

Just as he had restored the faith of some of his followers with *Jackie Brown*, Tarantino disappeared again. Two years later, film buffs were desperate for any scrap of detail about a forthcoming film reuniting Tarantino with Thurman.

The project in development was called *Kill Bill* and was actually born seven years earlier, while filming *Pulp Fiction*. During a casual conversation covering all film genres, Tarantino and Thurman happened to focus on revenge flicks and the latter came up with an interesting opening scenario: a heavily pregnant blood-spattered bride is left for dead on the floor of a church after an assassination squad murders the wedding party; the bride then seeks retribution and embarks on a killing rampage.

Tarantino loved the idea and counter-created the mastermind behind the massacre, Bill, whom Thurman describes as 'the pimp of all assassins'. With these ideas whirling around in his mind, Tarantino wrote some thirty pages of script during downtime on the set of *Pulp Fiction*, but then shelved the idea.

The pair didn't speak about their unfinished revenge romp until they met up at the Miramax Oscars party in March 2000. When Thurman enquired about *Kill Bill*, she rekindled Tarantino's interest. 'The best part of being a writer is that you write something, and it's not ready, [so] you put it in the incubator and wait till it's done,' he says. 'When I take it out, that's when it really starts.'

Although she had been the one to initiate the idea of such a strong female lead – the bride is actually a former assassin – Thurman suddenly became daunted about the role. 'He's writing it for me,' she said. 'I play somebody I don't even know if I'm capable of playing. I don't know why everyone casts me as these really tough chicks, these heavy chicks; it's tough to live up to.'

Thurman needn't have worried; Tarantino, ever the perfectionist, took his time writing and rewriting the script and was still 'just two weeks away from being done' over a year later.

'Quentin, I know you're "two weeks away from being done", but I just got offered this job and I think that maybe I should do it,' Uma would enquire on a regular basis.

'No, no, I'm going to need you,' came the response.

'OK, OK, I won't do it,' she conceded, turning down yet another role.

One such project that she rejected was Brian De Palma's return to form with *Femme Fatale*, ironically a similarly themed delve into the underworld about a small ring of jewel thieves led by a man known as Black Tie.

Femme Fatale would have been another gamble for Uma – clearly she was aware she had made several bad choices in the past and thought it wise to wait for her mentor to mastermind her second reinvention.

*

Fifteen months after Tarantino resurrected the *Kill Bill* script, he triumphantly called Uma to announce its completion. Unfortunately, as luck would have it, by the summer of 2001 she was several months pregnant and unable to undertake a demanding action role.

'I had been involved with the movie for so long and I was his sounding board for all his ideas as they got crazier and crazier, so not being in the film was an impossibility for me,' she says. While she felt emotionally involved in the project, she was still taken aback that Tarantino was prepared to wait for her.

'I felt very flattered,' she says of his decision. 'It showed that he truly believed in my talent, and that this film was exciting enough for him to put all his artistic energies into something with me.'

When questioned about the prospect of waiting for Uma not only to have the baby but also to get back into shape, Tarantino simply replied, 'When Josef von Sternberg was preparing to shoot *Morocco*, Marlene Dietrich fell pregnant – and he waited. So you wait for your Dietrich and film history will thank you.'

In actual fact, Tarantino continued to tinker with the script and began pre-production while Uma carried Roan. As Uma neared her due date, the production team started calling her daily to find out what her schedule was, until she apparently snapped and said, 'Listen guys, if you put any more pressure on me to drop this baby, I'm gonna hang on to it! He's going to be overdue, he's going to come out with dry feet!'

Tarantino himself was more patient and spent the time assembling the rest of the cast and crew. Oscar-winning cinematographer Robert Richardson was hired as he had proven his ability to create myriad different looks, including replicating photographic styles and techniques of the past, most notably under the great director Oliver Stone.

Film junkie Tarantino had long been an admirer of martial arts expert Yuen Wo-ping, and was honoured when the master agreed to choreograph the extensive fight scenes for *Kill Bill*. While modern audiences were familiar with Yuen's work in *Crouching Tiger, Hidden Dragon* and *The Matrix*, Tarantino was more interested in re-creating some of his kung fu craftsmanship from twenty years earlier.

Starting with the titular part of Bill, Tarantino approached Warren Beatty. 'I kind of sold it to him as a groovy guest-star part,' says the director, 'but as it went on, Bill became more involved with the movie.' Beatty had seen a glittering career over four decades come to a grinding halt in 2001 with the almighty flop *Town And Country*, and was excited about the prospect of benefiting from the Tarantino touch. There was some debate as to whether the delay waiting for Thurman caused problems for Beatty or whether he was concerned about the growing importance of the role, but either way the actor pulled out, suggesting instead David Carradine.

As soon as Beatty proposed the name, it seemed like kismet. Having mastered martial arts, Carradine was actually chosen over Bruce Lee to play Caine in the long-running television series *Kung Fu* in the 1970s (Lee became the programme's technical advisor). In the early 1990s he once again reprised the role in the updated series *Kung Fu: The Legend Continues*.

Carradine had also written his autobiography, *Endless Highway*, which Tarantino happened to be reading – and consequently revisiting tapes of *Kung Fu* – while writing *Kill Bill*. Having only appeared in straight-to-video or made-for-television movies for years, Carradine jumped at the role of Bill. 'I'm doing everything an actor could dream of doing: long monologues, fighting with swords, spaghetti western shit, comedy, romance,' he said. 'I am so hot for this movie, it's an incredible gift.'*

Bill's killers are members of the D.iV.A.S. (Deadly Viper Assassination Squad) and each has a codename: Vernita Green, aka

---

* Confusion reigned after the release of the movie as to exactly who was Tarantino's ideal and original Bill. Despite Beatty's link to the role, Carradine appeared on TV claiming the part of Bill had been specifically written for him. Then, in a further twist, co-star Michael Madsen alleged Tarantino had told him he had fired Beatty for not understanding what the film was really about. Tarantino's current relationship with Beatty remains unclear, although he says he would like to work with him in the future.

Copperhead; O-Ren Ishii, aka Cottonmouth; Bud, aka Sidewinder; and Elle Driver, aka California Mountain Snake. Collectively, and in chronological order, they form The Bride's revenge hitlist. Tarantino had a clear idea of who to cast as the assassins.

Vivica A. Fox made her screen debut as a hooker in Oliver Stone's *Born On The Fourth Of July* and attracted further notice as Will Smith's girlfriend in the 1996 blockbuster *Independence Day*. She continued building a diverse CV, but being offered the small-yet-feisty role of Vernita Green, The Bride's first victim in the new Tarantino flick, was too good an opportunity to miss.

For the commanding part of O-Ren Ishii, Tarantino turned to Lucy Liu, more commonly known for her verbal fights in *Ally McBeal* and her girl-power action in *Charlie's Angels*. Although she had broken into feature films, Liu was regularly seen playing second fiddle and the chance to play the complex character of O-Ren allowed her to shine in her own right. (It is interesting to note that the character's background is depicted by an extended *animé* section; Tarantino was keen to revisit this genre, in which Japanese gangster comics are brought to life, after dabbling in it on *Four Rooms*.)

For Bill's brother Bud, Tarantino returned to Michael Madsen. With *Donnie Brasco* his only really successful film since *Reservoir Dogs*, Madsen must have kicked himself for turning down the role of Vincent Vega in *Pulp Fiction*. His career had slumped sharply in the late 1990s and he did not hesitate when offered a second chance of working with Tarantino.

Finally, Elle Driver was a role for an older, more experienced actress; Tarantino surprised his prey in London, where she was playing the Marilyn Monroe role in the stage version of *The Seven Year Itch*.

'I was appearing at the Queen's Theatre and Quentin showed up in my dressing room after the play,' recalls Daryl Hannah.

'What the hell are you doing here?' she demanded to know.

Tarantino had intended to play it cool and just say that he had come to see her performance, but her rather aggressive reaction threw him. He gave Hannah a brief outline of the film and the role he had in mind for her, and left it to her to read the script.

Agoraphobic and diagnosed as borderline autistic as a little girl, Hannah amazed everyone by taking up first ballet and then acting. Achieving fame in *Splash* in 1983, her career since then had proved erratic; highlights included *Roxanne* and *Steel Magnolias*.

With little to show for much of the 1990s, Hannah marked the new millennium with a moderate comeback, starting with *Dancing At The Blue Iguana* and followed by *The Big Empty* and *Northfork*. The part of

Elle Driver piqued her interest, not least as it was inspired by Christina Lindberg's performance in *Thriller – En Grym Film*, in which the character's eyeball was sliced out with a scalpel, all shown in graphic detail.

Hannah was on board and the D.iV.A.S. were complete.

*

'I'll never learn to temper my excitement; excitement is something that should only ever be coveted. Especially now I'm back with Quentin. I trust him implicitly,' declared Uma as she prepared for *Kill Bill* in the spring of 2002.

'I've made so many period films, and so many kind of laced-up things, so his characters alone are very exciting for me.'

The Bride is certainly a force to be reckoned with. Having lost everything, including her fiancé and unborn child, she has nothing to live for and is only intent on seeking revenge. Tarantino stacked everything against Uma, making it hard for her to relate to The Bride as she embarked on her killing spree.

Uma drew on Clint Eastwood's iconic nameless spaghetti-western hero. 'He was an enigma,' she explains of her choice of inspiration. 'In those movies he had very little dialogue and it was a very internalized performance.' Contrary to Tarantino's usual fast-talking style, the dialogue in *Kill Bill* is minimal as he preferred to let the action speak volumes. Like *Pulp Fiction*, *Kill Bill* is narrated in a chapter format, making it seem more like a book than a film.

Starting with the opening scene created by Uma, Tarantino had fleshed out the background detail with the utmost care. 'You have a little bit of licence when you do such a basic story as a revenge story,' admits Tarantino. 'You know the story before going in: five people did this to her, she's going down the list to wipe them out. So, you can go off in all these other directions, but you're always staying on course with the objective of the movie.'

The Bride was originally a member of the D.iV.A.S., but chose to leave the squad when she got pregnant. Bill waits until her wedding day to let her feel his murderous anger, but makes the mistake of not completely killing her off. The squad know that she is in a coma, but will not kill a sleeping target. Instead, when she regains consciousness, she vows to avenge the deaths of her loved ones.

'This movie does not take place in the universe that we live in,' continues the director. 'In this world women are not the weaker sex. They have exactly the same predatory hunting instincts as the men, the same drive to kill or be killed.'*

'Females have to be more devious,' elaborates Uma. 'Every woman who can stand on her own two feet and hold her own place in the professional world and not become hardened by it, and still maintain her femininity with her success and in her strength, is doing her bit.'

Actually resembling members of an international assassin group required three months of hard physical training for all the actors. Even Tarantino himself joined in the gruelling sessions; partly as he was originally going to undertake a cameo role, but also so that he could relate to his cast. 'I'd be damned if I had these girls train and I couldn't!' he laughs. 'And if I hadn't, I wouldn't have had the authority to tell them, "Do it again!" They knew I knew how much it hurt.'

A training centre was set up in a warehouse in Culver City, south of Los Angeles. The programme incorporated several areas of learning: kenjutsu samurai sword techniques were taught by fellow cast member and venerable film veteran Sonny Chiba, and Chinese martial arts came from Yuen Wo-Ping, including the fancy wire work he used in *The Matrix*.

With each new art form the cast learned, they exercised a different set of muscles. 'Samurai swords are heavy and you constantly have to fight the tendency to bend over. It's an intensive workout on your thighs and forearms because of the weight of the sword,' explains Lucy Liu. 'But in Chinese martial arts you do bend your upper body. Each of them requires you to teach your body a new language.'

Incongruously, sword-fighting is a very intimate sport. 'It involves control of breath and eye contact,' says Sonny Chiba. 'You must know your competitor, how he breathes, what he's thinking. Sword-fighting is person-to-person, based on human relationships and emotional spiritual expression. It is about the heart and soul.'

Both Liu, who had recently undertaken similarly intensive training for *Charlie's Angels*, and Carradine, who had always practised Chinese Shaolin-style kung fu, were at an advantage over the other actors, but neither escaped without aches and pains.

Liu and Thurman also had to say a few lines of Japanese, so they studied using instructional CDs to get a grasp of the language. 'I was trying to get to the point where I could say my Japanese lines with feeling and conviction, as if I knew what I was saying,' explains Uma. 'They tell me my Japanese is comprehensible. That's what I was going for.'

---

* This promotion of 'girl power' as something new was actually a little behind the times, as films like *Charlie's Angels* and *Tomb Raider* had already paved the way for women to be physically strong on screen.

Of course, Uma had to undergo far more training than anyone else, as each of the D.iV.A.S. has a speciality, whereas The Bride has to fight each specialist in their own field. On top of the months spent learning Japanese, sword-fighting, kung fu and wire work with the others, she also mastered two different styles of each fighting method, along with knife-throwing, kickboxing and hand-to-hand combat.

'Uma had to fight alongside people who had been doing it their entire lives,' continues Chiba. 'I was especially struck by how she was willing to do something over and over until she got it down. She was absolutely professional.'

This was no mean feat for the actress, who had only given birth three months earlier and was still breastfeeding. 'They told me later that when I walked in 35 pounds overweight, nursing my newborn son, the whole fight team threw up their hands and said they would have to get a double for me,' laughs Uma. 'Little did I know that Quentin had it in his head that I was going to attempt everything that was done in the movie.'

The intense and relentless training was undoubtedly tough, especially when juggled with caring for her baby son, but Uma soon began to see physical results and improvement in her ability. 'I got this terrific rush in getting my body to be so lean and taut,' she says. 'They taught me to be co-ordinated. It was really, really hard work, I didn't know if I'd get there, but I couldn't believe what they helped me do . . . They changed me. It's really amazing.'

Through the life-changing experience of what she calls 'Chinese boot camp', Uma lost 2 stone and looked fitter than ever before. Working out from 9 a.m. to 5 p.m. every day from Monday to Friday for three months certainly played its part in her weight-loss, but, curiously, there were also reports that Uma indulged excessively in desserts, sometimes to the exclusion of normal food, a habit she alternately fuelled and denied.

Either way, her incredible transformation had serious repercussions. 'The entire wardrobe department had bloody fingers from taking that costume in every week, because I was slowly shrinking,' says Uma. 'It was like: "Is she going to make it, or is this going to be kind of funny for Quentin – this very large-bottomed samurai?"'

The Bride's outfit was an exact replica of the yellow jumpsuit Bruce Lee wore in *The Game Of Death* (the film left unfinished when he died in 1973 and released later), replete with a black racing stripe down each side. 'That was really inspiring. Putting that on made me feel as if I could really take on a whole bunch of guys single-handed,' smiles Uma.

That the costume was not overtly sexual in the same way as the *Charlie's Angels* outfits was appropriate, as The Bride is a no-nonsense woman uninterested in sex or romance. However, Tarantino insisted on using one feminine touch. The work of filmmaker John Woo was another source of inspiration for the director, and Tarantino showed Uma Woo's movie *The Killer*, starring Sally Yeh, to demonstrate Woo's signature slow-motion theatrics. Tarantino wouldn't let Thurman cut her hair as he wanted to re-create Yeh's mane flying in slow motion.

Finally, in preparation for her magnum opus, Uma carefully studied the incredible list of films Tarantino gave her to brush up on everything from Clint Eastwood, Sergio Leone, Jackie Chan and Bruce Lee to Japanese revenge films, all manner of exploitation films and endless Hong Kong cinema. 'I watched dozens and dozens and dozens of movies,' she says, 'such an amazing mix from highbrow to lowbrow. You kind of wonder what's going on in his mind.'

In spite of Tarantino's own exhaustive knowledge, he decided to hire Wu-Tang Clan's RZA to collect old Asian film themes and sound effects. 'RZA was invaluable,' says Tarantino. 'I felt sort of alone, because no one around me would get my movie references. But RZA knew everything I was talking about!'

Even the most ardent fans of the genre will be hard pushed to catch all the citations in *Kill Bill*. 'I'm making this film for me,' grinned Tarantino. 'Everyone else is along for the ride.'

*

In May 2002, following the gruelling training regime in Los Angeles, Tarantino took the cast and crew of *Kill Bill* to the Beijing Film Studios, China, where they would be based for the majority of the shoot. The studios in the northern section of the Chinese capital were originally built in 1949 and were once home to Mao Tse-Tung's propaganda machine.

It was very important to Tarantino to be in China while making this Asian-influenced film, so as to absorb the atmosphere and to have masters of various martial arts on tap. Additionally, he was able to take advantage of cheaper costs and the facility to work six days a week, rather than the standard five in Hollywood.

Once in China, on top of the daily exercise routine, rehearsals started and the actors had to concentrate on the intricate combat movements as much as, if not more than, the lines. 'I basically drilled choreography every single day, learning hundreds of moves and combinations,' says Uma.

After months of preparation, filming for *Kill Bill* finally started in

June 2002. It was originally planned as an eighty-nine-day shoot, predominantly in China but also on location in Japan, Mexico and America, but they ran into problems early on. 'We'd never made a fight movie before, and we just didn't realize how long it would take,' admits producer Lawrence Bender. Ultimately, it turned out to be a staggering 155-day shoot at a cost of $55 million.

The protracted delay was in no small part due to Quentin Tarantino's insistence on filming what he called 'the Chinese way'. This meant that all digital special effects were vetoed and most stunts had to be done as they were in the kung fu films of the 1970s, using replica devices and techniques. These methods certainly taxed the flexibility and experience of the 300-strong multinational cast and crew. Furthermore, although the director had spent the best part of two years fine-tuning the script with every fight scene laid out in intricate detail, he scrapped most of his plans and relied on collaborative improvisation with Master Yuen on the set.

'It's unusual for someone to be willing to think on their feet this way rather than to be hanging by their fingernails to their script, or to their little thing that they wrote, or to the decision that they thought was the right one yesterday in the shower,' marvelled Uma. The last-minute changes tested her skills to the limit.

'When we went onto the set to start shooting the fight, Quentin introduced this new idea, where all of that choreography could just go right out the window. He would change it on the spot and I would have to learn immediately five-, ten-, fifteen-point fights on the spot, while the camera was waiting.'

To the master's surprise and delight, he had taught Uma so well that she was able to take all unexpected on-the-spot changes in her stride. Pulling Tarantino aside, Yuen said, 'With some actors who look good in movies it's like, one or two moves, very well executed, and then you have to cut. Uma is doing four-, five-, six-move routines, and picking them up on the spot.'

Everyone felt the strain of the drawn-out shoot, and none more so than Uma. Not only was she required on set virtually every day, but she also had her children to look after; her husband's workload for 2002 had vastly increased and besides, Uma wanted both her children to be with her, particularly her six-month-old baby.

Although she had the help of a nanny, Uma was still breastfeeding Roan, a physically and emotionally draining task at the best of times. 'In the first week, I ended up in the bathroom crying,' she admits. 'There were a couple of moments when I was on my knees. I was breastfeeding and sleep-deprived because I'd been up all

Glenn Close unquestionably stole the show in *Dangerous Liaisons* with her portrayal of the scheming Marquise de Merteuil, seen here with Uma as the ingénue Cécile.

Uma's role as the girlfriend in *Johnny Be Good*, seen here with co-star Anthony Michael Hall, was one she wished to forget.

'She looks as though she floated down from the clouds,' said *Baron Munchausen* director Terry Gilliam of the actress, who so resembled Botticelli's Venus.

With Patrick Bergin in *Robin Hood*. Co-star Jeroen Krabbé said: 'Patrick and Uma play Hollywood on a non-Hollywood set.'

Uma finally got the opportunity to work with family friend Richard Gere on *Final Analysis*.

Top: Uma was transformed by Timna Woollard's incredible body art in *Where The Heart Is*.

Above: Smouldering with Maria de Medeiros in *Henry & June*.

Uma hitchhikes her way to adventure with the aid of her oversized thumbs in *Even Cowgirls Get The Blues*.

Uma with co-stars Robert De Niro and Bill Murray in *Mad Dog And Glory*.

'We were just completely immersed in the magic of the material for twelve hours,' says John Travolta of the memorable dance scene in *Pulp Fiction*.

Uma as the iconic Mia Wallace on the poster artwork for *Pulp Fiction*.

Uma's two striking appearances in skin-tight outfits as camp caricatures in *Batman And Robin* and *The Avengers* were less than successful at the box office.

Branching out into comedy: Uma with Janeane Garofalo in *The Truth About Cats And Dogs*.

Uma jumped at the small role of Blanche in *Sweet And Lowdown* in order to work with Woody Allen.

'We got to know each other before filming started,' said Uma of her *Gattaca* co-star and future husband, Ethan Hawke. 'I realized that this was someone I wanted to spend a lot of time with.'

As the desperate mother Fantine in *Les Misérables*.

Uma continued her return to period pieces with *The Golden Bowl*.

'She was open to my ideas, full of her own ideas, had great impulses, made things real, made things fun,' says Barry Edelstein of working with Uma on *The Misanthrope*. She is pictured with co-star Roger Rees (*above left*).

'*Tape* didn't feel like a normal film,' says Uma of her collaboration with Ethan Hawke and Robert Sean Leonard. 'It was relaxed and freeing and we were able to experiment with the performances.'

Above left: With Ben Affleck in *Paycheck*.

Above right: Reunited with John Travolta for *Be Cool*.

Left: With Juliette Lewis in *Hysterical Blindness*, Uma's first foray into producing.

As The Bride, Uma takes on the Crazy 88 in the House Of Blue Leaves scene from *Kill Bill Volume 1*.

Learning her trade from Gordon Liu Jia-hui as Pai Mei in *Kill Bill Volume 2*.

Top: Fighting Lucy Liu in *Kill Bill Volume 1*.

Above: The final confrontation with David Carradine in *Kill Bill Volume 2*.

night with the baby. I was exhausted. I'd never realized how hard it would be.'

Worse still, as the completion date was pushed further back, Uma found it hard to see an end to the daily grind. 'It was definitely a marathon . . . because it was supposed to be four months but the goal line kept moving. I was one of the only people there who had children and it was very difficult.'

There were other considerations, too, for Maya who had just turned four. 'My daughter was very brave. She would go off to school in Beijing and then come to see me at work,' says Uma, well aware of the parallels between Maya's transient childhood and her own.

Of course, Uma had never had to watch either of her illustrious parents get beaten up on a film set every day. The worried mother carefully explained to Maya that the blood she was covered in was fake and just like paint. She said that the squibs in her mouth tasted 'like sugar, full of syrup. For the mouth spits, they made a minty one, so my breath could be bloody fresh!'

'She seemed to take it quite well,' confirms Uma. 'I hope it's not too scarring or damaging.' Besides the hundreds of gallons of fake blood (three different types, apparently), the undeniable fact is that Uma and her children were on the set of one of the most brutally violent films in recent history.

The actress had been very explicit about her distaste for such gratuitous gore four years earlier: 'I close my eyes and cover my ears when people get hurt in movies. I hate frivolous suffering, and there's so much of it in films. I particularly hate it when I read scripts where violence is used in the same way as sexuality – as titillation for shock value.' Uma's involvement in *Kill Bill* was quite a turnaround.

Her justification is poetic licence: 'Violence is a big expression for [Tarantino] . . . I was surprised to see [in] *Pulp Fiction* that somehow his tone and his humour, the violence didn't disturb me the way it often does in a movie. His way is very unique, and way out of my control.'

*

No matter how finely choreographed *Kill Bill's* back-to-back fight scenes, if someone's concentration broke for a split second, the consequences were extreme. 'One day I put my head the wrong way and I took a sword right in the face,' remembers Uma. 'I thought my face had opened up. I ran off the set and checked to see if I was bleeding, which, miraculously, I wasn't. I cried by myself and then went back to do the scene.'

Uma relied on ice packs and tubes of arnica cream to reduce swelling and bruising, but she still damaged various tendons and areas of cartilage. 'It was a brutal shoot,' she recalls. 'I get buried alive. I walk through the desert. I take on eighty men at one time. I get shot in the head. I get shot in the chest. I get shot in the leg. I get stabbed with needles filled with drugs. The only things Quentin didn't do to me were set me on fire and drown me.'

One constant was The Bride's weapon: her sword. Sonny Chiba plays a small but key role in the film as Hattori Hanzo, a retired master samurai-sword maker. The Bride enters his small coffee shop, above which he stores his 'killing machines', and has to persuade him to step out of retirement and craft her a sword. 'I was using the Japanese that I had studied for months and he was struggling with English, so we had this incredible kind of balance of language handicaps in our scene,' laughs Uma.

The Bride is very possessive about her sword, and Uma was amazed at the very real path she embarked on to fuse with her weapon. 'I earned it, I became at one with it – and it took a long time,' she says. 'When I first had it I couldn't even swing it and I learned the hard way how to handle that thing. My favourite thing was the journey that took me to that sword.'

The real test of the instrument was at the massacre of the Crazy 88 in the House Of Blue Leaves. This sequence took a particularly long time to shoot, eight weeks in all, but it was designed by Tarantino to raise the bar for all future fight scenes.[*] 'I tried to think up every inventive and entertaining way I could to dismember and disembowel and put to an end to these bastards,' he recalls gleefully. 'It took me about a year to write that sequence.' It was undoubtedly his greatest directorial challenge.

Due to the numerous different languages spoken on set there was a team of Japanese, Mandarin and Cantonese translators in attendance, but Tarantino devised a better way of communicating his vision for the almighty bloodbath.

'For almost an entire day Quentin basically acted out the entire "House Of Blue Leaves" scene for Master Yuen Wo-ping and his crew,' remembers producer Lawrence Bender. 'He'd jump up, then fall flat on

---

[*] Quentin Tarantino has hinted at the mythology behind the Crazy 88: 'because O-Ren is half-Chinese and half-Japanese, so is her army'. As each half would consist of forty-four members, it is no coincidence that the number four is pronounced the same as the word 'death' in both Chinese and Japanese. Tarantino therefore intended O-Ren's army to consist of two lots of 'double death'.

his back. He'd flounder on a chair. They had never seen anything like it! But the end result was that they understood each other very well.'

Master Yuen then choreographed every step of the scene, adding grace to the action. The result is a mind-boggling combination of Tarantino's humour and Yuen's balletics as The Bride kills off seventy-six warriors.

As with the extremes he went to with *Pulp Fiction*, Tarantino again paid great attention to detail. Set designer Yohei Taneda elaborates, 'He is very visual and describes what he wants . . . I used really red tones for the hallway in which the sequence begins, then a traditional Japanese green in the main dining area.' (The Japanese expression 'blue leaves' evokes a very fresh shade of green.)

The outfits in this scene are also notable: a twist on the simple white shirts, black ties and black suits made famous in *Reservoir Dogs*. Here Tarantino added a small black mask as a homage to Bruce Lee's costume as Kato in *The Green Hornet*.

In among the anonymous crowd being picked off by The Bride are two distinctive faces. The first is the suicidally aggressive Go Go Yubari, played by Chiaki Kuriyama. The hauntingly beautiful Japanese girl started her career early as a model, but by the age of eleven she had broken into films.

Her chilling gaze tormented audiences in *Shikoku*, and, after seeing her in *Battle Royale*, Tarantino cast her as the manic Go Go. Fans of Kuriyama's performance in *Battle Royale* were thrilled to see her again dressed in a school uniform and re-creating her most famous scene by stabbing a Japanese businessman in the crotch.[*]

Rather than a knife, here Go Go's weapon of choice is an amalgamation of the lethal yo-yos brandished by the schoolgirls in the long-running Japanese TV series *Sukeban Deka* and the technique used in one of Tarantino's favourite martial arts films, *Master Of The Flying Guillotine* (1976). The instrument fashioned for Go Go resembles a mace with a buzz-saw attachment, and in Kuriyama's control it is not just threatening, but terrifying.

The other actor to be singled out is Hu Xiaokui, who explains how he was spared at the last minute: 'I was supposed to die, but when Uma was about to kill me, the director saw something in my face that made him change his mind.' Tarantino changed it so that Xiaokui is the last man standing at the end of the scene, thus affording The Bride an extra dimension as a character with compassion.

---

[*] Tarantino had the candy-pink plastic bar in which this scene was shot dismantled and shipped to his house in Los Angeles to replace his old bar.

The extended scene finally culminates in the long-awaited battle between The Bride and O-Ren Ishii in the beautiful formal Japanese snow garden at the back of the House Of Blue Leaves. While Uma is exhausted and bedraggled after slaying a roomful of fighters, Liu looks calm and serene dressed in her white kimono.

Although Uma had a height advantage over Liu, they were well matched physically. 'Lucy has excellent body movement,' praises Sonny Chiba. 'Her concentration and speed give her an edge. She's done a lot of action films, and it shows. She's got an excellent technique.' The ensuing sequence is as graceful as any ballet, until the gruesome climax . . .

Uma still had several big scenes to get under her belt, including face-to-face battles with Vivica Fox, Daryl Hannah, Michael Madsen and, of course, David Carradine. After eight months Tarantino eventually allowed The Bride go head to head with Bill, a scene which Uma infused with her own desperation. 'By the time I got there I was *really* ready to kill Bill,' Uma rolls her eyes. 'So when Bill came my way, I was like, "Bill, you're no longer in this world, buddy, because as soon as I get my hands on you you're outta here! You're so dead!" '

With the majority of filming in the can, the cast and crew shot on location at a Buddhist temple on Miao Gao Mountain for a week. After climbing a huge flight of stairs, they then had to film The Bride's Shaolin kung fu training sequences under the tutelage of Gordon Liu Jia-hui as Pai Mei.

Having discarded much of the script in favour of improvisation, it is no surprise to learn that Thurman's vicious scrap with Hannah was also altered at the last minute, inspired the day before, when Tarantino had seen the slapstick *Jackass: The Movie*. 'Suddenly it was like, "Let's flush your head down the toilet! Let's smash a lamp on your head!" ' recalls Hannah, who was left with one bruise that just wouldn't go away. Like Liu and Thurman, Hannah too was applauded for her grasp of martial arts, although much of their fight is more like a bar-room brawl. 'Daryl has the piercing eyes of a Samurai,' says Chiba. 'Very good and serious concentration. I nicknamed her "blue-eye samurai".'

Although important, Hannah's role was relatively small and filming did not take long, but she followed the team even when they moved on as they were so close-knit. 'I was helping with wardrobe, and then some gaffer stuff,' she laughs. 'I was even Uma's hand stand-in.'

The death of the first victim, Vivica Fox, was in fact one of the last scenes to be shot when they finally returned to America; suburban

Pasadena to be precise, and the home of Vernita Green. 'I have never been so happy to see wall-to-wall carpeting in my life!' says Uma. 'While it was so different that it felt almost like another movie, I knew it was the same movie, because we never left a set until we'd trashed it.'

*

'It's hard to describe someone that has realistically functioned as a muse because that's not a thing that you describe, it's a thing that you feel,' ponders Tarantino, who has often credited Thurman with being his inspiration.

As much as Tarantino has drawn creatively from Uma, he has encouraged and pushed her to new limits. 'He's had more faith in me than I've really ever come across,' acknowledges Uma. 'He believed in me enough to challenge me to do something to an insane degree beyond my confidence in myself.'

Conversely, as she took every test in her stride, Tarantino was left not knowing where to turn next. 'She takes your expectations and fucking destroys them,' he says. 'I didn't know that what she did was possible. It has altered my parameters forever.'

Of course, some things never change, and typical Tarantino shots were naturally present in his latest offering, including a bathroom scene where The Bride overhears Sofi Fatale on the phone shortly before disarming her, a shot from inside the trunk of a car (Fatale again), and countless close-ups of feet, notably Uma's size elevens. In fact, one whole segment is devoted to Uma's big toe as she wills herself to recover from her coma and regain her strength.

As close as they were, Tarantino recognized that there were some things he could not even ask Uma to perform. The infamous 'Fuck Buck' scene was originally much lengthier and the director wanted to run it past Uma first.

'I'm gonna read you something,' he said on the phone, 'and I feel really bad about it and you can have any reaction you want.'

'He just read me the goriest, most violent, multi-Frances-Farmer-style sequence complete with a fantasy sequence that went on and on . . .' recalls Uma of a disturbing scene in which the perpetrator who raped the comatose Bride receives his comeuppance as he is gangbanged by centaurs and minotaurs in hell.

'That's Quentin's conscience in action: he felt so bad about this raping of The Bride he had to add in, maybe just to get through the call with me, this hell sequence. My response to it was to be completely amused.' Thankfully, none of this sick fantasy vengeance made it to the actual film, although The Bride gives Fuck Buck the mother of all headaches.

It was this kind of discussion about the characters and plot, not to mention that the opening scenario was Uma's idea, that led Tarantino to make a touching tribute to his muse. Although he takes full screenwriting credit, he acknowledges in the title sequence that 'Kill Bill is based on the character created by Q and U'. It is a very personal form of recognition. Contrast this with the fact that he fought so hard *not* to honour his old friend Roger Avary for his contribution to *Pulp Fiction*, although Avary had far more input, with an actual script changing hands.

That filming dragged on should have been a sign that *Kill Bill* had taken on a life of its own and got out of hand. Towards the end of the shoot there were discussions about splitting the sprawling movie into two separate instalments, but nothing could be decided until the editing stage.

'We started talking about it,' explains Lawrence Bender. 'Quentin came up with a way of how to do it. Then we just dropped it and finished shooting. About six weeks into editing the movie, we called Harvey Weinstein in.'

With an open mind, they all watched the first chunk as put forward by Tarantino. They asked themselves, 'Is this the first half of a bigger movie or is it one movie unto itself?' The conclusion was the latter and accordingly *Kill Bill* was divided into two volumes.

'The movie always had an extraordinary, episodic, saga-like form,' explains Uma of the ease with which the film was separated by its chapters. 'This world was so thoroughly investigated by [Tarantino], if he had set himself to it, it could've been eight movies.'

Of course, sceptics didn't view the decision to produce two films as a result of Tarantino's obsession; it was pointed out that delays had caused *Kill Bill* to exceed its budget – what better way to recover the excess than to release two movies for the price of one? To be fair, geek that he is, Tarantino's motivation was more likely to be the desire to define film history rather than financially led. He had become so engrossed in the Asian movie world that he even considered producing a more extreme version for a separate release, along the lines of *Battle Royale*. Needless to say the subsequent DVD releases would contain exciting extras – a technique which can be viewed as either artistic or mercenary.

Indeed, Tarantino's problems did not end with the fuss over dividing the epic into two chunks. The censors had yet to see *Kill Bill* and a large swathe of critics were bound to take exception to the relentless violence. After it was rated R in America and 18 in England, one story suggested that the Motion Picture Association of America insisted sections should be run in black and white to help disguise the carnage, although that was probably more of a stylistic decision.

*

In August 2003 Tarantino organized a preview screening of *Kill Bill Volume 1* for the cast in New York. Unfortunately there was a communication mix-up over the date and Uma failed to attend. Regardless, the director and actress met the following day for dinner to discuss the imminent release and publicity strategy.

Uma was prepared for the onslaught. 'There will always be resistance,' she said matter-of-factly. 'Anything that is really brave and dynamic offers itself up to be battered down. It's very bold filmmaking and I'm sure it will alienate a good percentage of the population!'

In her bid to counteract the controversy that was bound to develop upon the film's release, Uma cut a holiday short to make herself available for the usual round of interviews in October 2003. The premiere took place on 30 September in Los Angeles, with a general American and British release to follow in mid-October. The film did not smash any box-office records, but made $60 million in America in the first month, thus covering the production costs.

So what can be made of *Kill Bill Volume 1*? The immediate answer is blood, blood and more blood. As promised, there was gallons of the stuff sloshing around the set, but the violence was actually couched in such a way that it was possible to see beyond the gorefest to the exquisite choreography and cinematography.

Moving past this obvious stumbling block, it is important to evaluate whether the long-awaited fourth film from Quentin Tarantino was up to scratch, and indeed if this was the vehicle to revive Uma's career once more.

The opening scene, as set out by Uma almost a decade earlier, certainly provides enough scope to form an intriguing plot, no matter how predictable a revenge flick is bound to be. The face-off with the first victim on The Bride's list, Copperhead, produces a clever, fast-paced piece of action with humour and drama rolled in.

A little more is then divulged about The Bride's journey thus far, her determination to recover cleverly expressed purely through her fixed stare at her big toe. There are also some lovely Tarantino touches of black humour, including Sofi's fate, Fuck Buck's retribution, and anything to do with Go Go. It seemed as though Tarantino had pulled it off.

From here on, however, *Volume 1* slides off course. The Japanese *anime* describing O-Ren Ishii's background, while undeniably interesting and bringing another dimension to the film, is the first sequence that feels too long. After that the plot fails to progress as The Bride undertakes a killing spree in her bid to fight O-Ren Ishii. The bloodbath at the House Of Blue Leaves, though spectacular, quickly becomes monotonous and predictable – as Tarantino said himself, it was just a challenge to think up as many ways as possible in which limbs could be severed. The vicious dance with Go Go Yubari stands out as the most thrilling section, but unfortunately the long-awaited execution of O-Ren Ishii almost falls flat in comparison.

Tellingly, when asked if Tarantino's latest film was any good, *Time Out*'s New York critic Mike D'Angelo responded, 'We'll find out in February' – the original release date for the second volume. The overwhelming feeling at the end of the mammoth first half was that the whole film should have been presented in one piece. While two-part movies or even trilogies are commonplace (*Lord Of The Rings*, *The Matrix*), so too are films in excess of three hours. Instead, it was exasperating to have watched an entire film and yet have so many questions unanswered and whole areas of the story untouched.

'In one of the first scenes of *Volume 2*, we'll actually see what happens at the wedding chapel,' offered Tarantino. 'And I've had people say, "I know you're saving the wedding chapel for *Volume 2*, but if I had seen that in *Volume 1*, I would have liked Uma's character more."'

Equally, the director's decision to bleep out The Bride's name as if it were a profanity baffled most people, including Uma. 'That one eludes me,' she said. 'You will definitely find out her name [in *Volume 2*], I can tell you right now, but that'd ruin it.'*

'Storywise, this is Tarantino's most slender film, and it suffers from being truncated at the halfway point,' expounded *heat*'s Charles Gant. 'We never learn much about any of the characters, and we'll have to wait until *Volume 2* to fill in the blanks.'

Viewers' frustration aside, *Kill Bill* as an entity will go down in history as one of the boldest films ever made, and Tarantino retained his reputation as a maverick director. For her part, Uma amply

---

* The Bride's real name is hinted at throughout *Volume 1*, with clues to be found in Bill's speech, on her boarding card to Okinawa, and within her verbal exchange with O-Ren Ishii. Tarantino's reasoning behind bleeping it out remains unclear, but possibly the childish reference is meant to be a precursor to the outcome of the film.

displayed her talents as both an actress and a dedicated craftsman by undertaking such a phenomenally physical project.

Throughout the spilling of gallons of fake blood, Uma never lets the viewer forget her mission. 'Her journey and her pain are for real,' Tarantino says. 'She keeps it on course, and she's not asking for any sympathy in this film.' It is a fine performance that proves her versatility and re-establishes her credibility. Her old friend and mentor had succeeded once again in showing what Uma could achieve given the chance.

As the release of the second part was pushed further back to April 2004, eagle-eyed critics noted that Miramax were allowing the two films to be considered for awards in different years. However, Uma sagely realized that the extreme violence was likely to prevent the film picking up any trophies.

The BAFTAs in February confirmed her fears: she was nominated for the Best Actress award but beaten by Scarlett Johansson for *Lost In Translation*. The film also lost out in the categories of Editing, Sound, Music, and Visual Effects. It was the same story at the Golden Globes, where Uma conceded the Best Actress prize to Charlize Theron for *Monster*.

Thurman didn't even receive a nomination at the Oscars, about which a rather biased Tarantino tellingly commented, 'As far as I'm concerned, the Academy should've just walked up to her door, knocked on it and put the Oscar in her hand.

'*Kill Bill Volume 2* – there's a whole other year, a whole other crack at it.'

26

A WALK IN THE PARK

'Sometimes you reach a point in your life when you're so happy with how things are going that you go through a second childhood . . . I'm not questioning my happiness for one moment.'

UMA THURMAN

During the mammoth shoot of *Kill Bill*, Uma had little time for a private life, but over the summer of 2002, reports emerged that she and Ethan had bought their very own private island.

The tiny 9-acre island was situated in Tracadie harbour, on the Gulf of St Lawrence, east of Antigonish, Nova Scotia. It came complete with two cottages, dating from the 1870s and 1990, and access to the mainland via a 60-metre land bridge. The older property, a farmhouse, had amazingly been hauled across the ice to the island in 1940. 'It's a spectacularly beautiful spot,' said the previous owner, Marie Kelly.

Kelly had first met the celebrity couple four years earlier through a mutual friend, and although they had fallen in love with the place then, she had only decided to sell her family's summer idyll in January 2002. Hawke visited the island again in June, and the deal was finalized. It was estimated the Thurman-Hawkes paid between $800,000 and $2 million for the island, joining the ranks of other celebrity land barons like Marlon Brando and Richard Branson.

Finally released from the set of *Kill Bill* in February 2003 (although she would return for reshoots and voiceovers on the second volume as late as December that year), Uma was thrilled to be properly reunited with her family.

'It's wonderful,' she sighed blissfully. 'I loved nurturing Maya so much that I was looking forward to going through the same experience with Roan. I find it fascinating to be part of his world and also how Maya is relating to having a brother.'

Uma encouraged her children to lead an active life and tried to limit their exposure to television and the movies, despite the fact that both parents worked in those fields. When asked whether she could picture her brood following in their footsteps to become actors, Uma always skirted round the issue, amusingly stating that she wanted them to have a college education first – not something her own parents had ever managed to enforce!

Having been with Hawke for more than five years, Uma thought they had ironed out a lot of issues around balancing work with raising children. Always she would stress that there was nothing special about their arrangements: 'We're just regular people. It's great when there are movies we believe in and stories we want to have told, but then we go home and schlep the baby around and eat ice cream.' She was pleased to see her husband get more involved with Maya as she busied herself with Roan, and asserted, 'Having two children is working out pretty well.'

But what of the strain such a complicated life must have placed on their marriage? One of the key attractions of Hawke had always been that he was someone whose dedication to his work not only matched hers, but nowadays even surpassed it. 'We're different,' Uma admitted. 'He's obsessive about needing to do a lot . . . constantly pawing the ground. He needs six projects ahead of him to feel calm.'

A comment made by Anjelica Huston, her co-star in *The Golden Bowl*, provided an interesting perspective on the pair.

'When you're as bewitching as she is,' said Huston of Thurman, 'the temptation to chase rogues is very intense. Her choice of Ethan is striking, because she's gone for somebody who really likes to communicate.'

Uma agreed. 'I can talk to Ethan in a way I could never have imagined talking to my past boyfriends,' she said. 'I can be who I am and he can be who he is. We have a good laugh together and I don't have to pretend I'm not as smart.' In interviews at this time she would allude frequently to not having to tone down her intelligence for her husband ('I don't have to purr for Ethan'), which was an interesting slant both on the match of equals in their marriage, and the balance in her previous relationships.

As two Hollywood A-listers, rumours were always bound to circulate about on-set romances with attractive co-stars, but on this front somehow the Thurman-Hawkes had been left totally and miraculously unscathed. Uma had no doubt anyway that her husband only had eyes for her.

'I'd never worry about him with a leading lady,' she insisted. 'I'm not even worried about him straying. I could torture the poor guy and drive him into some other situation . . .

'But he's not the kind of person whose behaviour would come unmotivated. If something happened in our relationship I'm sure it would be my fault. I'm 100 per cent sure of it . . . I feel really grateful to be with someone so nice.'

Uma felt so secure about her position that in March 2003 she apparently actively encouraged her husband to enjoy several stripteases by the burlesque dancers at the 40 Deuce nightclub in Hollywood. In fact, she practically joined in, egging the girls on, hollering and imitating their bumps and grinds. It was not the behaviour of a dominated or suppressed wife.

Uma admitted that 'marriage is hard work', but pressed the point that there was little in life so worthwhile that came easily. 'Marriage definitely requires commitment, discipline, love, self-investigation, and patience,' she said in all honesty, 'and all those things are the greatest qualities and the hardest to maintain.' She rightly believed that it was an ongoing process whereby each partner should be involved in the other's life with unmitigated support and dedication.

'The longer I'm married, the more I like it,' she said. 'It's been a wonderful journey so far and I think our relationship has worked out in such a way that we have a sound basis for it to keep unfolding happily.'

*

Noticeably much fitter after her time with Tarantino and *Kill Bill*, Uma was the unlikely subject of tabloid speculation that she had undergone plastic surgery to radically change her looks in February 2003.

Comparing before and after pictures taken when she had just given birth and was still breastfeeding and of her current martial-arts-honed appearance, reports claimed everything from fat transfers to skin peels, but the truth was her intensive training to play The Bride had reawakened a craving for workouts at the gym. The lazy side of Uma admitted this renewed desire to keep fit was going to be difficult to combine with her hectic schedule: 'Once you get out of it, it's so hard to imagine going back in.'

Uma's new-found love of action had clearly opened up a different area of her career. *The Avengers* and *Kill Bill* were both in their unique ways comic-book adventures pitching Uma as a conquering heroine.

When the script for the upcoming Paramount/DreamWorks project *Paycheck* landed on her desk, Uma readily accepted a part in the science-fiction action thriller.

It was the director who most attracted her to the project.

John Woo – one of Tarantino's pointers for Uma's *Kill Bill* research – was a Chinese director and screenwriter and former film editor specializing in action and crime movies. The first Asian filmmaker ever to oversee a major Hollywood feature, his style was as distinctive as his movies, combining graceful slow-motion sequences with choppy edits, jaw-dropping combat scenes and visual trickery.

Woo's reference field was almost as wide as Tarantino's, and he cited American musicals, French New Wave films and the directors Sam Peckinpah and Stanley Kubrick as his first inspirations. After his directorial debut, *The Young Dragons* in 1973, a host of low-budget kung fu pictures followed, and Woo also introduced an element of comedy into his work.

By the mid-1980s, it seemed that Woo's inspiration had dried up, until the release of 1986's *A Better Tomorrow*, which proved to be his commercial and critical breakthrough and introduced stars Chow Yun Fat and Leslie Cheung. Thereafter Woo expanded his talents and subject base, working with the likes of Jean-Claude Van Damme in 1993's *Hard Target* and John Travolta and Nicolas Cage in 1997's *Face/Off*. Further box-office success came with *Mission: Impossible II*, starring Tom Cruise, in 2000.

'I think his filmmaking style is masterful,' said Uma. 'It's breathtaking to me.' As far as *Paycheck* was concerned, she didn't really care about the content or the characters. 'I would have made a western with John Woo!' she laughed. 'After the intense gauntlet of work that *Kill Bill* was, when John called me it was like it was meant to be.' It was all about Woo.

Of course, it was necessary at some point to read the script. *Paycheck* was adapted from a 1953 short story by Philip K. Dick, whose writings had elsewhere inspired futuristic science-fiction hits such as *Blade Runner*, *Total Recall* and the previous year's *Minority Report*. Following similar lines to those stories with its themes of paranoia and questioning reality and identity, Dean Georgaris's screenplay captures the adventures of techno genius Michael Jennings. A specialist in 'reverse engineering', he is paid millions of dollars by powerful corporations to do hush-hush jobs, but always has his memory erased once his work is complete so he won't be able to divulge any company secrets. He loses years of his life in this manner, but is rich enough to buy whatever he desires.

Waking up after a three-year assignment for a man named Rethrick at Allcom Inc, Jennings discovers to his horror that he has forfeited payment in return for an envelope containing twenty seemingly useless and random objects. Upon leaving Rethrick's office, Jennings is arrested by the security police, who order him to reveal the nature of his top-secret work. Unable to believe his defence that his memory has been wiped, they prepare to arrest him. The prospect of a lifetime's imprisonment somehow reawakens a brief memory and Jennings uses one of the objects from the envelope – a wire – to escape.

Chased by the police, the FBI and his former boss for a crime he has no recollection of committing, Jennings soon discovers that his life is at stake. Each item in the envelope is a clue to his past. As time runs out he discovers he had fallen in love with Allcom's head scientist, Rachel Porter, during his assignment and only she can help him uncover the truth: a government conspiracy involving a time-altering machine and Jennings's ultimate innocence.

*

Uma was to play Rachel in *Paycheck*, and she was under no illusions as to her place in the pecking order of the movie.

'I went back to work with John Woo just to be in a normal movie and play "the girl",' she said, joking that she wouldn't see much action but she would get to wear cute biologist outfits. It was, she claimed, the best way she could think of 'unwinding' after the unprecedented rigours of *Kill Bill*.

John Woo was after Matt Damon to play the lead role of Jennings. Damon had just finished shooting the action film *The Bourne Identity*, in which he played a government agent suffering from amnesia. Damon understandably thought that the two projects sounded too similar to place side by side on his CV, and instead suggested his best friend, actor Ben Affleck, for the role.

In a scene reminiscent of James Ivory's first viewing of Uma in *Batman And Robin*, Woo was flying back from his meeting with Damon when he tuned into the airplane movie: *Changing Lanes*, Affleck's 2002 thriller.

'He dug it, and when he landed, they offered me the part, and I was like, "This is serendipity!"' Affleck later exclaimed.

Two years younger than Uma, Affleck was at that time as much renowned for his romance with the actress-singer Jennifer Lopez (their names forming his much-despised derisive moniker of 'Bennifer') as he was for his cinematic output. Beginning with bit parts in Ethan Hawke's slacker territory (one of his first appearances was in Linklater's *Dazed And Confused*), Affleck really broke into the Hollywood A-list when he won the Best Original Screenplay Oscar for *Good Will Hunting*, which he co-wrote and starred in with Damon.

Affleck's strong-jawed, matinee-idol looks consequently won him a long succession of high-profile parts, mixing big-budget blockbusters such as 1998's *Armageddon* and 2001's *Pearl Harbor* with more intellectual fare, like *Shakespeare in Love* in 1998 and *Dogma* the following year. *Changing Lanes* was one of his three films released in 2002, and pitted him against Samuel L. Jackson in a tense, thought-provoking thriller.

Like Thurman, Affleck had not read Dick's short story, but was in awe of Woo's genius. Prompted to pick up a book containing the original *Paycheck*, he was soon hooked. The author 'had a startling kind of prescience,' Affleck mused. 'There is something in the story about how we'll use technology to create alternate realities for ourselves and stuff that sort of seems to be coming true already.' It all had a definite ring of *Gattaca*.

Uma had met Affleck once before, on the night of the previous presidential election, when the two sat up awaiting the result with a group of mutual friends and fellow actors. She had instantly warmed to him. 'I was totally struck by his humour and his intelligence,' she said. 'We're both from Massachusetts and he really reminded me of the kind of people I went to high school with. He just seemed very easy and familiar and fun and gracious, like somebody from home.'

With Thurman and Affleck in place, Woo went on to cast Aaron Eckhart as Rethrick, and soon he was ready to commence shooting.

*

Paycheck was filmed from April to July 2003 at Vancouver Film Studios, and on location in Vancouver, British Columbia, which was doubling for Seattle in the story.

'We decided to design the production as a stylish mystery, not your average high-concept futuristic design that can have a tendency to look artificial,' said production designer William Sandell. 'Instead, we went with a slick, clean look, which we felt better served the sophisticated nature of the story.' Thus there was a second *Gattaca* comparison: a revolutionary but familiar world using 1950s suburban imagery as a backdrop.

From the outset, Woo's cast and crew were heavily influenced by their director's unique, fast-paced style. Knowing that his elaborate sets would be used to depict many wild action sequences, Sandell admits he 'got a little wild, making it possible for each set to break apart like a puzzle box'.

Revelling in the thriller genre, Woo was inspired by Alfred Hitchcock movies for some scenes, such as an exciting subway chase, which drew on the famous train sequence in *North By Northwest*. Elsewhere the movie was full of explosions, choreographed fight scenes and high-tech gadgetry, one highlight being a dramatic motorcycle chase through the streets of Vancouver.

In interviews promoting *Paycheck* Uma would often say that she had more fun in this movie than she had in *Kill Bill*. 'I had a really nice time,' she said. 'Ben did all the heavy lifting, I got to watch John Woo work, see Ben hit people and wasn't covered in blood!'

Uma especially enjoyed the comfortable banter she fell into with her heroic leading man. 'He was great to work with,' she enthused. 'I haven't done a lot of straight-up romantic things, so that was really fun for me, especially after *Kill Bill* where I had to do them all in! So I just really enjoyed it.'

Both actors were in awe of Woo, who had worked as an editor before his transition to direction. 'John knows exactly which piece of film he's going to use and where you should focus your efforts,' raved Affleck. 'It's an enormous luxury for an actor because you don't have to worry about doing 1,700 options.

'It shows that you can be a great director *and* be a sane, calm, normal person.'

*

Fortunately, Uma's role in *Paycheck* wasn't *all* about standing back and looking pretty. It being a John Woo spectacle, she had several 'kick-ass' fight scenes of her own. Unlike her last film, these took very little effort.

'Compared to *Kill Bill* it was a walk in the park!' she laughed. 'I was like, "Kick that person? Sure, no problem! What kinda kick do you want? Tell me the kick and I'll give you the kick!"'

Woo was naturally delighted when he saw what the actress was capable of, and he and the stunt co-ordinators rubbed their hands in glee. In a brief attempt to bring Woo back down to earth, Uma pointed out that she was playing a biologist, so realistically how technically proficient would she be?

'That's why the few things that I do in the action are very street, self-defence,' she says. 'But what I really did enjoy was I felt so entitled to comment on the action . . . I liked to slightly brag, I had the stunt lingo, and could deal with pretty much anything they wanted to throw me.

'I would never have thought that I would have that kind of self-confidence about a field that women are pretty much excluded from.'

Ben Affleck had no such training, and when confronted with a vision of the high-kicking Uma, he could be forgiven for wanting to run a mile. 'I don't think any woman in the history of cinema has ever done that much [physical fighting],' he said. 'So I just deferred to her wealth of experience on that subject. There were a lot of bloopers that mostly involved Uma being so much tougher than me . . .

'She was beating my ass and it wasn't supposed to come off that way, so I tried to correct that. I was like, "John, can you cut out the stuff where Uma's a lot stronger than me?" '

After the *Paycheck* shoot was in the can, Uma stopped by on her way home at Simon & Schuster's New York studio. There she narrated the audio version of the new satirical pop-culture novel about an L.A. gold-digger, *Maneater* by Gigi Levangie Grazer, the wife of *Paycheck* producer Brian Grazer. On its release, Uma was praised for her smart, sassy and thoroughly entertaining uninhibited reading, using different accents for each character and effortlessly capturing the shallowness of the hilarious anti-heroine.

27

WHAT KINDA KICK DO YOU WANT?

'I've spent my life searching for a man to look up to without lying down.'

FRANCES MARION, FILMMAKER

While Uma spent a couple of months in Vancouver on the set of John Woo's *Paycheck*, Ethan was busy filming on the other side of Canada in Montreal.

At the end of May 2003, production started on Hawke's next movie, D. J. Caruso's *Taking Lives*. Based upon the 1999 novel of the same name, the thriller follows an FBI profiler in her bid to track down a serial killer who assumes the identities of his victims. Angelina Jolie (*Tomb Raider*) undertook the lead part, Hawke was cast opposite her as a museum employee searching for a thieving art professor, and Olivier Martinez and Kiefer Sutherland took on supporting roles.

Being apart from each other for long periods so often in recent years had put a great strain on Uma and Ethan's relationship. But the down-to-earth couple had always maintained that a marriage required effort and compromise from both parties and they had worked hard to survive the ravages of fame and parenthood.

Before Uma finished work in July, reports began filtering through the grapevine that her husband was spending a lot of time in the company of Jennifer Perzow, a local model. Assuming that at worst it was just a one-night stand, Uma hoped they would be able to work through the alleged infidelity – after all, she had declared in 2000: 'When you're in a relationship, it's better to be with somebody who has an affair than with somebody who doesn't flush the toilet.'

Heartache struck when it seemed to be something more serious, and the harsh reality of a marital crisis sunk in.

Before Uma had a chance to deal with her own feelings and the future of her marriage in private, in August 2003 the press got wind of something, although they were a little off the mark. Having decided that Angelina Jolie was not seeing Kylie Minogue's latest squeeze, Olivier Martinez, journalists then paired Jolie up with Ethan Hawke, providing grainy photos of them kissing as proof. Hawke's praise of his co-star ('She's ravishingly beautiful and never gets old or boring') was definitely complimentary, but Jolie, a divorcée as of May that year, did not mince her words in refuting all the allegations. 'I haven't had sex in a long time,' she said. 'As a woman I miss certain aspects of an intense relationship, but right now I am not looking for that kind of love from a man or a woman.'

Then the story broke: Ethan Hawke had apparently begun an affair with Jennifer Perzow back in June. The twenty-two-year-old model, whose CV included adverts for Fructis shampoo, Diesel and Fornarina, also had a psychology degree and worked full-time as a buyer for her father's fashion company. She told the tabloids that she met Ethan in a restaurant in Montreal when he was out with fellow cast members of *Taking Lives*, including Martinez and Sutherland.*

According to Perzow, Ethan approached her for a chat, they hit it off immediately and she joined the gang as they hit a club. At the end of the night Hawke asked for her phone number. Over the next two months their relationship blossomed and they became a fixture in the local social scene.

'I'm no home-wrecker,' protested Perzow in a *News Of The World* exclusive. 'All this stuff that I broke up their marriage is just not true.

'The truth is, it's Uma who wanted out of the marriage, not Ethan . . . The very first night I met him, he told me he was no longer with his wife – that they were having problems and he was separated.'

If Perzow's story was to be believed, why had Thurman ended the marriage? Much had been made of the stiflingly close relationship between Quentin Tarantino and his muse over the years, and one story suggests that Ethan became convinced Uma was having an affair with her director during the prolonged filming for *Kill Bill*. This seems

---

* It was a bizarre coincidence that Kiefer Sutherland should be present at significant turning points during the collapses of both Thurman's marriages.

unlikely considering the pressure of the shoot and the fact that Uma had her two children with her constantly and was still nursing Roan; but Tarantino had recently given an insight into just how intimate the two friends had become.

'We love each other, but we're almost too close now to be a couple,' he said. 'We had our life together on *Kill Bill*. It was like a marriage in every way.' Hawke could be forgiven for getting the wrong impression, but once the trust in a relationship is broken, it is hard to retrieve.

The Thurman–Hawke dissolution was probably in large part the result of *Kill Bill*, although not an affair between Uma and Tarantino. Uma's renewed ambition to revive her career meant that she tolerated the extended shoot even though she hardly saw her husband for more than six months. Although they tried to get back into a routine after Uma returned from filming, they both then accepted work that once again kept them apart in different cities.

It was against this troubled background that Hawke reportedly started the affair with Perzow, claiming that he was separated from his wife. After *Taking Lives*, Hawke travelled to Paris to make another movie, a sequel to Richard Linklater's *Before Sunrise*, and on his return to Manhattan he stayed in a hotel rather than at the family home.

Hawke was wise to stay away from the Thurman household, as Uma's brothers were livid and eager to avenge their sister's wounded pride. 'It's a sort of dramatic family,' Uma has said. 'There's a lot of passion. We give each other hell, call each other on everything. It's merciless. Nobody is blasé about anybody else.' As expected, the backlash was quite something.

'I want to kill him. He's a piece of shit,' Mipam was quoted as saying on the Peoplenews website. 'I can't believe what he's done to my sister. Ethan is blaming Uma. He says the marriage wasn't great and that he was forced to turn to other people. He's compounded the problem with this affair.' Ganden was far more reasonable, saying, 'Anger may be the proper reaction to what Ethan's done. I side with my sister categorically, but this is a matter for Uma and Ethan. I really want to encourage them to come to an amicable resolution. I wish them all the best.'

Regardless of these outbursts, representatives for the teetering couple remained adamant in their refusal to comment on any allegations. 'At this present time there are no plans for a divorce,' was the joint statement made.

*

At the end of September Uma was called upon for some heavy-duty promotion for *Kill Bill Volume 1* as it premiered in Los Angeles. With so much media speculation, she finally cracked and admitted she was separated from her husband.

'My opening weekend of the number-one movie in the country was probably the worst weekend of my life,' she said shortly afterwards. 'It is a difficult time and I am not exactly sure what to make of everything myself. As it is I am just trying to figure things out.'

Going through such a personal plight, and seeing it simultaneously splashed so publicly across tabloids worldwide, naturally begged the question of whether fame is worthwhile. 'The attention doesn't piss me off anymore,' she said. 'You never get the disclaimer paper when you become a public person, no one ever explains what's going to happen . . . You trade this in, and in exchange, if you really, really love what you do, you get a beautiful life.'

Uma was in no doubt about the fact that her success meant she signed away her privacy and was very practical about the deafening Chinese whispers that were being repeated and distorted. 'Of course, there's going to be the reporting of unfortunate moments,' she reasoned. 'Most of it is true, and sometimes it's false. Often it's true but it's unkindly presented.'

It is interesting to note that Nicole Kidman went through a similar dilemma as *Moulin Rouge* (her own once-in-a-lifetime opus) was due to open, on the same weekend her husband Tom Cruise walked out on her amid speculation about his relationship with Penélope Cruz. Like Kidman, Thurman had to protect her family first and foremost. 'I have two children. The public space is not the place to air your issues when you're a parent,' Uma said matter-of-factly. 'It's just inappropriate for me to say anything. My children should never have to read any nonsense about their family in the papers.'

With this in mind, it was reported in October that Hawke and Thurman were attempting a reconciliation for the sake of their children, but rather than rekindling their marriage it was more a question of finding a practical way forward. Like Kidman and Cruise, the pair were unanimous in making Maya and Roan their priority. 'We share two children, some precious times and we'll have to find a way to carry on and take care of our kids,' said Uma. 'Ethan was really young when we had kids . . . I watched him grow into a very good father.'

However, Uma was not alone for long. She was first rumoured to have run back into the arms of actor John Cusack, the man who provided sympathy and distraction after her break-up with Gary Oldman. In fact, there was a man in Uma's life, but again the tabloids were off the mark, as it was not Cusack.

In November it emerged that Uma had tentatively begun a romance with an old friend, New York hotelier Andre Balazs. The owner of Chateau Marmont, the ultra-hip celebrity bolthole in L.A., and the Mercer in New York, Balazs had split from his wife, Katie Ford, and so was free to pursue the newly single Uma.

*

December was a busy month for Uma, whose first public engagement was at the Golden Globes on the eighteenth, where she announced the award contenders. One week later, *Paycheck* was released on Christmas Day.

The movie's main theme of memory-loss was certainly a hot cinema topic. The plot had abundant similarities to the likes of *The Bourne Identity, Memento* and *Minority Report*, while upcoming pictures already announced for the New Year included *Gothika, The I Inside, Eternal Sunshine Of The Spotless Mind* and *50 First Dates*. Had the audience reached saturation point?

Despite the upsetting developments in her personal life, Uma remained bright and breezy for the publicity interviews, laughing about her casting as a scientist. 'When it comes to technology, I am a borderline Luddite,' she joked. 'My washing machine overwhelms me with its options and its sophistication . . . I can manage the cell phone and e-mail, but a PalmPilot – forget it. I'm even afraid of the Cuisinart. I like to hand-chop my vegetables.'

When some canny journalist made the link between knowing the future and the unpredictable period Uma was experiencing in her private life, she cleverly countered: 'I think life is intense enough as it unfolds, so I quite like getting to have one day at a time myself. I wouldn't mind a few clues, if anyone had any great insight or advice for me, but a lot of that is intuitive.'

Paycheck is good clean fun, with no swearing or sex scenes, and never aspires to be deep and meaningful – just an entertaining night out at the cinema. Jennings's series of clues are predictable but fun – the envelope of mysterious items is a clever idea, if not exactly original. As audiences puzzle over what possible use he could have for hairspray, ball-bearings, an allen key, a wire, a ticket stub, a bus token and more, Affleck delivers a performance befitting a rather generic movie. Thurman was also fine – if a little frazzled – in the girlfriend role, and perhaps as a conciliatory gesture for her character being very much second fiddle, Woo gave her all the laughs.

Unfortunately, press coverage for the movie centred as much on its leading man as it did on its repetitive subject matter.

Ben Affleck too had experienced a run of bad luck that year: *Gigli*, a romantic comedy in which he starred with his then-fiancée, Jennifer Lopez, was one of the biggest bombs in recent cinema history. His wedding was postponed amid much tabloid mayhem, as embarrassing reports surfaced that he had been 'indiscreet' at a strip club in Vancouver. 'This one better pan out for me,' he laughed, knowing that *Paycheck* could make or break his career.

Reviews for the film were middling to poor. 'Unlike *Minority Report*, *Paycheck* doesn't take itself seriously other than as a rip-roaring adventure thriller and director John Woo hits all the right buttons,' praised *heat* magazine, also noting the 'terrific' action scenes and special effects, and 'delicious chemistry' of Affleck and Thurman.

But others weren't so convinced. 'Affleck must have signed on to this bloated action film to collect a fat check,' said *USA Today*. 'That would make more sense than if he claimed to be mesmerized by this ridiculous story.' *New York Daily News* bitched: 'You can't really blame [Affleck] for picking up his own fortunes for his film work. He's a good-looking guy with zero screen presence, and if the studios want to keep throwing money at him to play heroic figures, that's their problem.' The *Chicago Tribune* was perhaps the most cutting: 'Unfortunately, after watching *Paycheck*, you may wish you had the picture's gimmickry at your disposal, so you could erase your own memory of it.

Ultimately, *Paycheck* was aiming at a Christmas audience and so kept its references as wide as possible, providing a refreshing breather from the other seasonal offerings including highbrow epics such as *The Last Samurai*, *Cold Mountain* and *Master And Commander: The Far Side Of The World*.

*

There had been talk of a Christmas reunion for Thurman and Hawke, not least for the sake of the children, but Uma had moved on. She spent the festive period on the Caribbean island of St Barts with Andre Balazs and her children.

By the New Year, Uma was almost ready to reveal the romance. 'Yes, I'm seeing someone,' she said, confirming his name. 'It's been nice for me.' Even pal Quentin Tarantino was pleased. 'I just talked to Uma on the phone, and she told me she had a new boyfriend,' he said. 'I haven't met him yet, but I'm very happy for her.'*

---

* At the time of writing, two contrasting stories were in the news: the first that Thurman was preparing to accept Balazs's marriage proposal, and the second that the couple's ongoing fights looked likely to cause an imminent split. Uma's press office declined to comment on either report.

Hawke, on the other hand, was struggling to come to terms with everything that had happened over the last six months. Asked by one interviewer if he was hurt by Uma's budding relationship, he replied, 'That's a leading question. How am I supposed to answer that, man? Do you think it's tough? It's very tough.

'You gotta think about your kids . . . I'm trying to be a grown-up.'

28

TRIX ARE FOR KIDS

'I wish there was a whole salad bowl of opportunities that I could just flip through and always pick the best of the best.'

UMA THURMAN

Despite not being nominated for *Kill Bill*, Uma turned up at the 2004 Oscars in February – yet it was not her beauty for which her appearance was noted. Uma was crowned the worst-dressed star as she turned up in an outlandish, billowing Christian Lacroix evening gown befitting the nursery rhyme 'Little Bo Peep'.

'You get bored. That's when you have to say, "I will be worst dressed." I think I deserve it, and I can take it. I need a good panning every so often or I wouldn't really recognize my life,' she retorted, either tongue-in-cheek or covering her embarrassment.

Being a clothes horse was probably the last thing on her mind, as proposals for a divorce were circulating between her and Hawke. It seemed that with a bit of distance, both parties were trying to accept some of the responsibility, lay a portion of blame with the other person and set a few facts straight. 'The story of us breaking up over infidelity has been an annoying one,' defended Hawke. 'If our problems were that simple, we'd still be together. Uma and I were having troubles long before the press got a hold of us.'

In an interview for America's *20/20* news show, the actor said it was hard being married to 'a woman who wants to be a movie star', ultimately citing her professional drive as a key problem. 'It is very difficult for any couple who are married if both people are very ambitious.'

Uma, on the other hand, felt the physical distance between them was an impossible pressure to overcome. 'As anyone who's been in a relationship will appreciate, if you're selfish or go away for too long and force the other person to do all the travelling, the relationship will ultimately suffer,' she said early in their marriage, sadly something which they were unable to resolve. 'He was young. I wanted to have kids. I put a lot on him,' she later admitted.

Typically, Uma was hell-bent on putting a positive spin on the mess, whether it was for the benefit of herself, the media or her children. She viewed the enforced change as an opportunity for reinvention. 'I don't feel like anything was wasted,' she said graciously. 'I've had a really rich life and I'm grateful for the last eight years – they were so much better than the eight years before that.'

*

Despite the personal upheaval of the past few months, it was important for Uma to keep busy and working. She was approached by Terry Gilliam, sixteen years after *The Adventures Of Baron Munchausen*, to appear in his latest fantastical film, *The Brothers Grimm*. The biopic of the German storytellers exposes them as conmen who convince villagers that their town is haunted, then exorcize the spirits for a fee – but they meet their match when they are hired to do battle with The Evil Queen.

The cameo role of The Evil Queen was originally taken by Nicole Kidman, but she withdrew due to scheduling clashes and Thurman stepped in. Unfortunately, filming for *The Brothers Grimm* was set to start in Prague at the end of June 2003, just when Uma was struggling to save her marriage, and so she too pulled out. After Thurman vacated the position, Monica Bellucci did not hesitate to accept it and appears alongside Heath Ledger and Matt Damon as the titular brothers, with Jonathan Pryce and Lena Headey in supporting roles.

Uma was not out of work for long; soon something far more appealing caught her eye. Director F. Gary Gray was looking to adapt Elmore Leonard's sequel to *Get Shorty*. Gray had made the jump from an award-winning career in music videos to filmmaker in the mid-1990s, cementing his position with the big-budget action flick *The Negotiator* and the remake of *The Italian Job*.

Get Shorty is a comic crime caper directed by Barry Sonnenfeld in 1995. Chilli Palmer (John Travolta) is a gangster trying to give up dodgy deals and double-crossing clients, but he finds himself caught up in the movie industry working with low-budget horror-film director Harry Zimm (Gene Hackman), B-movie actress Karen (Rene Russo) and the demanding actor Martin Weir (Danny DeVito).

As Chilli gets drawn deeper into Zimm's high-class underworld, *Get Shorty* explores the peculiar nuances of the entertainment business with hilarious satirical swipes at its corrupt nature. Leonard's second outing for Chilli Palmer, *Be Cool*, follows his move into the music business in search of his next movie subject, offering Chilli a new woman to chase and a fresh set of complications.

Travolta was thrilled to reprise his role as the amiable gangster Chilli, especially as it had been his first part after *Pulp Fiction* made him hip again. Danny DeVito also agreed to play the egocentric actor once more. Although casting took place in the autumn of 2003, the shoot didn't start until January the following year, which allowed Uma some time to get her life back in order.

Uma's role is that of Edie, a widow who inherits her late husband's record label and finds herself in business with Chilli Palmer. Although still making movies, Chilli witnesses the murder of his music-industry friend by the mob and agrees to manage an up-and-coming singer, Linda Moon (Christina Milian), in his absence. The supporting cast reads like a *Who's Who* of Hollywood: Vince Vaughn, James Gandolfini, Harvey Keitel, Aerosmith frontman Steve Tyler, Andre 3000 of Outkast and The Rock.

Notably the work reunited Uma with *Pulp Fiction* partner Travolta, and the pair were even set to come together for another electrifying dance scene with a Latin twist. 'Uma's wonderful,' beamed Travolta on hearing the news. 'She's so much fun. I'm looking forward to it.'

Filming finally commenced at the beginning of February 2004, and for Uma it was a manageable thirty-five-day shoot in Los Angeles. It wasn't ideal in terms of trips back and forth across America to see the children, but Uma felt the film was worth the effort. Having failed to capitalize on *Pulp Fiction*, perhaps she felt the need to make the most of her second Tarantino-propelled stab at success with *Kill Bill. Be Cool* was set for release in February 2005.

*

Uma juggled work on the promising *Be Cool* with another upcoming movie, *Accidental Husband*.

Accidental Husband was a project Uma held dear, as it was to be the first movie she had produced since *Hysterical Blindness*. Described as a 'sweet romantic comedy', the script was written by Mimi Hare and Clare Naylor, and featured Dr Emma Lloyd as a self-help guru who is busy planning her wedding. Unfortunately, when she applies for a marriage licence she discovers that she is already married.

It turns out that the husband in question, Patrick Sheridan, has forged the licence as revenge, because years ago his own fiancée dumped him at the altar after listening to Emma's advice. As Emma tries to persuade him to grant her a divorce, she begins to wonder if she's marrying the right man after all, or if in fact she's already married to him.

Uma, fancying herself as Emma, took the project to Jason Blum, who had partnered her as executive producer on *Hysterical Blindness*. Together they took the heart-warming comedy to Graham King, the president of the production company Initial Entertainment Group, who fell for the story's charms and did not hesitate to take it on, granting the project full financing. 'It's great when you know right away that something instinctively feels right and that's exactly how I felt about this project and the people involved with it,' he said.

It was announced that Brendan Fraser (*The Mummy*) had signed up as Patrick and Hugh Wilson (*The First Wives Club*) would be directing. Although *Accidental Husband* was due to start filming in September 2003 in New York, Uma obviously had other things on her plate at that time, and the production schedule was pushed back until later in 2004.

*

The long-awaited second volume of *Kill Bill* was released in February 2004 in America, and two months later in April in the UK. It would answer all the questions left hanging over from the first volume (if you could remember them) and reveal much more of the plot, including The Bride's background as an assassin and the events leading up to the massacre at the wedding chapel. Handily for viewers, and lucratively for the producers, the DVD of the first volume went on sale just before the second film opened in the cinemas.

Despite the hype surrounding the release, the UK premiere was almost hijacked by some bitchy backstabbing. Rebecca Loos, the alleged mistress of David Beckham, turned up with her former girlfriend Emma Basden dressed up like the football hero. Given her own very public split from Ethan Hawke, Uma was horrified to see Loos courting the media so readily with absolutely no regard for the Beckhams. 'I don't know the facts – I wasn't there,' said Uma, horrified at the attention-seeking stunt. 'I'm not sure whether she's trash or a tramp. I'd say tramp, though. She can't get enough PR.' Unsurprisingly, Loos was noticeably absent from the after-party at the In And Out club on Piccadilly, attended by Uma and Andre Balazs.

There were also rumours of a clash between Uma and Daryl Hannah after they requested separate wings at the Dorchester in London. According to a source at the hotel, the two actresses would 'often bristle and snap at each other'. Fuel was then added to the fire at the Cannes Film Festival in May: again the ladies were reportedly allocated segregated accommodation and separate photo shoots in order to keep them apart.

Whatever the truth of the matter, it was all good publicity for the film. *Kill Bill Volume 2* surpassed its predecessor's first weekend's takings of $22 million in America by a further $3.6 million as fans queued up to see the grand finale. By the end of the first volume, The Bride has killed Vernita Green and O-Ren Ishii, but still has two D.iV.A.S. – Bud (Michael Madsen) and Elle Driver (Daryl Hannah) – to dispose of, plus, of course, Bill himself.

In the second half, the viewer is treated once again to some exceptional fight scenes, notably the catfight between The Bride and Elle Driver, but also much more dialogue and character-building drama. The Bride's backstory reveals a few surprises, such as her love/hate relationship with Bill and the fate of her unborn child.

Samuel L. Jackson pops in for a cameo, we travel back in time to witness The Bride's extraordinary training in martial arts, and there are some genuinely terrifying moments, notably when she is buried alive. But the highlight is undoubtedly the lengthy mental and physical showdown with Bill. Here Thurman really proved her worth as an actress; playing opposite David Carradine, the perfect man for the job, she truly shines.

Audiences were thrilled with the movie's satisfying conclusion and immediately rumours abounded that Tarantino was planning a third instalment or an animated prequel. When presented with the possibility of another *Kill Bill*, Uma replied: 'All of Quentin's characters are alive – unless they're dead – but if they're living at the end of his film, they're living in his mind.

'I know he has visions of [*Pulp Fiction*'s] Honey Bunny carrying on in another movie, and Mia Wallace, and yes, he has a very good idea for the plot of *Volume 3*!'

TURNING ON THE HIGH BEAMS

'If you're not looking forward, you're looking backward or to the side, and you're going to smack into something really hard.'

UMA THURMAN

When Uma Thurman was just eighteen, she received rave reviews for her brief appearance in *Dangerous Liaisons*. Followed by equally revealing performances in *The Adventures Of Baron Munchausen* and *Henry & June*, she was soon heralded as the latest Hollywood sex symbol and hounded by the press and public alike. Given that she had always been shy and uncomfortable with her looks, it seemed surprising that she would continue to pursue a career in the limelight.

Yet clearly she had found her passion and chose to carry on regardless. 'I really do love acting,' she stresses. 'I have a great time doing it, it's a deeply exciting profession. It is inspiring and tremendously satisfying when you get it right.'

Having grown up in the spotlight, Uma learned the hard way that nothing is private; she has had to take responsibility for her actions. 'You're so accountable when you're famous,' she says. 'You can't avoid things, you just have to face them.' This brutal reality was exactly the reason why Richard Gere attempted to deter Uma from entering the business, but in many ways it has made her the woman she is today. 'I'm not a shrinking, insecure, awkward eighteen-year-old any more, thank heavens,' she told the *Daily Mirror* recently. 'I think I've become comfortable with myself and accept my failures, successes, short-comings and struggles. I never gave myself any credit for anything . . . I guess it comes with age.'

Throughout her career Uma has made some unusual choices, and with the benefit of hindsight it is easy to see which decisions were successful and which were instantly disastrous. But it is vitally important to view her choices in the context of her thought processes at the time. At first she was typecast as a sex symbol, but in her rebellion against that image she inadvertently stranded herself in the wilderness. 'My attempt not to fit into a Hollywood niche may have been detrimental,' she admits. 'It affects your "castability". You do not seem an obvious choice for anything because you do a little of everything.'

Although it was unwise to alienate a large – if unimaginative – section of the industry, Uma showed the courage to try new genres and became a well-rounded actress in the process. 'Everybody always tries to look into the future of their career,' she says. 'You look at the script, you look at the director, you look at yourself – you'll read any tealeaf to try to make your efforts not be in vain. The situations that worked out well deliver you one thing. The situations that didn't taught you something really crucial.'

With this attitude Uma is able to give past failures a meaning, and unusually, she doesn't define her achievements by the obvious successes. 'A key moment is every time a great director casts you,' she explains, 'because you have the potential to make a great movie. Every director that melded with me has transformed me as a creative person.'

Regardless of her own reasoning, it cannot be denied that while Uma has indeed appeared in some critically acclaimed movies and worked with some of the greatest directors, she is more often than not a supporting actress and has appeared in more than her fair share of less successful vehicles. Equally, the few times she has tried to join the crowd in the field of obviously commerical fare, the movies have been unmitigated disasters.

Thurman's collaborations with Quentin Tarantino are without doubt her finest moments, yet she failed to capitalize on the success of *Pulp Fiction*, instead moving sideways and experimenting with new areas and directors. Her greatest overall triumph, the comeback double feature *Kill Bill*, has certainly revived her career once more, and perhaps this time she will seize the opportunity to build on this.

'I've never felt better about my work than I do now,' she said recently. 'It's a nice turning point. I'm thirty-three years old. I have two children. I'm glad I stepped away and had them.

'I grew a lot, I risked a lot. I found new reasons to want to work. I feel new passion for what I do.'

Never one to conform, it hardly seems likely that she will start now, which may be exciting for her as an actress, but tends to make her continued output unpredictable. 'My ambitions have been raised as I have less to lose,' she continues. 'I feel I could do anything. If people don't like it, I'll try something else . . . If you're a slave to the fame game then it's a really ugly universe.'

Uma Thurman has always been unashamedly more content to achieve personal goals rather than gain public approval. Having tried her hand at producing, Uma says she would like to experience directing: 'If I find a piece that really moves me. I don't know if I'd be any good, but I'll find out.' The steely determination that typifies her personality leaves one in no doubt that she will fulfil this ambition.

Undoubtedly Uma's heart has always been ruled by her nearest and dearest. 'That Uma has made it big time in the movies is a tribute not only to her own hard work and bravado, but to the natural charisma of the family,' says her brother Dechen, explaining the genetic repercussions of Robert's oratorical skills and Nena's beauty and intelligence.

Her upbringing was indeed paramount in shaping her desires and capabilities and should never be dismissed, but Uma's own experiences have enhanced the extraordinary grounding created by her parents. After two marriages, two children and one divorce to date, she is now experienced enough to differentiate between fame and real life, headlines and truth, and take all of life's bumps in her stride.

Wisely she states: 'All life is change, and certainly physical things are always transient. And yes, there are going to be some harsh cuts. But I think I'm poised to take them gracefully.'

Importantly, after struggling through her teens and fighting against stereotyping in her twenties, Uma finally feels comfortable with her age. 'I feel like I'm growing into myself. I've always been younger than my vibe,' she says. 'I always felt like my thirties would be where I'd kick into feeling the most at home. It's my decade of choice.'

Uma's late coming of age and achievement of inner peace is aptly described by Barry Edelstein, her director on the life-changing *The Misanthrope*. 'There's a figure of speech, "to turn on the high beams" – it means to switch your car headlights to bright, to put off more light when you're on a dark country lane. Uma can turn on the high beams, and it gets very bright around her when she does.

'What knocked us for six was her composure within that glare. Under the pressure of public scrutiny, inside the bubble of celebrity, we found a real person, a lovely girl, a concerned mother, a serious artist.

And her genuineness made us all love being around her even more. She's an extraordinary person and a major actress.'

Uma's own take on her success is simple.

'As I like to remind myself, I'm a girl from Massachusetts,' she says. 'Life's just one long learning process, after all.'

CURRICULUM VITAE

Films are listed in reverse order of production; the date is of release.

Accidental Husband	2005
Be Cool	2005
Kill Bill Volume 2	2004
Maneater	2003
Paycheck	2003
Kill Bill Volume 1	2003
Hysterical Blindness	2002
Chelsea Walls	2002
Tape	2001
Without Lying Down: Frances Marion And The Power Of Women In Hollywood	2000
The Golden Bowl	2000
Vatel	2000
The Misanthrope	1999
Sweet And Lowdown	1999
Les Misérables	1998
The Avengers	1998
Batman And Robin	1997
Gattaca	1997
Duke Of Groove	1996
The Truth About Cats & Dogs	1996
Beautiful Girls	1996
A Month By The Lake	1995
Pulp Fiction	1994
Even Cowgirls Get The Blues	1994
Mad Dog And Glory	1993
Jennifer 8	1992
Final Analysis	1992
Robin Hood	1991
Henry & June	1990
Where The Heart Is	1990

The Adventures Of Baron Munchausen	1989
Johnny Be Good	1988
Dangerous Liaisons	1988
Kiss Daddy Goodnight	1987

INDEX

1	28	121	192	250	308	351	386	417
2	35	123	193	251	310	352	388	418
3	39	124	195	252	311	353	390	419
4	40	132	198	257	312	354	392	421
5	41	136	203	258	317	355	393	422
6	42	148	208	259	318	357	394	423
7	54	149	212	262	320	359	395	425
8	55	154	216	263	321	360	396	427
9	61	157	220	268	322	361	397	428
10	64	160	224	269	324	362	399	429
11	68	164	227	272	326	363	400	431
12	69	166	232	273	327	364	401	432
13	78	167	233	274	328	366	403	433
14	79	168	234	279	331	368	404	435
15	80	169	237	285	333	372	405	436
16	84	172	238	288	336	373	406	437
17	85	174	240	295	337	374	407	438
18	90	175	241	297	338	375	408	440
19	99	180	242	299	341	376	409	441
20	100	182	243	301	344	377	410	442
21	101	183	244	303	347	379	411	443
23	110	188	247	304	348	380	413	444
24	119	189	249	307	350	383	416	...

447	470	493	516	539	562	585	608	631
448	471	494	517	540	563	586	609	632
449	472	495	518	541	564	587	610	633
450	473	496	519	542	565	588	611	634
451	474	497	520	543	566	589	612	635
452	475	498	521	544	567	590	613	636
453	476	499	522	545	568	591	614	637
454	477	500	523	546	569	592	615	638
455	478	501	524	547	570	593	616	639
456	479	502	525	548	571	594	617	640
457	480	503	526	549	572	595	618	641
458	481	504	527	550	573	596	619	642
459	482	505	528	551	574	597	620	643
460	483	506	529	552	575	598	621	644
461	484	507	530	553	576	599	622	645
462	485	508	531	554	577	600	623	646
463	486	509	532	555	578	601	624	647
464	487	510	533	556	579	602	625	648
465	488	511	534	557	580	603	626	649
466	489	512	535	558	581	604	627	650
467	490	513	536	559	582	605	628	651
468	491	514	537	560	583	606	629	652
469	492	515	538	561	584	607	630	653